EDEN

ON THE

CHARLES

EDÉN

ON THE

CHARLES

THE MAKING OF BOSTON

MICHAEL RAWSON

HARVARD UNIVERSITY PRESS

Cambridge, Massachusetts • London, England • 2010

Library of Congress Cataloguing-in-Publication Data
Rawson, Michael.
Eden on the Charles : the making of Boston / Michael Rawson.
    p. cm.
Includes bibliographical references and index.
ISBN 978-0-674-04841-6 (alk. paper)
1. Boston (Mass.)—History—19th century. 2. Boston (Mass.)—Social conditions—19th
century. 3. Boston (Mass.)—Environmental conditions. 4. City planning—Massachusetts—
Boston—History—19th century. 5. Human ecology—Massachusetts—Boston—History—
19th century. I. Title.
F73.44.R39 2010
974.4'6103—dc22   2010007038

CONTENTS

When I was growing up in the Boston area, one of my favorite views of the city was from a hilltop in a suburban forest preserve that lies north of the city. The hill places the observer at the boundary of two seemingly distinct environments. To the south, the view reveals five miles of increasingly dense development that culminates in the skyscrapers of Boston. To the north, the unbroken forest of the preserve stretches almost to the horizon. The sharp contrast between the urban and the wild, the "artificial" and the "natural," makes for a powerful visual experience. The viewer is overcome by the impression that cities and nature are completely disconnected from each other. It almost seems as if one can see, in sharp relief, the very line that divides them.

I still enjoy visiting that hill, but I realized in writing this book that the view is misleading. Like the residents of all cities, Bostonians maintain many connections with the natural world. They breathe air, visit parks, drink water, eat food, and sail on the Charles River. They burn fossil fuels to produce energy, and they consume goods made from wood, cotton, metal, and other natural sources, some of which enter the city through the large natural system that is Boston Harbor. Urban scholars recognize today that Boston and other cities are not detached from the natural environment. Rather, they are inextricably connected to it.

But such connections are not as straightforward as they might seem. Even simple actions, like visiting a park or drinking a glass of water, are structured by complex relationships between humans and the natural world that are social, cultural, political, economic, and legal in character. The residents of Boston, for example, do not simply "visit" Boston Common but relate to it entirely through leisure. Cultural norms and city ordinances restrict their activities to recreational pursuits, in contrast with prior generations who related to the Common through activities such as digging gravel and pasturing a cow. Bostonians also maintain a particular relationship with their drinking water. Unlike urbanites in many other parts of the world, they consider access to an abundant supply of clean water to be a moral and political right, rather than a privilege. As a result, they insist that it be dispensed to users—usually by a governmental agency—at a reasonable price. Relationships such as these are easy to overlook because they are so familiar, yet variations can be found in all American cities and play a central role in how urbanites organize their interactions with the natural environment. In a world increasingly dominated by cities, they could not be of greater importance.

There was a time, however, when many of America's most commonly experienced ways of relating to nature did not exist. They were invented in the nineteenth century with the construction of the nation's first cities, and many were invented in Boston. As residents of one of the earliest communities to urbanize in America, Bostonians helped to design some of the first canals, urban parks, waterworks, sewer systems, railroads, factories, residential suburbs, rural cemeteries, harbor facilities, and suburban forest preserves. We often think of such places and systems as the "infrastructure" that underpins urban life, and so they are. But this book also treats them as key points of connection between the human and natural worlds that structure how the two interact. By helping to create these connections, Bostonians also helped to invent the new environmental relationships that came to define what it means to be "urban." That process is the subject of this book.

The metropolitan world that emerged during the nineteenth century was based on different ways of relating to the environment than Americans had previously known. Technology mediated interactions with nature that had once been more immediate, sometimes to dramatic effect—the difference, for example, between fetching water from an outdoor well and getting it from an indoor tap was enormous. Scientific advances enabled urbanites to adopt more aggressive approaches to controlling the harbors, rivers, and other natural systems that support cities. Changing ideas about leisure led to the dedication of certain natural areas solely to recreational pursuits, and a new desire to moderate the disruptive effects of ceaseless urban change made it possible to permanently preserve such places. In the countryside immediately outside cities, a set of new relationships to nature based on a domestically oriented suburban ideal was replacing a traditional agrarian lifestyle. Linking these changes and countless others was the growing influence of government, which often encouraged, managed, and protected new ways of interacting with nature. By the end of the century, the transformation was complete. A new web of environmental relationships was in place, one that continues to characterize the American metropolis today.

Ideas about nature deeply informed the shape of these new interactions, and the work of cultural historian Raymond Williams helped me to appreciate how complicated such ideas could be. They often reflected contemporary thought about society, economics, politics, medicine, and science, and they were incredibly divisive. Almost without exception, the ideas of nature discussed by Bostonians were freighted with the baggage of class strife or ethnic tension and conveyed as much information about the human as they did about the natural. Williams recognized this when he famously wrote that "what is often being argued, it seems to me, in the idea of nature is the idea of man . . . indeed the ideas of kinds of society." Williams applied this insight to the creation of literary representations of the city, but I am exploring its implications for the creation of the city itself.

Since Boston was America's intellectual center for much of the nineteenth century, it provides especially fertile ground for exploring competing ideas of nature. In fact, one would be hard-pressed to find another place in nineteenth-century America where people were devoting more time to thinking and writing about the natural world. Much of this intellectual activity was responding to the process of urbanization, especially after 1822 when Lowell—the nation's first industrial "shock city"—was founded only twenty-five miles from Boston. The growth of Lowell and the early development of their own city prompted Bostonians to reexamine their relationships to nature earlier than most other Americans, and their reflections are recorded in everything from paintings and poems to government documents and engineering reports. If these sources reveal anything, it is the simple but powerful fact that controlling the environmental change produced by city building required controlling the meaning of nature as well.

What we call "nature," however, is neither wholly cultural nor wholly physical, but almost always both. That inherent complexity has made it difficult for scholars to write histories that give both aspects of nature their due. Urban and cultural historians, for their part, have tended to treat the role of nature in the city-building process as a largely intellectual one, with nature narrowly defined as the set of romantic ideas that influenced the design of pastoral places like parks, suburbs, and rural cemeteries. Material conditions and asymmetries of power are usually left unexamined. Environmental historians have launched their own sustained study of urban growth and its social and environmental consequences, but their work tends to emphasize material nature at the expense of cultural nature. This book brings both aspects of nature to the foreground with the conviction that engaging nature in all of its physical and cultural complexity produces a more nuanced understanding of its place in human history.

Since the new relationships between urbanites and the natural world emerged from specific social and environmental contexts, I have chosen to focus on several closely analyzed case studies. Early chapters explore how Bostonians transformed Boston Common from a pasture into the first public park, created one of the earliest city-wide waterworks, and helped to invent that enduring residential ideal, the pastoral suburb. Later chapters trace how Bostonians used innovative means to control the city's coastline, rivers, and harbor, and pioneered a new kind of suburban park system that preserved natural areas and provided a matrix for future development. Individually, each chapter details the creation of a familiar building block of the modern metropolis from a less familiar environmental perspective. Together, the chapters provide a topical and loosely chronological journey through the century-long process of city building, tracing through their stories the gradual accumulation of the relationships to nature that make up metropolitan life.

These chapters do not cover the full extent of this enormous transition. Only a volume of monumental size and scope could contain the entire story. But the relationships that I have chosen to highlight have either become central to urban life across a broad swath of American cities or are particularly revealing. Several also represent new stories about environmental change in Boston itself. The removal of the cows from Boston Common, the battles to annex the city's suburbs, the transformation of the harbor—all represent underexplored pieces of Boston's past that played major roles in its development. Of course, emphasizing some transitions necessarily means deemphasizing others. In making such choices, I was guided by the historical questions I was seeking to answer and by the history of Boston itself. The reason, for example, that I do not explore more fully the new ways of interacting with nature created by the rise of the factory system is that Boston industrialized a full generation after its neighbor, Lowell, and did not directly experience the earliest formation of those relationships. The chapters, then, strive to be true to Boston's distinctive history, and they find unity in thematic connections rather than topical coverage.

As the chapter topics suggest, I am treating Boston as both a discrete political entity that is separate from its suburbs and a more nebulous cultural and environmental region that includes them. This seemingly paradoxical characterization simply reflects the fact that cities have many different kinds of boundaries, and their political boundaries are usually different from their environmental and cultural boundaries. Where Boston's political control stops at very clear municipal lines that are traceable on a map, its environmental connections and cultural influence extend over a much larger area. Excluding Boston's suburbs from its environmental history just because they fall outside of its political boundaries would therefore be just as shortsighted as omitting Ralph Waldo Emerson from a cultural history of Boston because he lived in Concord.

Although my primary goal is to shed light on the historical relationship between nature and cities, I also remain fascinated by the history of Boston itself. As a native of the Boston area, I know firsthand that the city's past is always present, not just in countless monuments and historical markers but also in its sense of identity. In an age of cultural homogenization on a global scale, Boston has managed to retain an impressive measure of continuity with its past. The old adage that Boston is a "state of mind," a particular way of thinking, still resonates today. But it was never more relevant than in the nineteenth century, when Bostonians applied their distinctive state of mind to the creation of a distinctive city.

If we consider how much we are nature's, we need not be superstitious about towns, as if that terrific or bene-fic force did not find us there also, and fashion cities. Nature, who made the mason, made the house.

RALPH WALDO EMERSON (1844)

To Build a City

The life of Edward Everett Hale spanned much of the nineteenth century, and the older the noted author and minister got, the more he marveled at the changes to the natural world produced by the growth of Boston. Born on the corner of Tremont and School streets in 1822, the elderly Hale remembered the Boston of his childhood as "a large, pretty country town." His memory of free-standing homes with large gardens and orchards stood in sharp contrast to the brownstones and business blocks that he had watched replace them. Hale wondered whether people might now "buy their thread and needles, perhaps, where I have picked and eaten pears, or have aimed my arrow at a target a hundred yards away." The younger Boston had also been a city of hills, almost all of which had since been leveled. "Fort Hill has been entirely removed," Hale observed, "and a little circular bit of greensward marks the place where, in my boyhood, was a hill fifty feet high." As Bostonians were taking down the hills, they were using the excavated material to make new land by filling tidal flats. The neighborhood that Hale and his parishioners called home stood on ground where the sea had ebbed and flowed only a few years before. "I have sailed my bark boat on the salt waters where I now can sit in the parlors of my parishioners," Hale recalled. "I have studied botany on the marshes where I now sit in my own study."[1]

Rather than being unique to Boston, such wholesale rearrangements of the natural world lay at the heart of the nation's first great period of city building. In the same century, Chicagoans reversed the flow of their city's river so that it ran away from, rather than toward, Lake Michigan; the residents of Pittsburgh raised parts of their city by as much as ten feet to improve drainage; and the citizens of New Orleans surrounded their city with miles of earthen levies to hold back the waters of the Mississippi River and Lake Pontchartrain. Such changes might seem extraordinary when considered one city at a time, but taken as a whole they were routine. Across America, the building of cities promoted a complete restructuring of the natural world to accommodate larger populations and to fulfill new social and economic goals. Environmental change of this magnitude created the understandable impression among many Americans that a city is a place separate from nature, a place where the built environment has replaced the natural one. The educator Henry Tappan made the point succinctly in 1852 when he wrote: "Life in a great city is, at best, a war with nature."[2]

The result of all this environmental change, however, was not the severing of human relationships with the natural world but the production of new ones. In 1800, when Boston had a population of just 25,000 people clustered on the northeast side of its peninsula, its residents interacted with the natural world in ways that were largely rural, or at least pre-urban. Bostonians combined labor and leisure on Boston Common, grazing cows and beating carpets in the same space where they took strolls and admired the view. They provided their own water for drinking, cooking, and cleaning by pulling it from a well, if they had access to one, or buying it from a vendor. They made new land by filling tidal flats, with no fear of damaging the gigantic natural harbor and without any scientific understanding of how its hydraulics worked. They altered their physical environment constantly, with the expectation that what they had just created would itself someday be replaced. And the residents of the small towns surrounding Boston organized their lives around agriculture and husbandry and were not "suburban" in any modern sense of the word.[3]

By 1900, with the population at 560,000 and the city's political boundaries greatly expanded, Bostonians had established a radically different set of relationships to nature. They had banished labor from their Common and created a number of other green spaces devoted exclusively to leisure pursuits. They had exchanged well water for lake water piped directly into their homes, and they treated it as a right to be provided by government, rather than a privilege. They had learned to see their harbor through the lens of science, which they used to make dramatic changes in Boston's estuary. They had come to appreciate the value of environmental permanence and had preserved thousands of acres of open land from development. And many of them had moved out of Boston proper into nearby suburbs to live a romanticized and recreational version of country life. Through these and other transformations, Boston had become a modern metropolis, not just in its political and economic relationships but in its environmental ones as well.[4]

Since Boston urbanized very early by American standards, it helped to invent many of the places and systems that would structure these new relationships. After removal of the cows from Boston Common in 1830, the Common became the first public park in America devoted entirely to recreation. Mount Auburn Cemetery in nearby Cambridge was the first rural cemetery when it opened in 1832, and Boston's water system and suburbs emerged early enough to provide models for many other urbanizing communities. Later in the century, the city established the first metropolitan sewage system and the first suburban forest preserves, and it dug deep beneath Boston Common to construct the nation's first subway. The new ways of relating to the natural environment expressed through these places and systems remind us that cities did not replace nature as they expanded. Rather, city building was a process that not only altered the natural environment but also revolutionized the relationships to it that supported communities and their inhabitants. People still interacted with nature, but in fundamentally different ways.[5]

The transformation of the relationship between Bostonians and

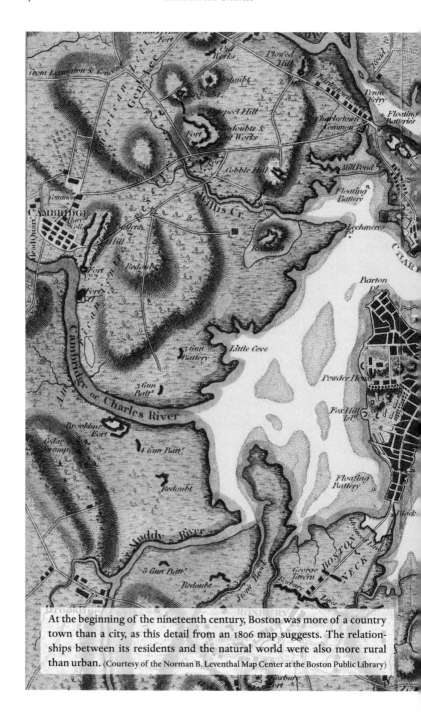

At the beginning of the nineteenth century, Boston was more of a country town than a city, as this detail from an 1806 map suggests. The relationships between its residents and the natural world were also more rural than urban. (Courtesy of the Norman B. Leventhal Map Center at the Boston Public Library)

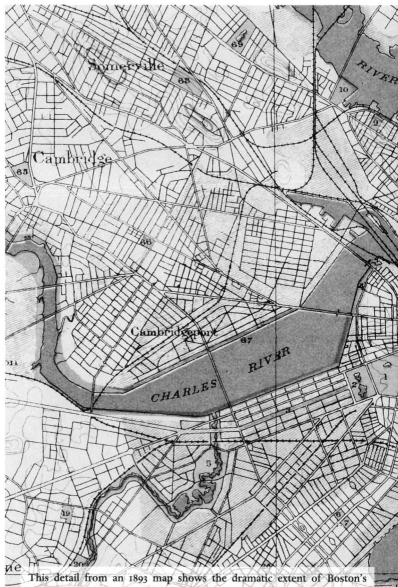

This detail from an 1893 map shows the dramatic extent of Boston's growth by the end of the nineteenth century and the incredible degree to which its natural environment had been transformed. Yet the relationships between Bostonians and the natural world around them had not ended. They had, rather, assumed new forms. (Author's collection)

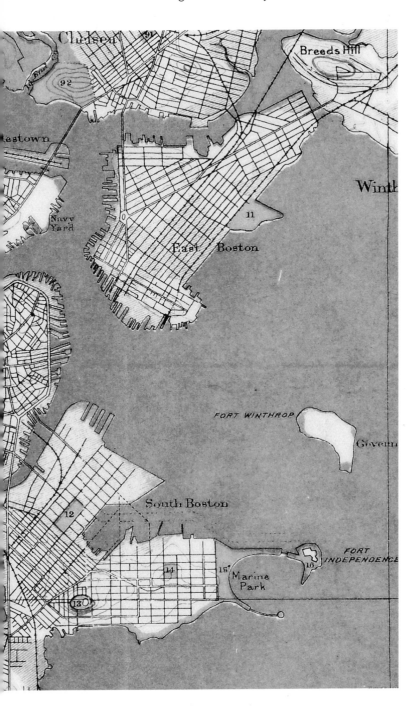

the natural world paralleled that of other cities in many important respects. But Boston also evolved in distinctive ways. When Bostonians got rid of their cows, they preserved rather than developed their common land; they chose a public water system when many other cities were building private ones; and they made more new land along their city's coast than any other city in America. Bostonians also worked to structure regional growth by building suburban parks and parkways long before other American cities were engaged in metropolitan planning. Yet, at the same time, the city failed to absorb its suburbs as many other large cities did and was left penned in by fiercely independent towns that feared the loss of their rural charm. Bostonians confronted many of the same environmental challenges as other cities, but they often handled those challenges differently and reshaped their city's natural environment and their relationships to it in unique ways. To discover why Bostonians made the choices they did, we have to probe beyond the standard narratives of urbanization in nineteenth-century America and look more deeply into the nature of city building.

The Nature of Boston

The new relationships that Bostonians developed with nature emerged in part from the natural environment itself, which traced many of its characteristic features to the end of the last Ice Age about 14,000 years ago. Having scoured existing hills and valleys on their way south from the pole, the glaciers withdrew to the northwest and left a changed world behind them. The melting ice produced enormous amounts of water that fed new ponds, lakes, and rivers, and it released the vast quantities of sand, gravel, and stone that gave northeastern Massachusetts the rocky soil that would later become the bane of area farmers. Boston was founded on a postglacial landscape that still exists today: after centuries of human development, the Boston area remains covered with hills called "drumlins" that are composed of glacial till and are oriented in the direction of the retreating glaciers. Among them are Breeds Hill, Bunker Hill, and Dorchester Heights, all of which are well known in American history for the roles they played in the Revolution but have natural histories that extend far deeper into the past. Even the islands of Boston Harbor, which seem to float serenely on the water's surface, are actually glacial drumlins that poke their heads above an otherwise submerged landscape.[6]

Once the ice was gone and the sea level had stabilized, the Boston region took on the shape that the first European settlers would encounter. They found a broad plain bordered by rocky hills on three sides and the ocean on the fourth. Four rivers drained what geologists now call the Boston Basin: the Charles, Mystic, Neponset, and Saugus. Within the basin were oyster beds and alewife runs, dense forests and open fields, small brooks and wide rivers, bear dens and beaver lodges, low-lying wetlands and lofty hills, and a dizzying variety of other landscapes and kinds of life. Boston's first settlers found themselves endowed with a natural environment that would both challenge and enrich them for generations to come.[7]

They would also find a climate that could tend toward extremes. "Who lives one year in Boston," claimed Ralph Waldo Emerson, "ranges through all the climates of the globe." At least it felt that way to locals. Emerson described Boston's weather as varying from "the splendor of the equator and a touch of Syria" to "a cold which approaches the temperature of the celestial spaces." But he also believed that such extremes had proven a blessing for Bostonians by giving them their distinctive character. Faced with a challenging climate, according to Emerson, they had developed a superior sense of ambition, a larger range of abilities, and a greater measure of wisdom than people who lived in more "luxurious" climates. For Emerson, as for many of his contemporaries, nature could shape society just as surely as society could shape nature.[8]

Natural forces had given Boston's environment its basic outline, but the first English settlers were not entering a landscape untouched by human hands. Rather, the area's Native American residents had been managing the natural environment to their own ends for thousands of years. They shaped the soil by growing corn, beans, and squash, manipulated the animal population by hunting deer, bear, and beaver, and influenced the fish population by using weirs to trap flounder, eels, and herring. Perhaps the most visible environmental imprint left by the Indians was a patchwork landscape of open and forested areas created through selective burning. The Indians used fire to clear land for farming and to encourage new plant growth that attracted deer. The results were plainly visible to the first settlers. "Though all the country be as it were a thick wood for the general," wrote Francis Higginson in 1630, "yet in divers places there is much ground cleared by the Indians." After European diseases decimated the Indian population, the English settlers became the beneficiaries of this subtly tended landscape. They built their towns on the sites of former Indian villages, planted their crops on abandoned Indian fields, and hunted animals that were attracted to the edge environments created by Indian burning. Rather than walking into a New World prepared by God for their errand into the wilderness, the Puritans walked into an old world groomed by the Indians to maximize environmental abundance.[9]

Near the center of the Boston Basin and jutting out into the harbor lay the Shawmut Peninsula, the clover-shaped piece of land that the Puritan settlers made their home in 1630. It was small—a little more than a square mile in extent—and was occasionally reduced to an island when storm tides overcame the narrow neck connecting it to the mainland. Five hills dotted a well-watered landscape that was largely clear of trees. Anne Pollard, who as a girl was the first of John Winthrop's group to set foot on the peninsula, remembered it many years later as "very uneven, abounding in small hollows and swamps, covered with blueberries and other bushes." The western side of the peninsula fronted on the Charles River, which snaked its way into the countryside, and the eastern side faced a well sheltered harbor that opened onto the sea. It was the best site in the whole region for a city, Emerson would observe over two centuries later, located "at the bottom of a deep and islanded bay, where a copious river entered it, and where a bold shore was bounded by a country of rich and undulating woodland."[10]

The area's natural environment began shaping the lives of its new residents from the moment they stepped off their ships. In fact, the scarcity of a key natural resource prompted an early change of locale that would forever alter the region's destiny. The group of Puritans that entered Boston harbor settled first not on the Shaw-mut Peninsula but on a site just across the Charles River that would become Charlestown. Shawmut, however, had superior water sup-plies—its name, in fact, meant "living fountains" in the Algonquin language. So about three months after landing, Winthrop and his followers crossed the Charles and re-founded the future metropolis of New England on a secondary site. But the influence of local envi-ronmental conditions did not stop there. Since the new site had few trees, the settlers were forced to hunt for wood on the mainland and harbor islands, and since the peninsula was almost entirely sur-rounded by water, they were compelled to establish a ferry service the year after they landed. It was the exceptional harbor, however, that made the largest impact on the community. The harbor made it possible for Boston to engage from a very early date in a lucrative coastal trade and an international market in fish and furs, with Win-throp building one of the first oceangoing vessels in America just a year after arriving.[11]

Even as Boston began its rapid growth in the nineteenth century, its residents never escaped the need to accommodate themselves to the area's particular natural setting. At every turn, Bostonians found both environmental advantages and disadvantages. The gentle slope of the tidal flats surrounding the city made them easy to fill, but that same slope also made it difficult to drain sewage away from neighborhoods. The harbor was perfectly suited to accommodate early seagoing vessels, but it required substantial dredging to service the huge ships that became the norm in later years. The abundant ground water made it possible to settle the peninsula, but the lack of adequate surface sources prompted a crisis when the ground water became polluted. The Charles and Mystic Rivers gave Boston water access to nearby communities, but neither one was long or deep enough to make the city master of a substantial hinterland. Boston's natural environment could be both an asset and a liability, but in either role it exerted a powerful influence on the city's development.[12]

As the city expanded over the Shawmut Peninsula and beyond its own political boundaries, it continued to encounter far less developed regions that were rural and sometimes wild. The urbanization of Boston's natural environment is therefore, in part, a story about border regions that gradually fell into the path of the growing city. Over time, remote agricultural fields, remnant stands of forest, and outlying tidal flats became attractive places to develop. Each would offer its own set of environmental advantages and limitations, and each would influence how Bostonians eventually shaped them. The natural world did not determine the area's history all by itself, of course, but it was hardly a passive stage on which the pageant of urban growth played out.

The Boston Ideal

If part of the explanation for how Bostonians developed new relationships with nature rests with the peculiarities of the natural world, another part lies in the distinctive characteristics of Boston's social world. To some extent, the city's residents were motivated by the same quest for status, power, and wealth as other Americans. Trying to draw sharp distinctions between Bostonians and the residents of other cities can therefore be a tricky business and has led different observers to opposite conclusions. Where Emerson considered Bostonians to be more driven toward success than other

Americans, Charles Dickens found the opposite to be the case. "The golden calf they worship at Boston," he noted during a visit in 1842, "is a pygmy compared with the giant effigies set up in other parts of that vast counting-house which lies beyond the Atlantic." Both descriptions might have contained some truth, or neither. The forces that drove Bostonians as a community remain difficult to disentangle from the capitalist ambitions that infused so much of nineteenth-century America.[13]

But Bostonians pursued those ambitions within a unique framework of values that illuminates some of the most serious tensions in the city's social landscape. Alone among America's urbanizing populations, Bostonians believed they had a divinely-sanctioned destiny to create a model community, one that would provide an inspiring example to others. This goal preceded the actual founding of the city. When Winthrop was leading his seven hundred Puritan followers across the Atlantic, he delivered the now famous sermon aboard the *Arbella* that articulated the sense of mission already felt by the group of dissenters. Drawing his imagery from the Sermon on the Mount, Winthrop advised the assembly that "we must consider that we shall be as a city upon a hill. The eyes of all people are upon us." He expected to build a community based on brotherly love, one whose members "must bear one another's burdens." That biblically based injunction to create an ideal Christian commonwealth lent Bostonians a sense of purpose that lasted long after Winthrop's Puritan faith had faded away. The meaning of that mission would change over the centuries, but even today Bostonians continue to use the metaphor as a yardstick for measuring their social and moral condition.[14]

The city's sense of purpose evolved in a more political direction when Boston played a leading role in the American Revolution, and it became more cultural in the early nineteenth century. Beginning about 1815, the city experienced an intellectual and literary flowering that led locals to dub it the "Athens of America" and the "hub of the solar system." One of Boston's most breathless proponents was Bronson Alcott, who migrated to the city from Connecticut in 1828. "There is a city in our world," he wrote shortly after his arrival, "upon which the light of the sun of righteousness has risen . . . It is the same from which every pure stream of thought and purpose and performance emanates. It is the city that is set on high. 'It cannot be hid.' It is Boston." If Alcott's enthusiasm seems a bit overwrought, it was nevertheless genuine and reflected the city's very real accomplishments in thought and learning. It also represented the widespread belief among Bostonians that the city was well on the path toward achieving its exalted destiny. Even Emerson, who had no love for cities in general or Boston in particular, considered Boston to have a preordained mission. "I do not speak with any fondness," he wrote in 1861, "but the language of coldest history, when I say that Boston commands attention as the town which was appointed in the destiny of nations to lead the civilization of North America." This sureness of purpose, this desire to create a model city, lay at the very heart of Boston's identity as a community.[15]

The problem was that the ideal society looked different to different people. From the very beginning, the effort to create a "city upon a hill" that everyone could agree on contained two important tensions that shaped Boston's social landscape and its future environmental relationships. The first was a conflict between the individual and the community. Although Winthrop had insisted aboard the *Arbella* that "the care of the public must oversway all private respects," the Puritan leadership found that keeping the settlers focused on common goals was often their greatest challenge. By the nineteenth-century, this tension had evolved into a struggle between private rights and the public good for control over ongoing environmental change. Urban historians have argued that a "culture of privatism"—the pursuit of individualism and personal wealth over broader, community-oriented goals—was one of the most powerful forces structuring American cities in the nineteenth century, and

Boston was no exception. Yet its residents pushed back harder than in other cities, perhaps because the spirit of reform that had brought the dissenting Puritans to America still flowed through their veins. Throughout the century, Boston consistently led the nation in developing progressive instruments of social and environmental reform, such as parks, model tenement houses, playgrounds, and water and sewer systems. The tension between individual and community was therefore particularly strong in Boston. As a result, the Reverend Theodore Parker believed that the battle to remake America by replacing selfishness with cooperation would be fought in the capital of New England, "for here the two extremes meet in closest contact, in sternest strife."[16]

The forces of government often mediated between public and private interests and played a leading role in structuring new environmental relationships across urban America. As the nineteenth century progressed, cities grew into larger and more complex entities that required closer management. In response, state and municipal governments acquired new powers and became more willing to regulate resources, build expensive infrastructure, seize private land for public purposes, and alter municipal boundaries to achieve larger goals. Governments in the Boston area often led the way in developing new institutions for managing environmental resources like tidal flats, water supplies, and open space, and they sometimes engaged directly in large-scale development projects. As early as the 1820s, Boston's government spearheaded the landmaking and construction that produced the publicly owned Quincy Market, and by the 1850s the state was overseeing the filling of the Back Bay and the building of a residential neighborhood on the new land. Projects like these lay beyond the traditional sphere of American government and fueled debates about the proper line between private and public activity. Yet wherever one looked—for better and for worse—the region's governmental leaders were actively involved in restructuring how Bostonians related to the natural world.[17]

The other major tension over what a "city upon a hill" should look like developed between competing social and economic classes. Winthrop had anticipated this problem as well. For all its appeals to Christian love and brotherhood, his message aboard the *Arbella* was also a plea to his followers to subject themselves to the authority of their leaders, who generally enjoyed higher status and greater affluence. The connection between class and power had changed little by the early nineteenth century, when Boston's leadership consisted of a tightly knit group of families that controlled the community's wealth, culture, and politics. Later dubbed the "Brahmins" by Oliver Wendell Holmes, this group contended with the developing middle and working classes for control over environmental resources, and tensions among the three groups infused virtually any attempt to change the urban environment. Debates over abolishing the right to graze cows on Boston Common, building on the newly-filled Back Bay, annexing growing suburban towns to Boston—all were influenced by class. The groups involved were not monolithic in their thinking, however, so that tensions within classes were almost as common as tensions between them. Members of the city's first families, for example, could often be found on opposite sides of an issue.[18]

The coming of the Irish to Boston gave existing class tensions an ethnic dimension that many feared might permanently divert the city from its path to perfection. From a trickle in the 1820s to a torrent in the 1840s, Irish immigration brought thousands of rural peasants into an urban world. Some native-born Protestants, like Edward Everett Hale, considered Irish Catholics to be the victims of British governmental policy and deserving of Christian sympathy and care. "We are," he wrote, "or ought to be, welcoming these last wrecks of so many centuries of retreat." Most others resented the Irish, sometimes enough to meet the newcomers with violence. Yet the flood of immigrants continued unabated. Just ten years after Ireland's potato famine of 1845, a third of Boston's inhabitants were

Irish. By the end of the century, the city's Yankee population found itself outnumbered nearly three to one by people of other ethnic backgrounds. In time, the Irish would challenge the political authority of the Yankee elite and by the early twentieth century had wrested the city government from its hands.[19]

This complicated social and political landscape ensured that whenever Bostonians tried to reshape the natural environment in order to build their city upon a hill, they always ran into the question of *whose* city upon a hill they were building. Battles between private and public interests and competing classes and ethnic groups invariably ensued, and it was no accident that the victors reaped not only the social, political, and economic rewards but the environmental ones as well. Throughout the century, Boston's wealthy lived in cleaner, better drained streets and had easier access to pure drinking water and recreational nature. Power had always structured environmental relationships, and it would continue to do so as America urbanized in the nineteenth century. "What we call Man's power over Nature," C. S. Lewis famously wrote, "turns out to be a power exercised by some men over other men with Nature as its instrument." Power over people and power over nature often turned out to be the same thing.[20]

State of Nature, State of Mind

The tensions inherent in the Boston ideal found a powerful outlet in social constructions of nature, which provide a critical third piece in explaining why the residents of Boston created the new environmental relationships that they did. Ideas about nature, as ethereal as they might seem at first glance, have a very real impact. Just like ideas about race, class, and gender, they represent important frames for structuring social thought, refract all kinds of other attitudes about the human condition, and deeply inform the ways in which we interact with the world around us. Yet it remains tempting to dismiss those who justify their causes through appeals to nature as using empty rhetoric, as not really meaning what they say. Sincerity of conviction, however, is not the point. Complex ideas, whether utilitarian or not, emerge from real social situations, and the importance of such ideas should be judged less by the integrity of their adherents and more by the extent to which they influence events. Ideas are not all-powerful, and they sometimes come laden with politics that we might not like, but they have undoubtedly played a major role in determining how we shape our environments. Emerson might have pushed the point even harder. "Nature is the incarnation of a thought, and turns to a thought again, as ice becomes water and gas," he wrote. "The world is mind precipitated." Even if he was only partly right, it becomes essential to understand the ideas about nature that Bostonians applied to the building of their city.[21]

The key lies in understanding that ideas about nature were never about the natural world alone but were always about human society as well. Any part of the natural world, or even the concept of "nature" itself, could be imbued with meanings about progress, community, democracy, science, reform, morality, social obligation, and much more. Pilgrim leader William Bradford's reaction in 1620 upon seeing the land that surrounded Massachusetts Bay—he called it "a hideous and desolate wilderness"—therefore tells us as much about the social world that he brought with him to America as it does about the place he was actually laying eyes on. Bradford's inclination to see the landscape of the Boston area as an embodiment of physical chaos was shaped by negative images of wilderness inherited from classical literature, European folklore, and the Judaeo-Christian tradition. It also reflected an anticipatory hostility toward the "wild men" that Bradford expected to meet. The wilderness that the first settlers encountered was therefore partly of their own creation.[22]

The social underpinnings of ideas about nature stand out in even sharper relief when one considers that not all of the early settlers to Massachusetts Bay saw the same thing when they looked at its landscape. Where Bradford and his Pilgrim followers perceived "a hideous and desolate wilderness," their neighbor and critic Thomas Morton saw "Nature's Masterpiece." "The more I looked," he wrote, "the more I liked it." Morton's more favorable interpretation reflected a different social agenda, one that rejected Puritan ideology and accepted a higher degree of integration with the local Indian population. The meanings that Bradford, Morton, and subsequent generations found in nature therefore contained much that was human, and Boston's best thinkers knew this well by the nineteenth century. "Say what some poets will," wrote Herman Melville from his home in western Massachusetts, "Nature is not so much her own ever-sweet interpreter, as the mere supplier of that cunning alphabet, whereby selecting and combining as he pleases, each man reads his own peculiar lesson according to his own peculiar mind and mood."[23]

Ideas of nature, and the social goals that infused them, became central to the building of Boston. Every time Bostonians moved toward a new relationship with a particular natural environment or facet of the natural world, they structured the relationship using ideas about nature that reflected the competing ambitions embedded in the Boston ideal. When, for example, Boston's residents debated whether to build a privately owned waterworks or a public system, they argued heatedly about the meaning of water. To some, fresh water was a "gift from God" and therefore a common resource to which all citizens had a right; to others it was simply a commodity like any other to be sold at market rates; and to still others it embodied all the wholesome powers of the natural world and offered a promising vehicle of social reform. Social goals and constructions of nature were deeply entwined in these different positions, and each standpoint suggested not only a different kind of water system but a different city upon a hill. The environmental relationships that emerged from such conflicts were therefore products of their time not only politically and technologically but socially and culturally as well. They could not have been created in these particular forms at any other historical moment.[24]

But ideas about nature are not only products of human culture. They have roots in the natural world as well, because the physical environment provides the stimulus to which people react. Simple town commons inspired some of the mystical experiences that transformed how Emerson thought about nature, and the heavily wooded Middlesex Fells in suburban Medford instilled a love of wild places in the young Francis Parkman that later found expression in his famous histories of the North American forest. Even within the more developed landscape of the city itself, Bostonians found their mental worlds reshaped by the physical nature they encountered. "We all carry the Common in our heads as the unit of space," confessed Oliver Wendell Holmes in 1861. The natural environment therefore played a role in the construction of its own meaning, giving nature a certain amount of agency in shaping human actions and intentions.[25]

Edward Everett Hale, the author and minister who lived to see a city emerge where a country town had once been, was himself engaged in applying ideas about nature to the restructuring of Boston's environmental relationships. As a prolific writer and a prominent reformer, Hale tackled a variety of social and environmental issues around the city. He employed contemporary scientific thought about water flow, for example, to warn that making too much land on coastal flats might eventually damage the harbor, and he drew on romantic ideas about rural nature to create detailed plans for building affordable working-class homes on undeveloped suburban land. In general, Hale combined ideas about nature with his social reform agenda to argue for environmental relationships that considered long-term needs, recognized environmental constraints, and spread environmental benefits to all classes.[26]

Yet despite his participation in a number of debates, Hale touched on only a small fraction of the battles for control over Boston's natural environment that pitted competing social and environmental visions against each other. The stakes were often high, with the outcomes determining where people lived, who had access to pure drinking water, and where the political boundaries of Boston ended and its suburbs began. Other conflicts would reshape the city's coastline and guide development in the larger metropolitan area. The social battles in which Hale and his contemporaries engaged, and the ideas about nature that they used to fight them, would be recorded in the new relationships that nineteenth-century Bostonians developed with the natural world, relationships that would come to define life in the city upon a hill.

Enclosing the Common

lthough modern Boston is filled with places that evoke the past, no part of the city seems quite as timeless as Boston Common. Its mature trees and peaceful pond appear to preserve a bit of Boston's environment just as the first settlers might have seen it. But looks can be deceiving. Not only is the Common's environment a product of the nineteenth century, so is the way that we relate to it today. The modern Common is exclusively a place of recreation, a stretch of green where Bostonians can sit on a bench, lie under a tree, walk along a path, or otherwise escape the demands of the working world. The Common of the early nineteenth century, however, was also a place of labor. Although many Bostonians at the time did enjoy strolling along its tree-lined edges, they also used its open fields for such decidedly unplayful pursuits as shaking carpets, training militias, and grazing cows. The dusty air, trampled turf, and animal droppings produced by these activities were as much a part of the Common for contemporaries as the grass and trees. Labor and leisure coexisted on Boston Common, just as they did in nearby neighborhoods where journeymen and apprentices both worked and lived in a master artisan's house. It would have been far more unusual if Bostonians had related to such a large urban green space through purely recreational pursuits. What we understand today as a public park did not exist in America at the time.

At the beginning of the century, the Common's natural characteristics did not seem to encourage one kind of activity over the other. A largely treeless expanse in the sparsely-developed west end of Boston's peninsula, the Common contained about fifty acres and had five unequal sides that gave it an irregular shape. Beacon Hill bordered it on the north, Boylston Street on the south, Park and Common (now Tremont) Streets on the east, and the shallow waters of the Back Bay on the west. Several low hills interspersed with small ponds gave the landscape a rolling quality as it sloped gently toward the Back Bay. Only one tree of any note stood in the whole interior expanse of the Common, the Old Elm, which rested near the center and was said to predate the first English settlers. The Common's open space made it a perfect pasture, and that same openness created the views over the Back Bay that made the edges of the Common such pleasant places to stroll. In the eighteenth and early nineteenth centuries, visitors were just as likely to praise the Common's usefulness as grazing land as to admire its attractiveness as a leisure space. The Common lent itself to both.

Transforming the relationship between Bostonians and their Common would require not only a change in land use but a re-imagining of the land's meaning. Many Bostonians, particularly the laboring classes, clung to a traditional interpretation of the Common embedded in the English common lands tradition. In this view, Boston Common was foremost a landscape of work where residents had an established legal right to graze their cows that dated back to the purchase of the Common in 1634. Since the pasture provided an important source of fresh milk to residents who owned a cow, extinguishing the right of pasturage—or "enclosing" the Common —would be a serious matter. By the early nineteenth century, however, wealthier Americans were widening the distance between their businesses and homes. They were also developing a preference for a more recreational relationship to natural landscapes, one that reinforced their social status by emphasizing leisure over labor. As a result, many upper-class Bostonians came to believe that productive activities like the grazing of cows were inhibiting their ability to enjoy the Common and making the space less refined. Pressure mounted throughout the 1820s to trade traditional grazing rights for the cultural cachet of a pastoral playground. When the movement finally succeeded, it transformed the way that Bostonians related to the city's most prominent green space. It also created something entirely new: America's first public park.[1]

Boston Common as Common Land

Boston Common entered the expanding world of English colonial settlement as private rather than public land. When Winthrop and the first wave of Puritans arrived on the Charlestown Peninsula, the neighboring Shawmut Peninsula was already occupied by a single inhabitant. The Reverend William Blackstone had been part of an earlier and failed English settlement on the southern shore of Massachusetts Bay, and he had wandered northward to the slope of Beacon Hill where he built a cottage, planted an orchard, and lived a solitary life. Five years later, when the Puritans began building their settlement across the Charles River, Blackstone invited them to join him on the Shawmut Peninsula to take advantage of its better water supply. He retained his house and a fifty-acre parcel of land, but after living with his new neighbors for four years, Blackstone decided to leave for less crowded ground in Rhode Island. In 1634, he sold most of his land as a single parcel to the settlers, who purchased it as a common pasture and military training field. This parcel became Boston Common.[2]

The relationship that the settlers established with this area was rooted in a centuries-old English common land system that regulated access to productive natural resources like pastures and woodlands. The character of common rights varied widely in England depending on the community and the resource in question, but they could include the right to graze animals, dig for stones or sand, take wood from a forest, remove turf, or catch fish. To prevent overexploitation of a particular resource, many communities restricted access to those people with a legitimate right in common, and limited use to personal rather than commercial purposes. If a resource was large enough, commoners might also permit those without common rights to use it. Such close management was essential, for the economy of an entire village might depend on the prudent use of its common lands.[3]

Access to a common was a legally protected property right in England, although it did not imply ownership of the actual resource. Rural lords or municipalities held title to the common, while certain property owners or renters enjoyed carefully defined uses. Such use rights did not adhere to a commoner but rather to his property, perhaps a nearby house with some land, and could not be sold or transferred separately from that property. The actual ownership of the common resource was therefore not absolute. A lord or municipality typically needed the consent of the commoners or an Act of Parliament to sell, develop, or cultivate common land.[4]

The Puritans carried the idea of common land from Old England to New England and used it to create a distinctive common land regime that influenced land use as far away as Long Island and northern New Jersey. The first English settlers, sometimes called "commoners" but more often "proprietors," initially owned all property in a given land grant as a group. They divided some of it among themselves, kept some for common use, and reserved other areas for future settlers. In the early years, to be a proprietor or a resident of a town was more or less the same thing, and decisions about common lands were made in town meetings. But as immigration increased and land became more valuable, proprietors stopped admitting new people into their select group and began guarding their rights more closely. In Boston, the freemen voted in 1646 to bar future residents from access to common land unless the newcomers rented or purchased the right from an existing commoner. The restrictions lasted until 1672, when a new vote extended the right of commonage to all residents of the town. After that, the power to regulate Boston's common lands was invested in the collected citizenry when assembled in town meeting. Common rights neverthe-

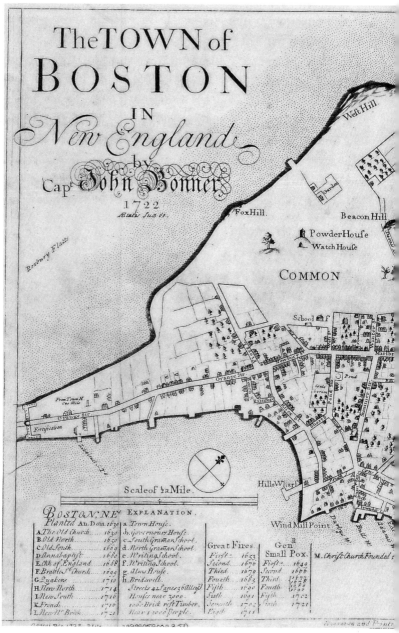

Boston Common, which appears on the upper left in this 1722 map, was originally on the western shore of the Shawmut Peninsula. The areas surrounding it

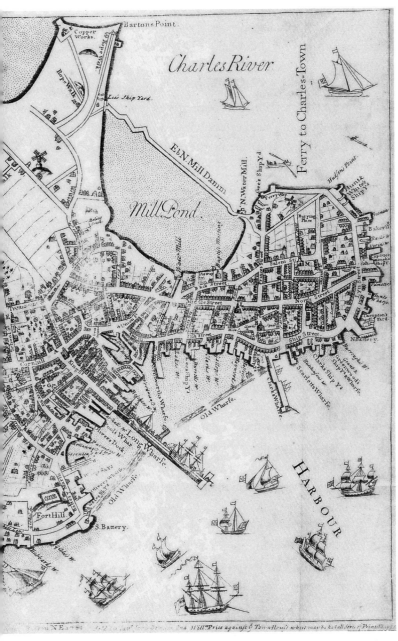

tended to develop later than other parts of Boston because they faced away from the sea. (Courtesy of the Norman B. Leventhal Map Center at the Boston Public Library)

less remained a valuable property right, with Boston's early settlers routinely buying and selling the right to pasture a cow on the
Common.[5]

Not all of the first settlers liked the idea of keeping land in common, however. In fact, Boston Common barely survived an early debate over the balance between public and private resources in the
new city upon a hill. In December 1634, just a few weeks after purchasing the land, the voting inhabitants of Boston selected a committee of seven to divide some of the town's property and assign
the parcels to particular families. To the surprise and consterna-
tion of the community's leading members, the inhabitants excluded
most of them from the committee. With the exception of a deacon
and one of the elders, the committee was composed of men "of the
inferior sort," as Governor John Winthrop reported. "This they did,"
he wrote, "as fearing that the richer men would give the poorer sort
no great proportions of land, but would rather leave a great part at
liberty for new comers and for common." The suspicions of the voters were well founded. With an eye to the needs of future settlers,
Winthrop had been a strong advocate of giving existing residents no
more land than they could work. After the Reverend John Cotton
convinced the assembly that God intended the elders to make such
decisions, the inhabitants scheduled a new election where they
chose a more balanced committee. Winthrop's views prevailed, and
Boston Common remained in the public realm.[6]

Mixing Work and Play

In its early years, the Common supported a wide variety of productive uses that reinforced its role as a landscape of labor. With special
permission from the selectmen, the residents of Boston could dig
clay and gravel from its Fox Hill section, build windmills on its high
points, and remove stones for use in building. In the late seventeenth
and early eighteenth centuries, the town constructed a complex of
municipal buildings on the eastern end of the Common that in-

cluded an almshouse, powderhouse, pound, prison, granary, and workhouse, and it used part of the Common as cemetery space. Women did their weekly washing under the Old Elm, first drawing water from the Common's Frog Pond and then heating it over a fire. The selectmen banned most forms of resource extraction as the town grew, but by the early nineteenth century the cleaning of carpets, grazing of cows, and drilling of militias still continued as daily evidence of the labor that had always defined the Common.[7]

The grazing of cows was one of the Common's earliest and most important productive uses, and the selectmen made regulating the animals and protecting the grass a priority. Over the years, the number of animals ranged from fifty to two hundred, and the selectmen restricted Bostonians to the grazing of only one cow per family from early spring to late fall. They also banned horses, sheep, and dry cattle from the pasture. The restrictions protected the pasture from overgrazing, ensured that residents used the Common for subsistence rather than commercial purposes, and reserved the space for milk cows. The selectmen watched nearby construction closely to ensure that no damage occurred to the grass, and they ordered the building of wooden fences to prevent carts and horses from trampling the turf. To help pay for improvements, the selectmen instituted a cow tax as early as 1638 that required anyone with cows pastured on the Common to pay a fixed tax per head. Residents were still paying a tax and grazing their cows as late as the 1820s.[8]

The presence of domesticated animals in a large and growing town was not unusual. In fact, the streets of most American cities served as a kind of "urban commons" well into the nineteenth century. Many Bostonians bypassed the Common and its cow tax by simply letting their cows wander the streets to snack on any tuft of grass they could find and any garden they could raid. In New York, the laboring classes routinely released their pigs into the streets to root through garbage, just as their country cousins let their pigs loose in the woods to search for acorns. Urbanizing America was still relating to its domesticated animals in a manner that was more reminiscent of the country than the city.[9]

In contrast to the chaotic urban common of Boston's streets, the Common was a heavily managed pasture and the site of constant labor from spring to fall. Residents of the workhouse spread extra dirt where needed to keep the turf in good order, and workers dredged the Common's small ponds to ensure adequate drinking water for the cows. A cowkeeper employed by the town monitored the cows and the bulls that the town kept for breeding purposes and had the unenviable job of collecting the cow tax. The owners of the cows led the animals each day from home to pasture and back again, a job often delegated to children. But the cows performed the most work of all. They grazed all day and did the biological labor of turning grass into milk. The process of making that milk relied on a highly structured system that integrated public and private needs through the labor of the cows, the families that owned them, and a number of town dependents, employees, and officials.[10]

Until the early years of the nineteenth century, the Common's labor-intensive activities coexisted easily with leisure pursuits. Children spent their days refighting the Revolutionary War in the eroding British battlements that still clung to Powder House Hill, while adults strolled through the pasture or along the tree-lined Malls that bordered the Common's eastern sides. One of the biggest attractions for those with leisure time was the view westward across the treeless Common and over the Back Bay. From almost any point on the Malls or the pasture, one could see the gently rolling water of the bay with the green hills of Roxbury and Brookline beyond. With the right wind, one might even catch the scent of the sea. Visitors to Boston never failed to mention the Common's beauty, and they never complained that carpet dust or cow manure had marred their experience.[11]

Everyday activities like grazing and strolling sometimes gave way to special or unusual events that were neither wholly work nor wholly play. Bostonians protested, celebrated, dueled, and brawled on the Common, and until the end of the eighteenth century the pasture hosted the huge gatherings that accompanied executions. Public festivals also marked the General Election of state officers in May, the Artillery Election in June, and Training or Muster Day in October. In Boston Common's first two hundred years, there were few kinds of activities that it had not accommodated at one time or another.[12]

This mixture of labor-oriented relationships with leisure ones was mirrored in the organization of American social life. Into the early nineteenth century, urban artisans routinely combined their homes with their places of work. A typical master craftsman's house would shelter not only his wife, children, and perhaps a servant, but also the journeymen and apprentices he employed. Those involved in the trade would live and work under the paternalistic guidance of the master. They toiled together in a shop that was most likely attached to the house, ate meals at the same table, slept under the same roof, and even went to church together. The line between labor and leisure was just as blurry in the day-to-day operations of the shop itself. Master and journeymen might elect one of their group to read the newspaper aloud while the others worked, or take impromptu breaks around a shared bottle of rum, or go fishing when business was slow. The mix of environmental relationships that defined Boston Common at the beginning of the nineteenth century fit perfectly into the larger framework in which many Americans lived their lives.[13]

Gentility Reaches the Common

As central as the Common was to Boston's social life, it was geographically remote from the center of population through the end of the eighteenth century. In 1790, Boston's population was about 18,000, only 2,000 more than in 1740. The town had grown very little in fifty years. That was in large part a legacy of the Revolution, when occupying British troops had heavily damaged the town and two-thirds of the local residents had fled. But the end of the war brought economic expansion, and between 1790 and 1810 the population almost doubled to 34,000. A wave of migrants moved to Boston seeking economic opportunities, and the need for more housing pushed the population toward the thinly-settled lands around the Common.[14]

Boston's wealthiest inhabitants led the exodus from the older sections of town and used the move to reinforce their status as members of the "genteel" classes. Since the beginning of the eighteenth century, America's elites had copied the homes, furnishings, clothing, and manners of the European aristocracy. By the end of the century, the desire to appear genteel was also spreading to the middle level of American society, which purchased symbols of refinement like carpets and clocks to distinguish their social status from the laboring classes. But the middling classes still followed the pace set by the nation's most affluent families, which used their wealth to replicate the geography of gentility they saw across the Atlantic. As upper-class residents of European cities built larger homes with gardens along tree-lined streets, their American counterparts followed suit.[15]

In Boston, neighborhoods of this sort first began appearing on High, Pearl, and Summer Streets. This district was just a few blocks from the wharves where merchants kept their offices, yet still retained the spaciousness of the country. While visiting from Philadelphia, Enoch Wines found Summer Street to be "the handsomest street in Boston. Town and Country seem here married to each other, and there is no jar between the husband and the wife."[16]

Later, Boston's gentility began migrating to the area of Beacon Street on the far side of the Common, which most locals considered to be the very edge of town. In 1790, *Massachusetts Magazine* referred to the Beacon Hill area as a "rural hamlet" in contrast to the town itself. The next year, when apothecary John Joy built a home on the hill so that his ill wife could benefit from the country air, she insisted that their stay away from the center of town be a short one. Even as late as 1802, when state senator John Phillips completed a home on Beacon Street, people wondered why he had moved so far out of town. What made Beacon Street a "rural hamlet" was, in part, its distance from the turmoil of the town center. But the adjoining Common's physical qualities—its expansive pasture and distant views—were largely responsible for the area's country-like atmosphere.[17]

Trailblazers like Joy and his wife did not have to wait long for company, for the Common had also caught the attention of state officials. In 1795, the legislature chose a scenic spot on Beacon Hill as the site for an elegant new State House designed by local architect Charles Bulfinch. At the same time, the town announced that it would sell the nearby east end of the Common, where the almshouse, workhouse, and other public buildings were located, to finance new facilities elsewhere. The news sparked a building boom around the Common that produced a large number of well-appointed residences for wealthy citizens, including a Bulfinch-designed block of fashionable row houses along Common Street and a number of homes for prominent citizens on Park Street.[18]

What drew these new residents to the borders of the Common was the aura of refinement that radiated from both the Common and the new State House. In the early nineteenth century, proximity to a garden or other well-groomed green space made a building site highly desirable, with the fashionable residential squares of London providing a model for American cities. Philadelphia began enhancing its Franklin and Washington Squares in the 1820s, and New Yorkers created the public Union Square and the private Gramercy Park in the 1830s. Boston preceded them both with the construction of Franklin Place and Louisburg Square, both private garden squares on Beacon Hill surrounded by expensive townhouses. Living across from the Common was beginning to provide the same kind of cachet as proximity to these parks. But the new State House added immeasurably to the Common's appeal, since America's upper classes also valued neighborhoods near elegant seats of government. They gravitated toward city halls and state houses the way that European elites clustered around royal palaces. The capitol buildings in Richmond and Philadelphia and the city hall in New York all attracted grand houses that basked in the dignity and power emanating from civic buildings, and Boston's State House did the same. Across urban America, beautiful houses near parks or squares and adjacent to stately civic buildings identified their residents as genteel.[19]

The same year that construction began on the new capitol building, a group of Boston investors began pursuing an ambitious residential development scheme that combined proximity to the State House with unequaled views of the Common. Leading Federalist Harrison Gray Otis teamed with several other businessmen to purchase pastureland on Mount Vernon, a hill bordering Beacon Street across from the Common. Operating as the Mount Vernon Proprietors, they cut the top fifty or sixty feet off the hill and began to transform the area into a neighborhood of grand houses with beautiful gardens and views of the Back Bay. Mindful of the Common's use as a pasture, but needing to preserve the new yards from unnecessary damage, builders left lanes between and even under the houses so that cows from the poorer neighborhoods north and west of the hill could reach Beacon Street and the Common. The development was a great success. Beacon Street, in the words of Oliver Wendell Holmes, became "the sunny street that holds the sifted few," and by the early 1830s more than a third of Boston's richest families lived on streets near the Common. Its scenery had drawn the new State House, and together they formed an irresistible magnet for the upper classes.[20]

The development of Beacon Street began during a period of unusual social fluidity in Boston's history. The departure of well-to-do loyalists during the Revolution had left room for people of more modest backgrounds to move up the social ladder. Into the first decades of the nineteenth century, a large number of newly rich families found themselves trying to demonstrate the high level of refinement that would win them acceptance in elite circles. The location of one's house was a prominent marker of refinement, as William Dean Howells vividly showed in his 1885 novel, *The Rise of Silas Lapham*. The title character is a rising businessman whose efforts to enter Brahmin society include the erection of a house on Beacon Street. The destruction of the house by fire at the end of the novel marks his failure to achieve the social acceptance he desired. Although the story is set later in the century, its use of a house near the Common as a metaphor for social ambition would have rung just as true in prior decades. But had Lapham been a man of fact rather than fiction, and a resident of Boston before the uppermost classes coalesced into the Brahmins about 1820, his quest for genteel status might have had a more positive ending.[21]

Nature and Gentility

As attractive as the Common was to wealthy Bostonians, the relationship between America's urban upper classes and nature was much more complicated than a simple desire for a view of grass and trees. The characteristics of refined life in the nation's growing cities were promoting a different kind of engagement with the natural world. Most Americans still lived in the countryside and related to their environments largely through their labor. They picked corn, mowed hay, chopped wood, and herded, fed, milked, saddled, and slaughtered their domesticated animals. Many urbanites had left various parts of that lifestyle behind, but only upper-class urbanites and some of the aspiring middling classes could avoid it almost entirely. In fact, evading such activities became a hallmark of gentility. Direct contact with productive nature receded into the experiential background of urban elites, and they began to derive more of the meanings they assigned to nature from what they saw with their eyes than from the feel and smell of wringing a living from the land.[22]

Most importantly for the future of Boston Common, the upper classes' distaste for manual labor inspired a landscape ideal that treated productive work as if it were inconsistent with nature. Early nineteenth-century romantics like Emerson embraced this sentiment. "You cannot freely admire a noble landscape," he explained, "if laborers are digging in the field hard by." The suppression of such productive activities could therefore enhance the uplifting effects of traditionally productive landscapes, like common pastures. In fact, Emerson had some of his greatest epiphanies while traversing them. "I do not cross the common without a wild poetic delight," he wrote in 1834, "notwithstanding the prose of my demeanour." Two years later, he described a twilight walk across a common that produced "a perfect exhilaration" and the transcendent state that he achieved when lost in the embrace of the natural world. In Emerson's experience, however, productive commons were at their best when no productive activities were taking place. Within this developing landscape ideal, nature abhorred a worker.[23]

The removal of work from the upper-class landscape ideal reflected a larger unraveling of the close relationship between labor and leisure in American society. By the early years of the nineteenth century, the expansion of manufacturing was producing large shops that functioned more efficiently when journeymen and apprentices lived on their own rather than with a master. Although the full separation of work from home would take decades to complete, many Americans were already finding that the two were drifting ever farther apart. Historians have long understood that the reduction of the old paternalistic system to a simple exchange of labor for money had enormous social consequences: the apprentice system would fade away, the rigor of industrial time would replace irregular work patterns, and masters and employees would lose their sense of mutual responsibility. But the sundering of job from home and work from play also reshaped how Americans related to the natural environment. An understanding of labor and leisure as best pursued in different landscapes had to precede the dedication of a public space to solely recreational pursuits.[24]

Since Boston's refined women experienced the greatest separation from the messy realities of working with the natural environment, it should not be surprising that they developed the most strained relationship to a central aspect of urban nature: cows. Rural women—many urban ones as well—had regular contact with cows because women usually managed the production of milk and dairy products within a family. But wealthy urban women had no such responsibilities. In fact, to exhibit alarm at the nearness of such large animals became a mark of refinement. "The fear of the cow," noted a local minister, "which prevails among the fair in cities and large towns, is one of the elegances of cultivated life." What refined Boston women thought about the local cows thus became deeply entangled with what they thought about themselves. But whether genuine, feigned, or simply imagined by men wanting to paint women as the weaker sex, the supposed fear of cows among Boston's ladies would become one of the chief arguments for their removal from the Common.[25]

Boston Common had not created the desire to gaze on a natural area free from productive activities, nor had it created the fear of cows among genteel women. But once enough elite families had moved around its borders, the Common gave Boston's upper classes a whole new landscape through which to express these particular cultural attitudes toward nature. As a result, a cow nuisance emerged where there had never been one before. As early as 1818, a lawyer, author, and great fan of the Common named Samuel Knapp voiced displeasure over the continued presence of the cows. Knapp expressed disbelief that a place so perfect for pleasure and recreation was still used for something as base as production. "Will it be

In this 1804 image of Boston Common, a woman and her children pose just a few feet away from grazing cows, while a figure with a wheelbarrow trundles by in the background. Such a mingling of labor and leisure in a natural setting was not unusual at the time, but it would grow increasingly objectionable to Boston's upper classes over the next two decades. (Author's collection)

believed," he asked, "that this enchanting common takes its name from its being a *common cow-pasture,* and is actually given up to that animal!" Although most of his contemporaries referred to the Common as a "field" or "pasture," Knapp called it an "extensive square." The choice was telling, for the term emphasized an urban and leisure-oriented relationship to the Common rather than a rural and productive one.[26]

From Town to City

The upper classes would have had a difficult time securing the necessary votes in a town meeting to end the right of commonage and remove the cows. Although wealthy Bostonians held many of the town's chief offices and provided much of the community's leadership, any policy that was unpopular with the laboring population could be blocked by a large turnout in town meeting. Closing the Common's pasture to cows would be a serious revocation of a traditional right, and the class benefiting most from that right—the poorer ones in this case—could be expected to defend it fiercely. That did not stop the upper classes from trying. Nathaniel Shurtleff, a physician, politician, and local historian, remembered years later that "those who were wont to perambulate the numerous bypaths and byways of the old common land" wanted to "remove the trouble" of the cows. He claimed that "many attempts were made, in vain," although he did not record their details. Such efforts to change how Bostonians related to their Common could find success only if the citizens gave up the direct democracy of their town meeting.[27]

Boston's government worked like most others in New England. Its heart was the town meeting, where qualified voters gathered periodically to make decisions directly rather than through representatives. A board of selectmen, board of health, and board of overseers of the poor met the town's daily governmental needs. Each body acted independently of the others, and their members served without pay. The system was cheap and reasonably efficient, and it gave direct input into the lawmaking process to every voting citizen.[28]

But a town meeting worked best with a small population bound together by a sense of community and mutual interest. By the turn of the century, that description no longer fit Boston. The number of residents was far too large for any one individual to know most of the people in the community or for a single building to hold the thousands of citizens who were qualified to vote in town meetings. As a result, the system was not as democratic in practice as it was in theory. Most town meetings had become exercises in apathy in which only thirty or forty people showed up to make decisions about town policies. The discussion of especially controversial issues, on the other hand, drew such large crowds that the gatherings overflowed Faneuil Hall and made it impossible for speakers to be heard.[29]

Since as early as 1784, Bostonians had made periodic attempts to adopt a representative or "city" form of government, but such efforts were always unsuccessful because residents remained emotionally attached to their town meetings. Part of the reason was that Boston's town meeting, like others around New England, conjured memories of patriotic voices calling for resistance to the oppressive policies of Great Britain. "This sentiment," remembered Mayor Josiah Quincy, Sr., "united with the natural reluctance with which every people part with authority they have long and successfully exercised, rendered all attempts at change, not so much unpopular, as hateful, to a majority of the inhabitants." But more than nostalgia was at work. Based on close to two centuries of experience, New Englanders had come to believe that their direct democracies were the ideal form of municipal government. For Boston to abandon it for something else must have seemed like a step backward rather than a step forward on its path toward perfection.[30]

Many Bostonians also feared that representative government

would increase the power of the rich. Upper-class leadership in town government was already well established. Wealthy citizens who believed they had an obligation to serve the town and had the leisure time to do so had controlled the town boards since Boston's earliest days. But many residents relied on the town meeting to check the power of this group, and some warned that without it Boston's upper classes could shift the burden of taxation to the poor. The fact that many of the wealthiest residents of the town, most of them Federalists, staunchly advocated representative government fanned the suspicions. Democrats denounced such proposals as aristocratic plots, while many working Bostonians condemned any plan to eliminate the town meeting as a thinly veiled attempt to encroach on traditional rights.[31]

Yet after decades of resisting change, Boston's citizens finally acknowledged the inherent limitations of town government. On January 7, 1822, they approved a representative form of city government by a less than overwhelming seven-to-five margin. The Town of Boston became the City of Boston, and its residents delegated their direct voting power to a mayor and a bicameral city council. Like the previous town boards, such offices would be filled almost entirely by merchants, bankers, businessmen, manufacturers, and attorneys rather than artisans and laborers. But the popular mistrust of representative bodies did leave its mark on the new city charter, which specifically forbade the City Council from selling Boston Common and Faneuil Hall. Those restrictions remain in place today.[32]

Boston's powerful new government began to reshape the city only a year after its creation, when the second mayor, Josiah Quincy, took office. Quincy was one of the most active reforming mayors of the antebellum period. With a zeal that stunned Bostonians, he rapidly consolidated power in his office at the expense of vestigial but still influential town boards and pushed through a number of reforms that changed the face of the city. Brushing aside all opposition, his administration removed thousands of tons of debris from the city's streets, built a new House of Industry, reorganized the fire department, and constructed the ambitious and costly Faneuil Hall Market. Always in the midst of the fray, Quincy combated prostitution and drunkenness by personally leading a squad of deputized draymen to the dangerous and vice-ridden northern side of Beacon Hill. He and his posse shut down a number of illegal establishments and regained control of an area that the authorities had previously feared to enter. Quincy believed that such changes were necessary if Boston was to achieve greatness, a destiny that was "too plain to be denied or misconceived."[33]

The new city government also made important changes to Boston Common. The cow tax had fallen into disuse after 1805, and the Common had suffered for several years from a general lack of regulation. The reasons for the inattention are unclear but the consequences predictable. With no method in place for monitoring the total number of cows, some people pastured several cows at a time, with one person having as many as eighteen. More than one offender established a commercial milk business and turned his entire herd onto the Common for free feed. To end the abuses, Quincy pushed through a new ordinance in 1823 that reaffirmed the restriction of one cow per owner, required the registration of each cow, and assessed annually the sum of five dollars for the privilege. Since that was a substantial cost increase over the seventy-five cents that owners had paid some twenty years earlier, the ordinance empowered the mayor and aldermen to waive the payment in cases of poverty. The new ordinance cut the number of cows from 200 to 119 overnight. It also restored the values that underlay the idea of common land—close regulation and subsistence rather than unrestricted commercial use. Given the chance to eliminate the system of common pasturage as corrupt and outdated, Quincy chose instead to confirm its relevancy by reforming it.[34]

But the ordinance also contained a clause that closed the larger urban commons. After much debate, the City Council outlawed the long-standing tradition of allowing cows to wander untended through the city's streets. Trespassing cows could cause considerable damage to yards and gardens, and the council decided that the accumulating harm outweighed the convenience gained by the owners of the cows. Although the clause did not affect the right to pasture on the Common, it did signal a shift in public feelings toward keeping domestic animals in the city. The reaction of everyday Bostonians to the new regulation went unrecorded, but similar ordinances in other cities revealed conflicting attitudes toward domesticated animals among different social classes. New York's police battled poor families into the 1830s to rid the city's streets of pigs, and when Atlanta's City Council finally banned cows from its streets in 1881, one critic considered it "an issue between flowers and milk—between the front yard of the rich man and the sustenance of the poor family."[35] By that time, a national movement to make cities more sanitary was categorizing domestic animals as not only an inconvenience but also a threat to the public health.

Defending the View

Once the city had brought the Common's pasture under control, it made a number of small changes that subtly altered the meaning of the Common by enhancing its leisure value. The city completed a promenade along Charles Street in 1824, edged Frog Pond with stone two years later, and replaced the poplar trees of Park Street Mall with more fashionable elm trees. Where prior aesthetic improvements, like the planting of trees along the Malls, had often relied on private funds, the most recent changes demonstrated a new willingness to dress up the Common at public expense.[36]

But the new city government's commitment to the Common's leisure value was not yet absolute, for it did not extend to the pasture's scenic views over the Back Bay. In 1824, the City Council announced plans to develop hundreds of yards of mud flats that extended from the Common into the bay. The flats were ten feet below the level of the Common, which was supported by a retaining wall, and they were mostly visible at low tide when the water receded to a deeper channel. Part of the flats had already been developed: six ropewalks—long, low, wooden buildings where workers treated fibers and twisted them into lengths of rope—rested on stilts plunged into the marsh at the base of the wall. Thirty years before, the ropewalks had been located in a different part of town where a fire had destroyed them. Motivated by the desire to preserve a vital industry and an obligation to move a persistent fire hazard away from populated areas, the selectmen had permitted the owners to rebuild on the flats. The decision made sense at the time, since the Common was a place of work and the height of the new factories would not obstruct the view. But after thirty years of urban expansion, the flats had become valuable real estate that bordered the increasingly popular Common. So with future development in mind, the City Council bought back the rights to the flats.[37]

The council envisioned an affluent new neighborhood on the site that would completely block the view over the Back Bay. Plans exhibited in Faneuil Hall showed the flats filled to the level of the Common and covered with 321 four-story row houses. Spacious, tree-lined streets divided the houses into blocks, and the ambitious size of the project promised many years of work to those in the building trades. It was hard to find fault with such a thoughtful and tasteful design—unless it threatened to obscure one's view. The plan became a test of how important such an intangible element of leisure enjoyment was to the population. The views of calm water and distant hills were impressive and widely enjoyed, but were they important enough to derail a project that would bring so many other benefits to the community?[38]

The council's 1824 plans coincided with a nationwide increase in the appreciation of natural landscapes. Just the year before, James Fenimore Cooper had published the first installment of his Leatherstocking tales, which chronicled the wilderness adventures of a noble woodsman on the ever-receding western frontier. Cooper's books were among the most popular produced during the nineteenth century and inspired a host of others that used the natural landscape as a richly symbolic setting for their stories. The year after the council announced its plan, the artist Thomas Cole would take America's burgeoning interest in landscape painting to new heights. Drawing his initial inspiration from the Catskills, Cole imbued his dramatic creations with themes about God and Nature and the destiny of the American nation. His work soon inspired the enormously influential Hudson River School. Although Cooper, Cole, and their literary and artistic descendants did not create America's love of beautiful scenery, they encouraged a more widespread appreciation for it at a critical point in Boston's development.[39]

From this context emerged a champion who was willing to fight for the Common's vistas. Andrew Eliot Belknap, a local merchant, used the city's newspapers to launch a one-man crusade against development. By claiming that the flats were and always had been an integral part of the Common, he framed the debate as an attack on the Common itself and therefore the public interest. Under the signature "Watch" and the heading "Look Out for the Common!" Belknap penned several editorials that argued for preserving the flats. He appealed to his readers' sense of nostalgia, reminding them of the formative role that the Common had played in their childhoods and confessing that, when just a boy, he had felt pride in the thought that "the *Common* belonged to *us all.*"[40] He appealed to their respect for the law, maintaining that the flats all the way to the middle of the Back Bay channel were part of the Common and therefore not saleable under the city charter. He appealed specifically to the genteel "Ladies of Boston," because they had the ability to rise above the greediness of men. And he appealed to his audience's aesthetic sensibilities, warning that they would exchange distant vistas for the sight of houses and trade the smell of fresh air for a lungful of coal smoke. The views and breezes, he believed, were as much a part of the Common as the grass and trees and deserved the same level of protection.[41]

Belknap was forced to address objections that wealthy residents seeking leisure were already beginning to monopolize the Common. "It is attempted to make us believe," he wrote in an 1824 editorial, "that this ornament of our city is reserved for the enjoyment of the rich alone, and that there exists amongst us a mean spirit of jealousy between the poor and the opulent. This is base calumny." Belknap saw himself as an advocate for the less fortunate classes and therefore proof to the contrary. To those who favored development of the flats for the jobs it would provide to the poor, he countered that income from sale of the land would be used to lower property taxes on the rich rather than to help the less fortunate. And to those who claimed that the Common was being groomed for the recreation of the city's wealthiest members, he emphasized the importance of the Common as a leisure space for the laboring classes. "The common," Belknap concluded, "is emphatically called the poor man's inheritance; and it is, for all may enjoy it."[42]

The City Council appointed a committee to study the proposed project, but Abbott Lawrence thought he could foresee what its report would say. Lawrence was a wealthy merchant and would go on to become a major figure in the state's textile industry, a representative to Congress, and minister to Great Britain. He was familiar with certain key members of the committee and knew that they were opposed to development. Lawrence predicted that these members, "together with what has been called the Aristocracy of the Lawn will without doubt stifle this speculation in embryo." He seemed unmoved by such a potential outcome, however, which might seem surprising since he had made the original suggestion to develop the land. The reason for his indifference was that Lawrence predicted a second and equally satisfying possibility. He believed that the committee would propose instead that the city preserve the flats as open green space in the form of a lawn or park. "To this," he concluded, "I will most cheerfully give my vote."[43]

Lawrence read the situation correctly. After three months of meetings and deliberations, the committee issued a report arguing that the construction of buildings on the flats would destroy the value of the Common as the healthiest and most beautiful area of the city. Drawing on prevailing medical beliefs in the miasmatic theory of disease, the committee warned that cutting off the current of fresh air that blew in from the west would invite pestilence into the city. The committee also insisted that a block of buildings of any height would "wholly obstruct the view of the country, from a spectator in the Mall," forever destroying "one of the most splendid Panoramas in the world" and compromising the recreational usefulness of the Common. The laboring classes, the committee cautioned, would be hurt most by such a project because "the rich man can procure shelter and accommodation every where; BUT THE COMMON IS THE POOR MAN'S GARDEN." Considering the extensive damage that the project would do to the Common and the city as a whole, the council's plan was "madness" even if it resulted in a large financial profit for the city.[44]

The one kind of development that the committee would sanction—and indeed strongly recommended—was a cemetery. It would provide citizens with opportunities for contemplation in a green environment and, most importantly, avert future threats to develop the site with buildings.[45]

The editor of the *Columbian Centinel* denounced the report and reserved his most biting remarks for the committee's idealized depiction of the flats. A plainspoken man and the friend of several committee members, Benjamin Russell marveled at the committee's ability to romanticize a marsh of sedge and mud that produced noxious odors and clouds of dust at low tide. He also criticized the importance that the committee placed on the view over the Bay and mocked their overwrought descriptions of it. "Something more solid than this fine imagery," he wrote, "will be necessary to convince me of the impolicy of erecting buildings on that vacant land." Russell wondered why the committee members were not also protesting the simultaneous filling of flats at the southern end of the city. "I know of but one reason," he decided, "and that is, these encroachments do not interfere with, nor hide the magnificent prospect of *'one of the most splendid Panoramas in the world'* from the view of a number of the members of the committee."[46]

Joseph Buckingham, editor of the *Boston Courier*, agreed with Russell and criticized the attitudes toward labor and the poorer classes that underpinned the committee's recommendation. In its effort to disparage development of the flats, the committee had noted in its report that they were remote from more developed parts of the city and lacked a convenient source of fresh water. Such conditions, they warned, might prompt builders to cover the flats with cheap houses rather than the stately homes pictured in the plans. Buckingham found the concern self-serving given the wealth of the committee members. In response, he advised his readers not to give away six million square feet of public land "for no other reason than to gratify the pride of a few rich men, who dread nothing so much as the neighborhood of honest industry."[47]

Bostonians had never battled so fiercely over the Common's aesthetics. There had been no serious fights over building a complex of municipal buildings on the Common in the early eighteenth century and no uproar when the town allowed the construction of ropewalks on the flats in the 1790s. Work to grade the pasture or plant the Malls had always gone forward with little fuss. In fact, with the exception of small changes, the Common itself was substantially the same as it had been a generation before. But Bostonians were not. An emerging middle class was reaching out for markers of gentility, and they joined the upper classes in attaching substantial value to the Common's recreational amenities and the sense of refinement that they conferred. More residents of Boston than ever before looked at the Common and saw a park before they saw a pasture.

By the end of 1824, the debate over the flats had turned so contentious that the new City Council abandoned its responsibility to make difficult decisions for the city and called for a public vote on the matter. In December, citizens gathered to decide on five competing propositions drafted by the committee. Its two most significant recommendations met with different fates. In a spectacular snub, ninety percent of the voters rejected the committee's proposal for a cemetery. Rarely were Bostonians so near to being of one mind. The rejection might have influenced the suggestion made just a year later to establish the nation's first rural cemetery outside the city limits, an idea that came to fruition in the eventual establishment of Mount Auburn Cemetery in Cambridge in 1831. In a much closer vote—fifty-five percent to forty-five percent—the citizenry decided against a sale of the flats. Belknap's entreaties had paid off, and admirers of the view over the Back Bay could celebrate a major victory.[48]

The Last Shake

Once the battle over the flats had ended, the city government—still only three years old—turned its attention to restricting activities on the Common that inhibited genteel forms of recreation. The first target was carpet beating. In 1825, the council considered an ordinance pertaining to the Common that largely restated regulations dating to the eighteenth century. The ordinance forbade residents from dumping refuse, injuring trees, removing gravel, sand, or dirt, pasturing animals other than milk cows, and riding horses except when part of a military exercise. These were familiar rules designed to protect both the productive and recreational uses of the Common. But the ordinance also contained a new section that forbade shaking or beating carpets within one hundred and ten yards of the

Park and Tremont Street Malls. If passed, the new ordinance would severely restrict the areas in which such work could take place.[49]

Edward Everett Hale, who lived near the Common as a child in the 1820s, remembered carpet cleaning as one of the primary uses of the space in these years. In an age before vacuum cleaners, carpets had to be removed from homes to be cleaned. The work was heavy and dirty, so Bostonians with sufficient resources often paid others to do it. Men with hand carts would trundle the carpets onto the Common's open spaces, where they shook and beat the dust out of them. Doing the work any closer to residences would have constituted a nuisance. The practice was a very old one in Boston and well sanctioned by custom.[50]

The council's debate over the carpet cleaning clause revealed an important shift in the perceived balance between labor and leisure on the Common, for council members focused on how far rug cleaners should stay from the Malls rather than whether they should be asked to move at all. In fact, the discussion opened with one council member calling for a complete ban on rug cleaning. Only a few people living near the Common benefited from this use of the space, a newspaper reported of his position, while most citizens "desired to enjoy the air unaccompanied with the dust of carpets." The council member seemed to be saying that shaking or beating rugs was entirely inconsistent with proper use of the Common, although a large majority of councilors disagreed. They not only rejected his proposal but even voted to reduce the distance in the draft ordinance by half. The compromise might have looked like a victory for both sides, but it represented a net loss in traditional privileges. The business of cleaning rugs on the Common hung on until mid-century, when the council finally banned it outright. "Then the Common became less dusty," wrote Hale, "and more grand."[51]

Some of the other activities that jarred with a more refined vision of the Common's natural landscape did not involve labor at all but rather laboring-class leisure. These activities tended to be associated with large public holidays observed on the Common, and city officials began looking for ways to regulate them. Hale had participated in such celebrations as a boy and remembered the Tremont Street Mall lined with the booths of vendors selling coconuts, sugarcane, tamarinds, dates, raw oysters, ginger beer, and a wide variety of candies. "Why we did not all die of the trash which we ate and drank on such occasions," he asked years later, "I do not know." But what Hale experienced as days marked by fun and adventure, others experienced as an insufferable intrusion of grog shop behavior into the public sphere. To at least one viewer, holiday festivities reduced the Common to a "camp of wickedness, where gambling and intemperance, profanity and lewdness, will meet the eye or the ear wherever you turn."[52]

The crowds at such events could in fact become rowdy, and reform-minded citizens wanted to control them. In the mid-1820s, a group of prominent citizens convinced the city to pay for a band to play on the Common during holiday celebrations. According to one observer, the music had "a tendency to promote order, and to suppress inclination to riot and intemperance."[53] But more importantly, temperance-minded citizens convinced the city council in 1828 to prohibit gambling and the drinking of alcohol on the Common on public holidays. The banning of such long-enjoyed activities from the Common was a powerful indication of how much control the new city government exercised over customary rights, and it established a small but important precedent for those who wanted to remove the cows.[54]

How to Enclose a Common

Most Bostonians would have put the right to graze cows in a better-protected category of traditional rights than carpet cleaning, drinking, and gambling. At least in the English common lands tradition that gave birth to Boston Common, terminating rights in the use of a common's natural resources required that the common be formally "enclosed." Since as early as the thirteenth century, English lords had been working to free their country estates from the rights claimed by commoners. To establish sole control over their holdings and increase agricultural production, lords enclosed them by extinguishing common rights through legal means and then fencing the land. Large numbers of commoners and landless peasants had eked independent livings off these commons, but once a common was enclosed they lost access to the pastures that fed their cows, the woodlots that provided fuel for cooking, and the fields where they planted their crops. Effectively forced off the land, many found work in the factories of Manchester and other industrializing cities where they traded a degree of freedom from the market for dependence on wages.[55]

Most enclosures in England took place far from urban areas, but growing cities also participated in the process. In search of land for new buildings and open space for leisure activities, England's cities enclosed nearby commons by purchasing them from the owning lord and buying out the rights of commoners. As the pace of city building quickened, Parliament began to actively encourage the creation of parkland out of enclosed commons. In the Enclosure Act of 1836, Parliament exempted commons within a ten mile radius of London from enclosure to ensure adequate recreational space for the city, and the General Enclosure Act of 1845 required that every enclosure set aside an amount of land for recreation proportionate to the size of the local population. Some of London's largest and best-known parks, including Wimbledon Common, Hampstead Heath, and Epping Forest, are former commons enclosed primarily for recreational purposes.[56]

Although Boston Common was born of the same legal tradition that governed common lands in England, it occupied a different legal space. The grazing rights in the Common were based not in the ownership or rental of a particular piece of land as in England, but simply in residence. That was rare throughout Europe, and by 1830 it was unrealistic in Boston because thousands of people presumably had the right to graze a cow on the Common pursuant to the regulations and limitations adopted by the city. But how well protected was that right? Could Boston's new representative government revoke it without the consent of the city's citizens? If the city did enclose the Common, would it have to reimburse residents for any resulting financial losses? The answers were unclear. But there could be little doubt that it would take an act of enclosure to transform the relationship between Bostonians and their Common.

The first step toward enclosing the Common was not a legal one, however, but an act of imagination. In the 1820s, with the neighborhoods bordering the Common firmly established as elite enclaves, printed images began to pair the State House and Common in scenes that evoked a parklike country estate with genteel citizens wandering its grounds. Earlier published views had shown Boston Common from a variety of angles and included figures representing a cross-section of Boston society. But almost all of the newer images appearing in books, magazines, and pocket diaries offered a more formulaic picture. A brightly illuminated State House shone in the background like a manor, and a darker Common sprawled in the foreground like a carefully groomed park. Only well-dressed people on leisurely strolls populated the pictures.[57]

The images carried multiple meanings. According to the reviewer of a lithograph by James Kidder, such images perfectly captured the ideal relationship between humans and nature. "The mall fences, the intersecting paths, and the trees scattered about, are in just proportion," he wrote of the picture. "The people promenading, and the dogs sporting about, and the cows grazing at leisure, appear like nature herself." The images also presented an idealized representation of Boston, painting it as a city that had reached its destined potential by transcending its less-refined elements. Finally, it carried the message that Boston Common was more park than pasture. In the imaginations of the literate and affluent Bostonians who were most likely to see and display these images, the Common's transformation from a place of mixed labor and leisure to a more refined place for upper-class play was well under way.[58]

Although working people had vanished from the images, cows remained. Some images pushed cows to the margins of the frame, and others placed them at the very center, but cows were almost always present. Their contribution to the composition was largely symbolic. They represented an idealized countryside free of labor, where even cows, in the words of the reviewer quoted above, spent their time "grazing at leisure." The cows also played a political role. By enhancing the rural feel of the State House's surroundings, they validated the existing political establishment. Antebellum Americans linked democracy and political virtue to the countryside, which was one of the reasons that so many Boston elites maintained country houses outside of the city. An image of the State House growing out of a rural field represented a powerful claim to political legitimacy and helped to make the country estate theme immensely popular. In fact, it was so well liked that many wealthy Bostonians set their tables with plates, platters, pitchers, and creamers adorned with renderings of the State House presiding over a Common dotted with cows.[59]

Such images reflected similar artistic trends across the Atlantic, where English landscape painting had become deeply embedded in the process of enclosure. Most enclosures in England reflected the desire to increase agricultural profits by consolidating land holdings, and this more capitalistic relationship to the land inspired new ways of thinking about nature. After enclosing common lands, lords often applied new and more efficient agricultural methods to one part of the property, while constructing a huge pastoral estate on the other. Through their design, these estates promoted a more gen-

The depiction of Boston Common in this lithograph by James Kidder was typical of the 1820s, the decade before the removal of the cows. It suggested that the most appropriate relationship to the Common was one defined by the passive recreation of a refined population. Note, however, that cows still make an appearance on the left edge of the image. (Courtesy of the Boston Public Library, Print Department)

teel version of nature. Landscape gardeners avoided formal garden elements and screened estates from the agriculture that supported them, creating vast areas arranged to please the eye but largely devoid of productive activities and any mark of the shaping hand. England's newest country estates obscured rural reality and the working poor by design, and landscape painters reinforced the change by creating scenes with more idealized natural settings than the real countryside offered. With common land so central to the life of the English countryside, enclosing it became not just a social, legal, and environmental act but a cultural one as well. The same was true in Boston.[60]

The War on the Cows

Although refined Bostonians welcomed representations of cows in their art, embracing real ones was a different matter. In early 1829, a number of women asked Mayor Harrison Gray Otis to cancel the upcoming grazing season. Otis had recently replaced Quincy in an unexpected electoral upset that would prove to be very bad news for the cows. The scion of a prominent family, Otis made his fortune through real estate speculation and investments in manufacturing. He became a respected politician who served as Speaker of the House and President of the Senate in the legislature and sat in both the United States Senate and House of Representatives. By the 1820s, Otis was one of the three principal leaders of the Federalist establishment in Boston. But those wanting the cows removed found his self-interest more useful than his political influence: Otis was one of the owners of the Mount Vernon Proprietors, the real estate firm rapidly transforming Beacon Street into an upper-class residential district. Otis himself lived at 45 Beacon Street, directly across from Boston Common. Since the Common was the primary attraction to prospective buyers, Otis's real estate interests would benefit from removing the cows. Otis acted quickly, although indirectly. That April, his son-in-law William Foster sponsored one of two petitions to the City Council requesting that the cows be removed from the Common.[61]

Supporters of keeping the Common a pasture quickly filed a counter petition arguing that the cows should stay because they fulfilled an important public purpose. Anyone who was too poor to purchase decent milk, claimed the signatories, could better support their families through owning a cow, and the children and families of the rich profited just as much from the freshness of the milk. The counter petitioners also insisted that the quality of milk produced by cows allowed to run free was higher than that produced by cows penned in the city's stables for the hottest months. Providing for the practical needs of the community, they argued, was the true purpose of this natural area. They concluded that as long as no person or business was being injured by a use that had existed "from time immemorial," it should continue. The City Council was persuaded and voted to allow the cows onto the Common as usual.[62]

But the council's decision only delayed the issue until the following spring, when those opposed to grazing took a different tack. In March 1830, Abbott Lawrence's brother and business partner Amos teamed up with a group of ten other wealthy individuals that included several residents of Park Street. Together, they petitioned the council to ban cows from the Granary Burying Ground, which was a short distance from the Common and had formerly been a part of it. The practice of renting grazing rights in public cemeteries was an old one that carried the twin advantages of keeping burial places mown and providing the city with a small income. The petitioners claimed that they wanted to beautify the cemetery with trees, which they found to be "highly salutary and necessary in large towns." Left unsaid was that those petitioners who lived on exclusive Park Street —a doctor, a lawyer, a Harvard professor, and several merchants— would also be beautifying their backyards. Their Park Street townhouses not only fronted on the Common but backed onto the cemetery, where cows grazed right up to the walls of their homes. Under the pretense of beautifying the city, they might rid themselves of an irritant. The City Council accepted their petition and even went a step further by banning cows from all of the city's cemeteries.[63]

With the cows gone, the Granary became a private recreational area for the Park Street abutters. By day, their children played and picnicked on the grounds, and on warm evenings the residents held outdoor suppers and spread champagne and strawberries over the flat-topped tombs. More importantly, the petitioners had success-fully transformed the city's cemeteries from pastures into parks and further restricted grazing space within the city.[64]

Opponents of keeping the Common a pasture lost no time in capitalizing on the precedent. A week after its decision, the City Council received a coordinated barrage of petitions requesting that the cows be removed from the Common. The merchants, owners of dry goods stores, and other well-to-do Bostonians who comprised the majority of the petitioners made the leisure needs of the com-munity the crux of their argument by claiming that the cows seri-ously impeded the recreation of refined women and helpless chil-dren. "Instead of a clean, open lawn as it might be easily made and kept were the cows excluded," they argued, "it is now rendered use-less to females and children from the filth and the natural fear that so many animals occasion in them." They insisted that the conve-nience of a few dozen cow owners should not take priority over the health and comfort of the city's most fragile vessels. "Not a day now probably passes," lamented the petitioners, "without some ap-prehension being occasioned to females passing in consequence of [cows] being pastured there."[65]

Their complaints were exaggerated at best. Edward Everett Hale was romping over the Common as a boy during these years, and he later remembered seeing little of the cows and never expressed any fear of them. The cows played an equally small role in the life of Caroline Dall, who was playing on the Common in the same years and claimed to have never seen more than two of the animals. But expressions of concern about the health and safety of women and children resonated deeply with refined sensibilities.[66]

The petitioners also argued that the cows were ruining the attractive natural qualities of the landscape. They claimed that the cows damaged the bark of young trees recently contributed by generous donors, spent so much time shading themselves beneath the Old Elm that no grass would grow there, and destroyed the lushness of the pasture as soon as grazing began in the spring. These charges were legitimate, and the impact of the cows real. The petitioners could reasonably have spent more time bemoaning the large quantities of waste dropped by the cows each day, and they never even mentioned the offensive smells produced by the animals. Perhaps addressing such issues too directly seemed unrefined. But there remained something ironic about valuing cows as symbols while criticizing their actual impact on the environment, and idealizing the country while avoiding the rural production that created and defined it.[67]

Faced with a jarring discrepancy between the physical Common and their vision of it, the petitioners tried to realign environment with ideal. To their way of thinking, this was no longer just the town pasture but "one of the greatest ornaments of the City." It had been fully incorporated into the geography of gentility, and the city's relationship to it needed to change accordingly. "The time has arrived," the petitioners claimed with suggested inevitability, when the Common "should no longer be used as a *Cow pasture.*"[68]

A large number of Bostonians disagreed. One hundred and fifty-eight signatories, most from the laboring classes, filed two counter petitions. Far more numerous than the group of sixty-five people who had actually grazed cows the previous year, they acted in defense of a custom that benefited some of them individually and all of them, they believed, as a community. One group of counter petitioners expressed dismay that "the cows could, in any way, discommode any citizen," while another stated the case more bluntly, claiming that "the principal reason assigned by the remonstrants against the cows going there is that they annoy their daughters who otherwise might walk and play there."[69] Where those against grazing had argued that a few cow owners should not deprive the many of their recreational needs, the counter petitioners argued that the recreational needs of the few were no reason to deprive the many of an "ancient privilege." They also met the aesthetic complaints of the petitioners with their own arguments. "The Common," the counter petitioners asserted, "is more beautiful and more convenient for the purposes for which it is improved than it would be if allowed to run to grass."[70] The counter petitioners remained convinced that the Common could meet the resource needs of production and the aesthetic needs of leisure at the same time.

The City Council convened a special committee to study the problem, but with Mayor Otis serving as chair its conclusions were predetermined. In his report, Otis claimed that the total number of cows grazing on the Common had been declining and predicted that the number would grow still smaller in the future. Sixty-five owners had grazed as many cows on the Common the prior year, too small a number, Otis believed, to hold hostage the recreational needs of the rest of the citizenry. He reiterated the petitioners' claim that the cows inhibited the full use of the Common by women and children, and he suggested that a pasture was inconsistent with urban life. "It is believed indeed," Otis wrote in the report, "that a public square in a City whose population exceeds sixty thousand, enclosed and preserved as a pasture for the accommodation of sixty five cows, owned by the same number of individuals, is an anomaly for which it will be difficult to find a parallel in any City in the world."[71]

In effect, Otis was claiming that he wanted to rid the city of a slice of the country that rested inappropriately in its midst. But he was really swapping one version of the country for another that had a similar look but not the objectionable feel and smell. In May 1830, with dozens of city residents expecting to pasture their cows on the Common as usual within a few weeks, the council adopted the committee's recommendation and brought the grazing of cows on the Common to an abrupt and unceremonious end.

This sudden change in the city's relationship to the Common took quite a few Bostonians by surprise, and a flood of new petitions deluged City Hall demanding to know how a common right could be so easily revoked. The 231 petitioners—overwhelmingly working people—protested the cavalier manner in which they had been "denied the privilege which has been enjoyed since the town was inhabited." They located the source of their right of pasturage in the original purposes for which the city had set the land aside in 1634 and in the ensuing two centuries of custom and tradition that upheld that usage. The right was a "privilege," "advantage," and "immunity" that had been "left them by their fathers," and they were not about to be robbed of it.[72] One group of petitioners reviewed the legal history of the Common and challenged the City Council's authority to pass and enforce such an ordinance. They insisted that Boston's citizens could only be deprived of the right of pasturage "by their own consent, manifested in some lawful and constitutional manner." The elected members of the council could not revoke it through a simple ordinance.[73]

Otis and the council refused to back down, but to quiet the continuing protest they made a small concession. They granted a right of pasturage on the Common's flats west of Charles Street for the remainder of the season, the same flats that Andrew Belknap had fought so hard to save from development. Since the land was not fenced, those people choosing to pasture a cow would have to hire a full-time keeper at their own expense. The ordinance banning cows from the Common would stand.[74]

Representative city government had made the victory possible. Looking back on the events of 1830, Nathaniel Shurtleff remembered that the change from direct democracy to representative democracy had "completely subjected the poor beasts, as well as their owners, to the mercies of a new regime." Defenders of the right of pasture had demanded that a town meeting be called so that the issue could be debated in a public forum, but the days of gauging the majority's will in such a gathering had ended eight years before. Without a town meeting to check their power, Boston's wealthiest residents were able to impose their environmental values on Boston Common.[75]

The impulse to enclose common land for recreational purposes also materialized in neighboring Cambridge, where during the same days of early June 1830 the state legislature considered a request to enclose part of Cambridge Common. A small group of gentlemen wanted to fence off about half of the Common's sixteen acres to create a public park with trees and walks. Over time, Cambridge Common had acquired two public highways and fourteen other informal roads that left it a maze of streets and a dangerous place to walk. Creating the park would require rerouting the public ways, an action that some residents and nearby towns protested. Rather than petitioning town officials, however, those desiring a park sought assistance directly from the legislature. On June 5, the governor signed a law entitled "An Act to Authorize the Enclosing of a Part of Cambridge Common." The act stood despite the claim by some opponents that the legislature had no jurisdiction over the land. In the rapidly urbanizing America of the early nineteenth century, there was more than one way to enclose common land in the pursuit of genteel recreational space.[76]

Making a Pasture into a Park

The removal of the cows unleashed a rapid series of physical changes to Boston Common intended to elevate it from a pasture to a park. Under the direction of the City Council, workers removed the wooden fences that had separated the cows from the Malls. They filled the marshy Horse Pond, which had served the cows as a watering hole, graded the Common west of Powder House Hill to eliminate low areas that accumulated water, and planted over two hundred trees. In 1836, physical enclosure followed legal enclosure when the city paid in excess of $82,000 to encircle the Common with over a mile of ornamental iron fence. In a token acknowledgment that owners of property around the Common would benefit more than other residents of the city, private contributions defrayed about $16,000 of the cost.[77]

More changes to the Common were to come. Always with an eye toward enhancing the value of his real estate, Otis suggested that Beacon Street be widened at the expense of the Common to create a promenade. He wanted the city to use a strip of the Common that lay outside the fence to create a paved walkway that would essentially serve as a private promenade for the residents of Beacon Street. "It would be a part of the Common," Otis assured a friend, "though left outside the railway."[78] Otis got his wish when the City Council ordered the construction of a brick walkway that not only extended along Beacon Street but encircled the entire Common.

Issues of class and status continued to shape how Bostonians related to the Common, even to the point of making specific areas the purview of particular social groups. After winning the battle to remove the cows and convincing the city to spruce up the landscape, the most fashionable members of Boston society took their strolls on the new brick walk and largely abandoned the old Malls and the Common itself to the less refined. The shift was visible to careful observers like the author Nathaniel Hawthorne. While strolling along the Common early on an April evening in 1840, Hawthorne noticed that mechanics and shopkeeper's clerks with their wives made up the majority of the Mall's patrons. But not everyone was happy with the trade. Nehemiah Adams, pastor of the Essex Street Church, migrated with his social peers onto the walkways outside of the new fence, even though he found the new paths less pleasant than the tree-lined Malls. He nevertheless accepted the reigning cus-

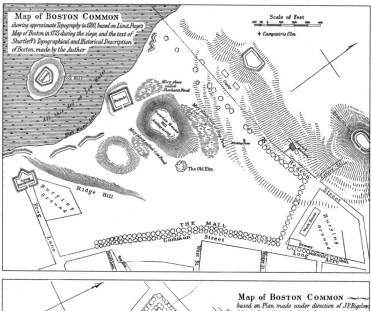

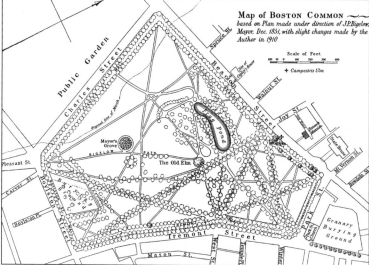

Boston Common in 1780 (top) and 1851 (bottom). In the earlier map, the juxta-position of a large pasture with tree-lined walkways reflects the Common's use for both work and play. In the later map, which shows the Common twenty-one years after the removal of the cows, the proliferation of trees and formal paths suggests a landscape devoted entirely to leisure. (Reproduced from Joseph Henry Curtis, *Life of Campestris Ulm*, 1910, author's collection)

tom, explaining it simply as "the propensity of cultivated and fashionable life in our republican country to separate itself from the common and plebeian world."[79]

The search for refinement also produced efforts to change some long-established place names. "Common" seemed an unsuitable title for a pleasure ground frequented by the city's most cultivated classes. An urban park needed an urbane name, and those advocating a change suggested that "Washington Park" might be more appropriate. A loud public protest ended the effort, however, and the Common's simple, descriptive name remains the last reminder of the labor once done on its pasture. The name remained confusing to some foreign visitors, however, like the Londoner who left Boston believing that "Common" had only been used in colonial times and that the space "is now dignified by the title of Mall." The fight to rename Frog Pond would not end so quickly. For the next twenty years or more, movements continually surfaced to change its name to Crescent Pond, Quincy Lake, or something equally refined. But time proved the older name more durable, and Frog Pond it remains today.[80]

The Common of the Mind

With the completion of these physical changes to the Common, its value rose even higher in the minds of the upper classes. In 1838 and 1842, Nehemiah Adams published two short books about the Common that described a pastoral paradise where the light of spring was softer and the hues of autumn milder than any other place on earth. On the Common, according to Adams, one could experience the peaceful, benign, healthful, and holy attributes of nature through morning walks, agreeable conversation, and pleasant thoughts. Leaving no doubt that God was the source of these uplifting qualities, Adams described the Common as "one of Nature's noblest palaces, or rather temples, where the devout mind can worship God more fervently than in houses of wood and stone."

With the cows gone, he was able to proclaim the Common "consecrated ground."[81]

Adams's words reflected an unusually intense attachment to the romantic idea that the natural and the divine are one. They also probably tell us more about Adams than they do about the Common. But he was not alone in holding such sentiments. Oliver Wendell Holmes described the Common as "that sacred enclosure," and Sophia Hawthorne, the wife of Nathaniel Hawthorne, confessed her enchantment with Boston Common to her diary. After walking amidst the Common's trees, hills, and water, she noted that the experience made her feel so "bubble-like" and "balloony" that she thought she might float right off the path. "O that Common," she wrote with reverence, "that Eden in miniature."[82] Writers had been applying lofty language of this type to natural landscapes for decades, but it only appeared in reference to the Common after the cows were gone. The newly refined pasture was encouraging a certain degree of reverence that was, in turn, promoting further efforts to refine the space. Nature and society were shaping each other within the close quarters of a growing city.

Printed images also responded to the Common's altered environment and purpose by foregrounding natural elements even more thoroughly than before. Views of the 1820s that had carefully balanced the Common with the State House gave way to images that emphasized the natural environment over the built environment. The images continued to radiate authority, however, if in a more subtle way. One of the most popular views of the Common produced at this time shows the State House and Park Street Church peaking above the newly planted trees. The buildings are clearly subordinate to the Common's natural environment, yet they serve as reminders of elite authority in the political and moral realms. Together, they sanction and bless the newest addition to the city's geography of gentility.[83]

The only image that showed any kind of labor on the Common employed a popular motif in landscape painting to evoke an idealized agricultural scene. In the 1830s, the British watercolorist George Harvey captured the scythe-wielding workers who took over from the cows the job of keeping the Common's grass trimmed. In a painting entitled *Afternoon Rainbow*, three neatly-dressed workers occupy the center of the scene, two of them resting to sharpen their scythes as they make their way up Powder House Hill. Two more workers pitch hay into a cart off to the side. Pedestrians stroll by, but they are untroubled by such wholesome agricultural labor. For contemporaries, the tidy-looking reapers lacked the objectionable qualities of Emerson's real-life laborers because they were engaged in a select group of activities used to conjure the peace, beauty, and bounty of an idealized countryside. Painters often composed similar scenes set in other landscapes that showed cornhusking, maple sugaring, and the gathering of apples and pumpkins. All served the same artistic purpose as the Common's cows had a few years before. Proximity to such activities was not undesirable, a point Harvey makes by having a woman and her young daughter stop near the scythe wielders to observe the rainbow. In fact, the central place that these workers hold in Harvey's painting suggests that they are worthy of contemplation themselves. Nehemiah Adams would have agreed, for he claimed that watching the scythe wielders on the Common could relieve the kind of "nervous headache" produced by urban life.[84]

Once shaped into a genteel park, Boston Common assumed a prominent place in the identity and culture of Boston's upper classes. "The 'noble place' of the Common," writes geographer Mona Domosh, "was a direct reflection of Boston's aristocracy." When they looked at the Common, they saw themselves: cultured, free from work, and "natural." They identified particularly closely with the Old Elm, the gigantic tree that had greeted the first settlers two

hundred years before and still dominated the center of the Common. For decades to come, they would celebrate it in books and poems because, as the monarch of the Common, it embodied many of the characteristics they prized most highly in themselves. Noble, deeply rooted, and seemingly permanent, the Old Elm became a

The Scottish artist George Harvey produced this painting of Boston Common shortly after the removal of the cows. Although the image portrays a harmonious relationship between work and play, the type of work shown—mowing grass—was one of several that contemporary viewers associated with the leisurely pace of rural life rather than hard agricultural labor. (Courtesy of The New-York Historical Society, accession no. 1952.411)

symbol of the upper classes that elites imprinted on everything from book covers to tabletops. Later in the century, Brahmin historians awarded the Common a central and formative place in the city's past, where earlier works had hardly mentioned it at all. Wealthy Bostonians wrote entire books about the Common and led efforts to protect it from industrial exhibitions, road widening schemes, and a host of other threats. Defending the Common came as naturally to the city's gentility as defending itself.[85]

Upper-class identification with the Common remained strong into the twentieth century. In 1910, the Boston landscape architect Joseph Henry Curtis wrote a history of the Common from the perspective of its oldest tree. The Old Elm had died years before, and Beacon Hill residents had transferred their affections to an English Elm planted in front of the State House in 1795. At one point in the book, Curtis imagines a conversation between himself and "Campestris" that served as a social and political allegory. Impressed by arguments for "greater equality and fraternity" among the classes, Curtis approached Campestris and demanded to know why he treated the "mean-looking, sickly" tree and the "little Runt of a tree" on either side of him so poorly. Curtis argued that land grew scarce as trees multiplied, that "the world owed every tree a living," and that Campestris could no longer expect to monopolize such a prime location on the Common. But the old tree countered that he had been there first and had a right to as much ground as his branches covered. When Curtis continued to press the matter, Campestris became agitated and shook its leaves so violently that Curtis retreated in fear. "I will not be a brother to that mean sucker," retorted the tree, "under any conditions whatever." Curtis dropped the subject, for he recognized that Campestris, an obvious symbol for Boston's aristocracy, had claimed the Common for itself and was prepared to defend its domain.[86]

The impact of enclosing Boston Common, of reinventing the human relationship to it, went far beyond the reinforcement of upper-class identity and the alteration of the Common itself. The transformed Common would influence the future development of a large swath of the city, beginning with the construction of a botanical garden on its flats in 1837. In time, the garden became so popular that the state preserved it as the Boston Public Garden. Though separated by a street, the Common and Public Garden served as extensions of each other and informed the subsequent development of the neighboring Back Bay as an elite enclave. Together, the Back Bay, Public Garden, Boston Common, and Beacon Hill formed an unbroken chain of refined spaces. The Common was the original link in that chain and inspired the development of the others. Its presence also thwarted less desirable forms of development. Like a natural bulwark defending the neighborhoods of Beacon Hill, the Common blocked the northward expansion of the commercial district and rerouted it in new directions. Altogether, a sizeable part of Boston's built environment traces its roots to the pastoral allure of the Common and a determined group's effort to conform the Common to their social needs and genteel views of nature.[87]

The new relationship between Bostonians and their Common also had an impact beyond the boundaries of Boston. When the Common shed its cows in 1830, it became the largest municipal green space in America dedicated entirely to passive recreation. That was fourteen years before Philadelphia began purchasing land for its Fairmount Park and twenty-three years before New York City began acquiring land for Central Park. The beginning of America's great park-building age was still over thirty years away. But by the time these landmark events in the history of park development had occurred, Boston Common had already taught a generation of urban Americans that they could assert their social status by relating to urban green spaces through recreational pursuits. The Common had also taught urbanites that such relationships represented a public good that government should bear the responsibility for maintaining.[88]

The transformation of this simple pasture therefore embodied the key intellectual shift that had to take place in order for parks to become possible: labor and production had to be banished from nature in favor of leisure, at least in certain public places. Boston Common's example would encourage the residents of other cities to preserve their own natural areas at public expense, and to do so not for the value that accrued when humans and domesticated animals mixed their labor with nature, but for leisure alone, and a particular kind of leisure at that.

It might be tempting to think that Boston Common avoided controversy after 1830, but it did not. Twenty years after the removal of the cows, the *Evening Transcript* published a biting letter suggesting that "there ought to be a rotation in the occupancy of all the houses fronting on the Common; otherwise it will always be a bone of contention." The author, who called himself "Ethan," also proposed that the city surround the Common with an eighty-foot fence filled with peepholes and charge citizens "fourpence a peep." But his tirade over the Common obscured the real source of his anger. "Ethan" was grasping for ways to pay down the four million dollar debt that the city had recently incurred to build its first public water system. The debt was a festering wound to those who had wanted a privately funded, for-profit waterworks, rather than a public one constructed at incredible municipal expense. To "Ethan" and the many others who had favored a private system, the debt was also a constant reminder that the majority of Bostonians had rejected their efforts to structure the city's relationship to water around the profit motive, and had instead adopted a more socially inclusive approach to "nature's nectar."[89]

2

Constructing Water

On a perfect fall day in October 1848, thousands of people from all over New England gathered in Boston to celebrate the completion of the city's first municipal water system. Crowds lined the narrow streets for over two hours and watched a massive parade wind its way through a sea of decorations that proclaimed the coming of water. Spanning Tremont Street was a specially constructed arch inscribed with William Shakespeare's words, "There will be a world of water shed"; the Reverend Francis Parkman's church displayed a flag declaring "Pure Water the Gift of Heaven"; and dignitaries spoke from a stand by the Frog Pond festooned with biblical passages, one of which drew on Genesis to assure the crowd that "The water is ours." At the end of the day, the delighted crowds watched in awe as a new fountain on Boston Common shot a silver stream eighty feet into the air. The celebrating did not stop there, for over the next several years local poets and illustrators would continue to venerate water as one of the greatest gifts the city had ever received from nature.[1]

It can be difficult to imagine a time when urban Americans reacted with that kind of excitement and wonder to something as commonplace as water. But the urban relationship to water in the first decades of the nineteenth century was entirely different from what it is today. The residents of most American cities, including Boston, New York, Baltimore, and New Orleans, still drew the water they used for drinking, cooking, and cleaning from wells and cisterns, most of them privately owned. Water was most commonly obtained through strenuous labor at an outdoor pump, and even the well-off were more likely to bathe in cold seawater at public baths than in fresh water at home. Already a scarce resource, water was also becoming an increasingly degraded one as leaky privies polluted groundwater and coal smoke contaminated cisterns. The relationship to water was a bit different in Philadelphia, where the city had built a large public waterworks in 1801 that dispensed clean water to certain parts of the city. But since the system operated at a loss for the first thirty years, few other cities followed Philadelphia's expensive example. Into the 1840s, most urban Americans still interacted with water through simple and age-old technologies, and they continued to debate the best ways to quench the growing urban thirst.[2]

Boston's water was as scarce and polluted as that of any other city, if not more so, but the geography of the city's water resources was complicated and presented no obvious solution. Although some of the city's wells produced better water than others, virtually all of them gave only "hard" water, which contains naturally occurring minerals like calcium and magnesium that enter the water from dissolved geological sources. The minerals make hard water less effective for washing than "soft" water, which some residents captured by directing the rain that fell on their roofs into privately-owned cisterns. But the quality of cistern water depended on the cleanliness of the roof, and the technology did not lend itself to a city-wide solution. Other sources of soft water would be expensive to develop, such as the Charles River or nearby country lakes, and none of them was problem free. Some were below grade, others were privately owned, and several contained microscopic life forms, the mere thought of which unsettled urban stomachs.[3]

For Boston, the road to a solution would stretch through two decades of contentious debate that began a few years before the city enclosed its Common. Urban reformers and their working-class supporters fought for a public system, while many wealthy and tax-averse Bostonians opposed it. The two groups disagreed on the quality and quantity of existing groundwater supplies, clashed over the level of purity that an acceptable supply of drinking water should possess, and argued above all else over the role that government ought to play in building a new system. Should Boston trust development to private corporations that would provide water only to those who could pay for it? Or should the city take a less traveled road by borrowing heavily to construct and manage a public system that would distribute cheap and abundant water to everyone? The choice was the single most important decision the city had to make, since it would determine everything from the size of the works, to the source of the supply, to who would have access to the water.[4]

Private and public systems embodied different ways of thinking about the relationship between water and society. Since a public system would deliver water more equally among a city's citizens (at least in theory), it seemed to imply that water should be abundant and a right. A private system would treat water as a commodity and sell it only to those who could afford the cost, suggesting instead that water was limited and a privilege. Boston's reform community, which supported a public works, brought yet another set of meanings to the water debates. Provoked by rising levels of social disorder and inspired by a deep belief in nature as a force for good, reformers claimed that an abundant and inexpensive supply of water from the wholesome countryside would transform the health and morality of the city's working classes. Together, these overlapping and competing ideas deeply shaped Boston's water debates and demonstrated how complex something as simple as water can become once it gets mixed together with human culture. When Bostonians finally settled on a municipal works, they were simultaneously helping to create a key component of the modern city and embracing a whole set of ideas that suggested a particular way of

relating to water. They were constructing not only a water system, but water itself.[5]

The Water Problem

In the early nineteenth century, most Bostonians—especially poorer residents of the city—took their daily supply of domestic water

Tens of thousands of people attended the Water Celebration in 1848 to mark the completion of the new water system and to celebrate their new relationship with water. (Courtesy of the Boston Athenaeum)

from wells. Some used public pumps, although the city maintained only a few for firefighting purposes. Like most other American cities, Boston assumed no responsibility for providing its citizens with drinking water. Many other residents relied on private wells that had assumed a public character over time. The Waltham Company, for example, allowed unlimited access to its water, and some wealthy residents intentionally left their wells unlocked for certain parts of the day or when leaving the city for the summer. Although some well owners guarded their water supplies more closely, an entire neighborhood might patronize a single well. Many better-off residents also used wells, most of them privately owned, but their greater financial resources also gave them easier access to soft water. Some obtained it by constructing private cisterns that collected roof runoff, as Harrison Gray Otis did for his Beacon Street home. Others purchased it from entrepreneurs who collected soft water from country lakes and sold it door-to-door by the bucket. These were expensive solutions, however, available only to a minority of Bostonians. Most residents met their daily needs as best they could with hard water secured from whatever well was close by and open to the public.[6]

In some antebellum cities, Boston included, residents who had enough money and lived in the right location could also have water piped directly into their homes by a private water company. Since the late eighteenth century, states had chartered corporations in cities from Portsmouth, New Hampshire, to Charleston, South Carolina, to meet part of the growing demand for clean water. The companies developed a source of water into a saleable commodity and then dispensed the water for a price. The Boston Aqueduct Corporation provided such a service to a limited part of Boston. Since 1798, it had drawn water from Jamaica Pond in neighboring Roxbury and transported it through pipes to better-off neighborhoods in the southern part of the city.[7]

Providing water only to those who could afford it reflected the common belief that urban residents should get only the services for which they paid. If property owners in an antebellum city wanted certain kinds of improvements to their neighborhoods, such as paved roads, sidewalks, or sewers, they often had to pay special assessments to get them. The levies could require the owners to cover a portion or even the entire cost of construction. When pushed to an extreme, as it was in Chicago, this system could produce a kind of government by personal interest, in which private responsibility was maximized, public responsibility minimized, and the redistribution of wealth avoided. But most cities relied on special assessments to one extent or another, including Boston, and much of nineteenth-century America's urban infrastructure was built by asking private citizens to share the costs of public works from which they derived a direct benefit.[8]

By the 1820s, however, Boston's patchwork system of private wells and cisterns and a single water company was failing. Like the residents of other rapidly urbanizing areas, Bostonians had begun to experience problems with the quantity and quality of their water supply. In April 1825, a large fire consumed fifty-three houses and stores before firefighters could find enough water to bring it under control. Forced by a lack of well water to use seawater, they had to drag their engines a thousand feet to the nearest dock and then back again, losing half the water in the process. It was a well known and pressing problem, but there were hints of another as well. Later that same year, the city's consulting physician and former dean of Harvard Medical School, Dr. John C. Warren, questioned the quality of Boston's water and claimed that the health of the city's residents required a new supply. He had noticed many cases in which the substitution of pure water for well water relieved illnesses, and he deduced that the city's well water was causing the ailments. Mayor Josiah Quincy responded to both problems by lobbying the City Council to find and develop a more plentiful and pure source of water. But he encountered stiff resistance because of the high cost of a municipal system. Quincy reluctantly concluded that such plans would have to wait until the desire for water outweighed the fear of increasing the city's debt.[9]

In 1834, faced with growing public dissatisfaction over the quality of the groundwater, the City Council commissioned a study of Boston's wells. Based on interviews of people who used the wells, the

survey showed that only seven of the city's 2,767 wells produced water that was sufficiently soft, or free from minerals, to be used for
washing. A full thirty percent gave water that nearby residents considered undrinkable, many of them giving off offensive odors that
suggested they had suffered contamination from privy vaults. Privies were holes dug beneath outhouses to store human waste, and
they frequently leaked and poisoned nearby water sources. After
two centuries of settlement, Boston's small peninsula was shot
through with privies. One builder, in the process of removing six
old residences to make way for new construction, found not only
the six vaults used by the most recent inhabitants but twenty more
that former residents had covered over. Cistern water had begun to
deteriorate as well, especially since the recent introduction of coal
as a household fuel. Roofs collected the ash discharged by neighborhood chimneys, as well as leaves from nearby trees and dust from
the streets, and rain washed the material directly into cisterns. Water contaminated with coal ash discolored clothes washed in it and
had a smoky taste.[10]

Despite the accumulating evidence of deterioration, the actual
extent of the water problem was hard to gauge. Some Bostonians,
from a cross-section of neighborhoods, insisted that their well or
cistern water was fine and that they were unaware of any general
want of water in the city. Josiah Knapp, an eighty-six-year-old resident of the South End, defended the city's well water by claiming
that he had "lived as long as any body" after a lifetime of drinking it.
Thomas Cushing, who lived near the State House, admitted that the
rainwater he collected in his cistern tasted like soot, but insisted that
his family had grown used to it. Reasonable people could disagree
about how bad water needed to be before it became unusable, especially since no scientific standard existed.[11]

It was more difficult to deny the water problem in the poorest
neighborhoods. Landlords made no provisions for access to water,
and the few wells in working-class areas tended to give water of

poor quality. But with few other practical choices available, residents continued to use them. Some areas had no potable water at all, and people had to walk as far as a third of a mile to find a well and then carry the water all the way back home. Desperate immigrants in the Broad Street neighborhood near the city's wharves sometimes paid as much as six dollars a year—more than a week's pay—to gain access to a private well, or smaller amounts if they simply wanted to fill a pail. When one property owner in the area decided to remove his cistern and offered its remaining water without charge, poor women and children carrying containers of all shapes and sizes overwhelmed his basement in an effort to collect every drop. The poor also descended on unguarded private wells. Benjamin Willis, a long-time inhabitant of Fort Hill, had been told by residents of Broad Street that they routinely sucked all the water they could out of his well when he closed his house for the summer. The quantity and quality of water available to the city's residents depended heavily on their individual social and economic status.[12]

Well into the nineteenth century, the most common solution to water problems in American cities was for a legislature to charter a private company to develop a water system. Proponents believed that private companies could provide water more cheaply than municipalities because a profit-driven entity would always search for the most inexpensive solution. They also claimed that cities empowering several companies rather than just one would enjoy more water and, due to competition among the companies, lower costs to consumers. Advocates often expressed admiration for London, which drew its water from eight different companies, although London's water companies had resolved their competition by dividing the city among themselves into monopoly districts and then raising prices. The water business could be very profitable, so finding interested entrepreneurs was rarely a problem. After upgrading its infrastructure, the Boston Aqueduct Corporation consistently paid its stockholders an annual dividend of ten percent.[13]

A municipally constructed and managed waterworks was also an option, although it was less common and swam against the tide of privatism. Opponents in Boston warned that a public system could lead only to disaster. The city, they argued, could not undertake such a large-scale project without a special legislative act that would enhance its powers with unpredictable results. Such an expensive public works project would also cripple the city with an unmanageable construction debt. Entrusting water to a private corporation instead, they claimed, would avoid such drawbacks. A pamphleteer writing under the name "Prudence" painted a rosy picture of private development in which "the city will avoid an everlasting pecuniary embarrassment, the citizens will happily escape the fiery ordeal of the tax gatherer, while the capitalist will cheerfully advance the means of accomplishing the desired object." Unless the city committed to private water, cautioned opponents of a municipal system, poorer residents might force a public waterworks on the city, secure in the knowledge that they would get the jobs and cheap water while the largest property holders shouldered an unjust tax burden to pay the debt.[14]

But private water companies had limitations. Always conscious of the bottom line, they avoided expensive public commitments and resented municipalities that forced them to repair streets after laying pipes or insisted that they provide water free of charge for fighting fires. Water companies also had well-deserved reputations for unreliability. Customers of the Boston Aqueduct Corporation frequently complained that the supply of water was inadequate and even nonexistent for extended periods, and similar distribution problems remained common wherever private water companies plied their trade.[15]

For these reasons, many Bostonians doubted the ability of private corporations to deliver an adequate supply of reasonably priced water to the entire city, especially to working-class neighborhoods. Samuel Eliot, who pushed for municipal water during his two terms as mayor from 1837 to 1839, insisted that the profit required by private companies would offset any savings. That same quest for revenue, he claimed, would encourage corporations to trade the long-term benefit of the people for short-term financial gain. Eliot explained that water companies would never invest more in a system than they absolutely had to, and the need for profit would effectively shut out the poor. This was, in fact, the case throughout the nation. Water companies rarely laid pipes through tenement districts, since they knew that most of the landlords would be unwilling—and the tenants unable—to purchase their product. The Boston Aqueduct Corporation, for example, refused to supply streets unless enough residents contracted to take the water in advance. As a result, many Bostonians hoped to build a public system like the one in Philadelphia. They believed that municipal control was the only way that the city's working classes would ever see a drop of water.[16]

Public Water as Social Reform

The debates provoked by Boston's water troubles were deeply rooted in the turbulence of the times. Beginning in the 1820s and accelerating into the 1830s, antebellum cities experienced the rapid commercial expansion and population growth—along with the social and economic disruptions—that accompanied the market revolution. America's cities suddenly found themselves overwhelmed by their own development and riddled with unprecedented levels of poverty, prostitution, drunkenness, and crime. They also were beginning to absorb a rising tide of foreign immigrants that would leave American cities more ethnically and religiously diverse than ever before. The newcomers, mostly Irish and German Catholics, were often met with hostility and even violence by native Protestant populations who feared that the Pope was plotting to take over America. Although the nation's cities had only just begun to grow beyond the size of large towns, the long list of troubles already plaguing them seemed to herald a future of social and moral break-down.[17]

Boston was suffering from an alarming level of ethnic and religious strife even before Irish immigration increased in the wake of the 1845 potato famine. Although the newcomers provided muscle for the new industrial order, their presence increased the cost of managing the poor, created enormous housing pressure in native-born neighborhoods along the wharves, and increased religious tensions in a city that retained a strong Protestant identity. In the late 1820s, when the number of Irish in the city was still comparatively low, riots regularly broke out between Catholics and Protestants in Irish neighborhoods along the waterfront and in South Boston. In 1834, a Protestant mob ransacked and burned the Ursuline Convent in nearby Charlestown, while nuns and female students narrowly escaped with their lives out the back door. Three years later, the city's ethnic and religious tensions sparked one of the worst cases of mass violence in Boston's history. The Broad Street Riot erupted when a company of Protestant firemen and the participants in an Irish Catholic funeral procession refused to share the same street. The confrontation escalated into a battle that eventually involved thousands of people and required the state militia to suppress it.[18]

Americans responded to their new urban problems with a series of moral and humanitarian reform movements in which Boston played a leading role. As early as 1813, Bostonians formed the Massachusetts Society for the Suppression of Intemperance, one of the first temperance organizations in America. In 1825, the deplorable condition of the county jail inspired the formation of the Boston Prison Discipline Society and the subsequent construction of more humane facilities. In 1841, a group of local literati organized the utopian community of Brook Farm in the rural suburb of Roxbury. Other reform-minded citizens devoted their time to abolitionism, women's rights, charity associations, and the improvement of public schools. Bostonians brought an enormous amount of energy to reform and pursued it on a dizzying number of fronts. "We are all a little wild here with numberless projects of social reform," quipped Ralph Waldo Emerson in 1840. "Not a reading man but has a draft of a new Community in his waistcoat pocket." Boston's zeal for constructive change had everything to do with its mission to serve as a city upon a hill. "They meant to make Boston a model town," wrote historian Van Wyck Brooks of the city's leading families. "They meant to make New England a model region."[19]

In the 1830s, Boston's reformers put public water in the same category as other campaigns for social improvement. A decade earlier, Mayor Quincy had called for municipal water largely to improve the city's ability to fight fires. Later reformers, however, believed that water could do much more. Dr. Walter Channing, a professor and dean at Harvard Medical School and an avid supporter of several reform movements, discussed water in the same context as temperance, abolition, and prison reform. Like these better-remembered causes, public water represented more than a solution to a narrowly defined problem. Water advocates believed that a plentiful supply of pure water could better the health and morals of the urban population, especially the working classes, and thereby transform society. Once reformers pinned such high expectations to water, they found themselves opposing privately owned systems of delivery that denied the fruits of nature to those who needed it most. Social reform and public water were natural allies.[20]

But that was not true in all cities. Philadelphia, the one American city with a large public waterworks before the 1840s, built its system largely in reaction to severe yellow fever epidemics in the 1790s. The city lost ten percent of its population to the disease in 1793 alone, and although there was disagreement over the cause of the fever, the consensus was that cleaner water would promote a healthier city. Philadelphia was less concerned with extending its water to the neediest residents of the city, even when it made later additions to the system. "The goal," writes historian Sam Bass Warner, "was never to help raise the level of living of the poor." New York City completed a public water system in 1842, just six years before Boston, and although it shared Philadelphia's concern about disease, it was also responding to a series of devastating fires that had highlighted the inadequacy of existing supplies. And like Philadelphia, New York was not as strongly influenced by the reform impulse as Boston.[21]

Boston's reformers and their working-class supporters would eventually win the public water system they wanted, but to understand the kind of relationship to water that they thought they were building, we have to examine the water debates closely. Reformers made three sets of arguments linking society and water: they claimed that an abundant supply of pure water would improve health; they maintained that it would promote moral behavior; and they insisted that access to clean water was a right rather than a privilege. These arguments were strongly contested by opponents, and the resulting debate opens a revealing window onto the many meanings that nineteenth-century Americans assigned to water. It also provides an essential guide to understanding why Bostonians chose to restructure their relationship to water in the way that they did, and what they hoped that new relationship would do for their city.

Water and Health

Perhaps foremost, Boston's reformers believed that a public water system would improve public health in at least two ways. The first was by promoting cleanliness. Although Boston had avoided the kinds of devastating epidemics that had swept through some other cities, it had suffered its own bouts with smallpox, cholera, yellow fever, and other diseases. Public health experts claimed that such illnesses were born of filth, and they maintained that most filth clustered in the streets and homes of poor neighborhoods and on the bodies of the poor themselves. As early as 1796, Noah Webster insisted that until more Americans recognized the connection between disease and environment, they would "wallow in filth, croud [sic] their cities with low dirty houses and narrow streets; neglect the use of bathing and washing; and live like savages." The introduction of pure, abundant water therefore promised to be an important preventative health measure: wash away the filth, and you wash away the potential for illness.[22]

The influential work of Edwin Chadwick, a leading public health reformer in Great Britain, crystallized the connection between disease, environment, and class. In 1842, after three years of research at the request of the House of Lords, Chadwick published his famous *Report on the Sanitary Condition of the Labouring Population of Great Britain*. He argued that the filthy, poorly drained environments in which the poor and the working classes lived caused diseases that then spread to more affluent social groups. Chadwick claimed that an adequate supply of pure water could cleanse both environments and inhabitants and, together with better sewers, dramatically reduce the development and spread of disease. Public health advocates and social reformers in urbanizing countries like the United States embraced his analysis with great enthusiasm.[23]

Chadwick's effort to change the public's relationship to water was informed by a strong desire to reform the poor. Although intended as a sanitary survey, Chadwick's report devoted more space to character, crime, and other social issues than it did to disease and cleanliness, which in his hands had clear moral valences. He wrote in the middle of a severe economic downturn that saw a dramatic increase in the suffering of the English working classes and a large increase in the costs of poor relief. By explaining these problems through environmental determinism, Chadwick masked the social and economic causes of the misery. Steady employment, high wages, and abundant food, he assured his readers, would not prevent workers from developing diseases. They simply needed to learn to clean themselves and their surroundings, and cheap public water was necessary to do it. Like other kinds of reform, public water could be just as much about social control as it was about helping the poor.[24]

Boston's reformers embraced these ideas about cleanliness and consequently found the hardness of the city's groundwater to be among its greatest shortcomings. Dr. Walter Channing, who emerged as the principal spokesman for Boston's water reformers in the 1840s, believed that hard water made cleaning almost impossible, since soap did not lather well with water that contained impurities. "It cheats you every day into the idea of being cleaned because you are 'washed,'" he asserted, "when the truth is, but for the ceremony of half wetting yourself, you are hardly a whit cleaner after the process than when you began." Samuel Eliot was of a like mind. He believed so strongly in the power of personal cleanliness that he thought it unnecessary to prove that existing supplies of water were "poisonous, or actively deleterious" in order to replace them. It was enough to know that an abundant supply of soft water would clean better than hard well water, since a city cleansed of its filth would endure less disease.[25]

The second reason that Boston's reformers thought cleaner water would promote better health was that they believed existing water supplies were actively causing illness. This argument brought Boston's physicians even more solidly into the debate, and they became the city's most prominent advocates of public water. Although Dr. John C. Warren's 1825 letter to the mayor had failed to stir much public discussion, he found a more receptive audience ten years later. In 1835, Warren organized a committee composed of five of the city's leading physicians to sponsor a petition urging city authorities to bring water to the city. Seventy other Boston physicians, all compelled by "a sense of duty . . . to the public health," joined the committee in signing the petition. They claimed that much of the city's groundwater was impure "either from its chemical composition or from the mixture with it of offensive foreign substances" and warned that it might contribute directly to the production of disease. The city's physicians recognized that leaky privy vaults and cesspools were poisoning the city's groundwater, and Channing had experienced the consequences firsthand. The contents of a neighbor's cesspool had leaked into Channing's cellar, ruining some stored vegetables and exposing his family to potential disease. The accident had also contaminated the cistern of the cesspool's owner, who had to purchase water from the Aqueduct Company thereafter.[26]

Although some doctors claimed that the hardness of Boston's groundwater was also contributing to illness, its true health effects remained a source of disagreement among the city's physicians. Where Dr. George Hayward claimed to have successfully treated patients with long-standing stomach and bowel problems by having them switch to soft water, Dr. B. P. Randall thought that the hardness of the city's water would affect only new residents, since the local population was probably used to it. The same range of interpretations plagued other cities. In 1831, a committee of the New York Lyceum of Natural History blamed hard water for dyspepsia and bowel disorders in children, only to have one of the city's doctors repudiate its findings in light of his own experience to the contrary. Water reformers in London endured the same uncertainty. In the absence of adequate scientific research, doctors had to draw on their individual experiences and came to different conclusions as a result.[27]

In Boston, advocates of private water quickly exploited the lack of a scientific consensus. Elias Derby, a lawyer representing groups opposed to a municipal system, defended the hardness of the city's groundwater as a positive attribute. He asked whether "a little lime and a little salt" could possibly be harmful. The body could not live without salt, he noted, and lime might actually prove to be beneficial. "The chemists told us that the bones of the body were made up of phosphate of lime," Derby argued, "and if we got a little with our water, it could not be very deleterious." Representatives of the

Boston Aqueduct Corporation also defended the chemical composition of the city's well water, since the introduction of cheap municipal water would likely destroy their business. In particular, they ridi-
culed chemical tests that pronounced local well water to be "not
pure." Since only distillation could produce truly pure water, they
maintained that the tester's standard of purity was unreasonably
high.[28]

Water and Morality

Boston's reformers not only insisted that a cheap and abundant supply of water would enhance public health, they also maintained that
it would improve morality, especially among the working classes.
Most reformers wanted to cleanse the city of both environmental
and social impurities, to reform both body and spirit, and they believed that water could shape an individual's moral condition just as
surely as it could affect one's physical wellbeing.

The moral argument for water made three distinct claims. The
first was that the higher level of cleanliness promoted by water—
the same cleanliness that reformers believed would result in better health—would also improve human behavior. By the nineteenth
century, more than ever before, personal and environmental cleanliness had become widespread markers of social position and moral
standing. It was obvious to Bostonians, as it was to urbanites across
the Western world, that the dirtiest neighborhoods were almost
invariably centers of disease and vice. Reformers concluded that
filth and immorality must therefore share a causal relationship. "The
condition of a population," wrote one British reformer, "becomes
invariably assimilated to that of their habitations." In short, dirt promoted immoral behavior. To those interested in improving morality, the logical course of action was to clean up the areas in question.
This conviction, which scholars sometimes call "moral environmentalism," suggested to Boston's reformers that giving the poor access

to an inexpensive and plentiful supply of water would be worth the high cost of a municipal system.[29]

In the eyes of these reformers, Boston's tenement districts seemed like cesspools of sin. Channing described the sanitary condition of the city's poor like an American Dickens: "The dark lanes and alleys they live in are rarely cleaned," he wrote. "They are never washed. Their wretched, dark, ill-ventilated rooms are scarce ever washed. Their persons are foul. Their clothing dirty." Channing was convinced that such miserable environmental conditions would breed degradation as easily as disease. "Every thing about them is most wretched," he continued, "most unfit to minister to self-respect, or to promote physical health, or moral progress. They become—are they not made—intemperate by such hard trial of virtue."[30]

Even those poor who wanted to rise above their circumstances faced certain failure without a clean environment. Channing wrote of a personal visit to an impoverished family of eight crammed into a single room in a run-down tenement. The father of the family, who claimed to have drunk "more rum than any man in Boston," had taken the temperance pledge four years before and intended to remain faithful to it. But the room remained a filthy and demoralizing place. Without convenient access to a well or cistern, the mother washed the floor only when a neighbor was willing to share dirty laundry water. Channing believed that the poor living conditions forced upon the family by a lack of decent water impeded the father's future moral improvement and even threatened to rob him of the gains he had made. If the man sank again into immorality, he would take his family with him.[31]

The second part of the argument for water as an agent of moral reform rested in the hope that a glass of clean water might replace alcohol as America's drink of preference. Temperance, the most popular reform movement of the antebellum period, sought to address a very real national drinking problem. Alcohol consumption swelled in the first two decades of the century as wage earners tried to cope with the anxiety and sense of powerlessness that social and economic displacement had produced. But temperance was more than just an effort to help those enslaved by demon rum. It was also an attempt by the middle and upper classes to control the growing sea of workers who no longer lived under their employer's roofs. Freed from paternalistic constraints, these workers were busy creating a distinct working-class culture beyond the influence of their former masters, and alcohol occupied a central place. The temperance movement was therefore as much a kind of social control as social reform, and its roots could be traced directly to the same separation of master from wage earner, work from home, and labor from leisure that had helped to produce the new relationship between Bostonians and their Common.[32]

Many temperance advocates believed that bad water was itself leading drinkers to the bottle and that clean water could be part of the solution. Faced with a foul-tasting glass of water, ran the theory, even the most ardent opponent of alcohol might turn to drink, or at the very least offset the bad taste by adding some spirits. Anecdotal evidence supported this claim. A Boston artisan named Joseph Tilden, for example, confessed that he "used to mix spirit with water, when it was so bad I could not drink it without." Other evidence suggested that an abundant supply of pure water could alter such behavior. Walter Channing knew a resident of Philadelphia whose drinking habits had changed dramatically after the construction of the city's waterworks. "Before this supply of pure water," explained Channing's friend, "I was in the daily habit of using intoxicating drinks, and scarce ever drank water without mixing them with it. Since the introduction of that water, I have almost abandoned the use of such drinks . . . *I do not want them.*" Impressed with such testimony, Boston's temperance advocates hoped to entice people away from alcohol with a glass of cold, pure, wholesome water. They enthusiastically threw their support behind a municipal system that would guarantee large amounts of water to all corners of the city.[33]

Intent on removing alcohol from every table, temperance reformers across America made water the rallying symbol and chief icon of their movement. Advocates referred to their membership as the Cold Water Army and pledged to drink nothing but water. John Pierpont, a Unitarian minister in Boston and a strident advocate of temperance and other reform causes, edited a collection of celebratory poems and songs that included lines such as "May pure cold water e'er abound" and "Cold water is the drink for me." Another of Pierpont's songs, written for the Friends of Temperance in 1838, encouraged the listener to plant the temperance standard near a well and to sing the praises of brooks, rain, and cisterns. "Yea, give a chorus loud and long," it concluded, "To aqueduct and spring!"[34]

Temperance reformers also looked to Christianity for proof that water was the most moral of beverages. Boston's water debates took place during the Second Great Awakening, a period of nationwide Christian revivalism that provided urban reform in general, and temperance in particular, with much of its fervor. Drawing on evangelical faith and biblical texts, temperance advocates argued that water had been the only drink in Eden and would be the only drink in Heaven. They also claimed that the Bible attested to water's central role in the unfolding of God's covenant. Was it just a coincidence, they asked, that human longevity decreased after Noah planted the first vineyard? Would the Israelites have found their way out of the desert if Moses had not released water from a rock with his staff but instead had built a still?[35]

Influenced by romantic tendencies to equate the natural with the divine, Boston's temperance reformers portrayed water as the creation of God and cast alcohol in the role of water's antithesis, the corrupt invention of humankind. One temperance writer contrasted the two by juxtaposing the environments that produced them: "Not in the simmering still, over smoky fires, choked with poisonous gases and surrounded with the stench of sickening odors and rank corruptions, doth our Father in heaven prepare the precious essence of life—the pure cold water." Rather, one would find the birthplace of water in the Edenic pastoral landscape: "In the green glade and grassy dell, where the red deer wanders, and the child loves to play, there God brews it."[36] While alcohol was antithetical to God and nature, water was a "drink divine" and "nature's nectar."[37] Through their writing, poetry, and song, temperance reformers used romantic ideas of nature to transform the most mundane of beverages into a powerful moral elixir.

Opponents of public water resisted efforts to link the movement to the temperance crusade. A pamphleteer who called himself "A Selfish Taxpayer" insisted that blaming the poor quality of the water for a brandy drinker's behavior merely provided an excuse for bad habits. "By recognizing such a pretence, as a legitimate apology," he declared, "we authorize the tippler to tipple on." A believer in total abstinence, "Selfish" feared most for moderate drinkers. If temperance leaders permitted them "to imagine, for one moment, that they are justifiable in their attempts to improve bad water by the addition of rank poison," then the claim that all alcohol consumption was born of moral bankruptcy would lose credibility. Besides, he predicted, an abundance of pure water would change nothing. Drinkers would simply find another excuse for their behavior.[38]

The third way that reformers believed water could promote moral reform was through its appearance in fountains, where its beauty could soften the hearts of the city's citizens. The Reverend Nehemiah Adams maintained that the possessor of a troubled mind, even someone whom doctors and ministers had been unable to help, could find relief by "lingering around a playing fountain, and seeing its vigorous, graceful stream mounting into the air, waving in the wind, and falling back into its bed." The benefits for the community could be just as great, since fountains could "leave a soothing and refreshing influence, and stir the social, kind feelings of the people." Channing and Eliot agreed that the restorative power of public fountains made municipal water all the more essential.[39]

Adams recognized that large fountains required cheap municipal water, but he also argued that the water must be exceptionally pure in order work its moral magic. He was therefore troubled by suggestions that the city should collect salt water or roof runoff for fire protection and then divert a portion to feed a new fountain on Boston Common. For a fountain to soothe the mind, temper passions, and improve morality, Adams believed its water had to be as virginal as his romanticized and feminized version of Nature—free of all impurities and unstained by previous use. The two proposed plans were unacceptable to Adams because in both cases the water did not meet that lofty and heavily gendered standard. "Nymphs of Helicon and Arethusa!" he lamented in 1842, "shall the Athens of America treat you to salt water and second-hand rain?" Adams suggested that patience would be a wiser course of action than rushing to complete an inadequate fountain. "We must wait," he concluded, "for that lingering project of supplying the city with pure water!"[40]

The connection between urban fountains and social reform was of recent vintage. Traditionally, fountains had played utilitarian, aesthetic, and civic roles in Western culture. They brought water to thirsty people, beautified cities, and celebrated the power of the government that had commissioned them. No one expected a fountain's water to improve the morality of a city's residents. That changed when romanticism's vision of a benevolent nature provided reformers with a new set of ideas that they could apply to fountains. Andrew Jackson Downing, America's first great landscape architect, added modest fountains to the country estates he designed. Downing claimed that no country seat was complete without a view of water, and he considered a simple series of jets emerging from a pool to be the only kind of fountain appropriate to natural settings. When New Yorkers completed the Croton waterworks and built a large fountain in City Hall Park, they chose this "natural" design over the ornately carved stone fountains so common in European cities. Bostonians would select a similar design for their fountain just a few years later, embracing Channing's conviction that nature in the form of simple sprays of water could "give tone and purity to the public heart."[41]

One critic of municipal water, who called himself "Anti-Humbug," doubted that fountains would work well for the city. But he did not question their ability to temper urban passions. Rather, he claimed that few residents would be around to enjoy them, since the fountains would play only in summer when many fled the city for cooler climes. More importantly, he insisted that New York City's magnificent fountain—made possible by its municipally owned water system—only played "when [the city's] democracy will permit the hundred hydrants which flow gratis for them to be occasionally locked up." New York's street hydrants serviced the needs of the working-class parts of the city, and "Anti-Humbug" believed that a finite supply of water meant that hydrants and fountains could not have water at the same time. He feared that Boston's laboring classes would likewise hold the city's water hostage while the public fountains sat idle.[42]

"Anti-Humbug" facetiously offered another plan instead. Suggesting that "those who don't pay taxes" would benefit more from a proposal that was better adapted to the city's climate, he advised that city officials introduce a new tax and use the proceeds to buy coal to warm the poor. "Which will make them most comfortable when they shiver with the thermometer at zero," he asked, "a frozen water-fall, or a grate full of live embers?"[43]

Clean Water as a Right

In addition to arguing that water would bring health and morality to the city, Boston's reformers also embraced a third argument for public water that suggested a radically different relationship to it from the prevailing one. Reformers claimed that access to sufficient clean water was a right rather than a privilege. This was the argument most welcomed by the working classes, and it was the most controversial. It was probably the most heartfelt as well, for the city's doctors were among the few upper-class Bostonians who routinely visited the city's slums and saw firsthand the consequences of an inadequate water supply. Dr. John Ware, commenting on one of the city's poorest neighborhoods in the North End, confessed: "I have rarely been more moved than I have been in Ann street, during a rain, in seeing the children, with all sorts of vessels in their hands, catching the falling drops, themselves literally soaked through in the labor." Another of the city's leading doctors, Henry Bowditch, knew of two Irish families in the Fort Hill district who had abandoned their side business of taking in laundry when soft water became impossible to procure. He also observed a physical altercation among several Irish women on Broad Street over the use of a pump. Even when Bowditch himself needed a small quantity of soft water to bathe a patient, he found it completely unavailable in poor neighborhoods. "No body knows," concluded Channing, "and no body can learn what deprivation means, who does not see the actual workings of a system which denies to the people the use of water."[44]

Reformers often based this argument on a deceptively simple analogy between water and other parts of nature to which humans seemed to have a clear right, particularly air and sunshine. "Avarice cannot withhold it, cannot stay it in its mission to all mankind, to bless all conditions of men," wrote Boston author John Stowell Adams. "It comes down from above like sunlight, and like that is free to all." Water's essential qualities made the comparison seem reasonable. Rain, air, and sunshine seemed to come unbidden from the sky to form a trinity of resources without which humans and many other forms of life could not survive. They also renewed themselves with unfailing constancy and without human assistance: one could always trust breezes to freshen the air, sunlight to reappear each morning, and rainfall to refill depleted ponds and lakes.[45]

The reality, however, was that most Bostonians worked much harder to get water than to get air and sunshine. They might not have paid for it, but they still pumped it by hand and lugged the heavy buckets all the way home. While there was no question that water was qualitatively different from the other necessities of life, like food, clothing, and shelter, and that it differed fundamentally from other saleable resources, like hay or coal, water was not quite as free to the taker as air and sunshine. But the very nature of water made it easy for reformers to argue otherwise and to connect water's physical characteristics to the social and cultural values they most wanted water to represent.

Reformers then built on this analogy to argue that a right to water could not be defended if water were managed by a traditional market. In an address before the legislature, a representative who favored a public water system articulated the worth of water within a moral economy rather than a market economy. "The value of an article depends, in a great measure," he claimed, "upon the inconvenience and suffering occasioned by the want of it. Water is as essential to life and health as bread; and, like air, it should be had without stint or measure." If the want of a particular good caused widespread suffering, then supply-and-demand mechanisms did not apply and people should have it "without stint or measure." Henry Williams, a friend of Walter Channing, embraced this vision of water and dismissed the idea of a privately constructed and maintained system as "preposterous in the extreme." To Williams, selling water for profit made no more sense than "farming out the pure air of heaven, of placing it in the hands of a few men among us to be stintedly doled out *at a price.*" Water advocates from New York City to Paris had made identical arguments against subjecting water to market forces when considering systems for their own cities.[46]

It was a short step from imagining water as a right that should not be managed by market forces to advocating a public water system. Reformers likened water to other essential human needs that they deemed to be best served by public institutions. The city "does not entrust the public education to private corporations, that men may speculate in individual culture, or popular ignorance," wrote Channing. "It does not entrust the care of the public health to private companies, which may grow rich upon disease." If the city did not entrust these essential functions to the private sector, then "neither should it for a moment admit the thought that the water men may, yes, must drink, should be doled out to them as it may suit individual caprice, or corporate enterprise." Whatever a society judged to be essential to the health and happiness of its people, Channing argued, must never be the responsibility of a profit-driven entity. It must, instead, be made the responsibility of government.[47]

There was a very different conversation about water rights taking place simultaneously in Boston's hinterland, where America's first industrial revolution was reshaping the human relationship to water around corporate needs. Entrepreneurs had discovered that New England's rapidly falling rivers could generate enormous amounts of power by turning turbines connected to large factories. Since the early part of the century, a collection of Brahmin families known as the Boston Associates had been building water-powered textile mills on the Charles and Merrimack rivers, with many of the mills concentrated in the new industrial city of Lowell. Although the owners of property along the rivers had long enjoyed traditional use rights to the water that flowed past them, the Boston Associates worked through the courts to gain rights to all of the river water they needed for their factories. Supported by jurists who believed that private industrial development was the greater public good, the "lords of the loom" built dams that altered the flow of water downstream, flooded nearby agricultural fields, and destroyed fisheries. They also took the unprecedented step of dividing flowing water into discreet units of power that could be bought and sold separately from the land through which it passed. With the rapid growth of the city and the industrialization of the countryside happening simultaneously, Bostonians became leaders in the evolution of not one but two new sets of relationships to water. One was urban, domestic, and trending away from the market. The other was rural, industrial, and dominated by private corporations whose control of the water supply cemented the fortunes of the most prominent Brahmin families.[48]

The claim that urban water supplies should stand outside of market forces did not go unchallenged. Some feared that the entry of municipalities into a traditionally private arena would turn the entire economic system on its head. Elias Derby painted municipal water as the first step down a slippery slope. "There were other necessaries of life which [the city] might as well undertake to supply, as water," he cautioned. "There were air, light, heat, clothing. Next year the city might come in there and ask for powers, under a vote of the citizens, to carry out some new project for supplying heat and gas from the interior of the earth; or to borrow money at four per cent to supply clothing for the poor, that the manufacturers need not charge them thirty per cent."[49] For Derby, making water a public responsibility would set a dangerous precedent that might undermine society's commitment to free enterprise.

Even more frightening to those who opposed a municipal system was the suggestion that the city distribute the water without charge. In the fall of 1844, a local merchant named John Wilkins published two articles in the *Boston Courier* arguing for the free distribution of water with the cost paid by a general tax. He hoped that supporting the system with a tax rather than water rents would encourage more people to use the water, since they were paying for it anyway. The poor would be exempted from the tax and receive the water like charity.[50] Opponents of municipal water saw Wilkins's plan as the logical but disastrous end point of any attempt to insulate water from market forces. The "Selfish Taxpayer" warned that Wilkins's plan would force enormous tax increases on property owners. He believed strongly that, whether a private or public system emerged, Boston should hold faith with the reigning municipal philosophy that every user should pay for his own services.[51]

Wilkins's position remained a minority one even among reformers who supported a municipal system. A number of influential public water advocates rejected his idea, although some accepted the possibility of giving water to the poor at no cost. Edward Everett Hale's father, Nathan Hale, supported a municipal system but drew on the arguments of his opponents to discredit the Wilkins proposal. The precedent set would be a dangerous one, he advised, that could lead to the adoption of "the same expedient for the supply of fuel, light and every other necessary of life." The notion of free water crossed a line beyond which few reformers were willing to go.[52]

Many working-class Bostonians, on the other hand, held out the hope that the city might distribute water without charge after it had paid down the construction debt. From the perspective of a capitalist, this was a radical proposal. But from the perspective of a laborer, it was conservative because his family probably did not pay for much of the water it was already using. L. M. Sargent, the principal stockholder of the Boston Aqueduct Corporation, claimed that he had "been told by more than one respectable mechanic of this city" that he supported municipal water "on a presumption, that he would have the water, as he has the high way, for nothing." To a mechanic whose family patronized a public well, free water would be business as usual, but to Sargent it heralded the end of free enterprise and the eventual loss of his company's customers. "When this demand shall have been obtained," he warned, "competition must cease, and we shall endeavor to contemplate the ruin of our property, as philosophically as possible."[53]

When the arguments made by Boston's reformers regarding health, morality, and the right to clean water are considered together, it becomes clear that they represented an appeal for a fundamentally different relationship with water. Rather than scarce, polluted, and a privilege, water would be abundant, clean, and a right. What made that agenda so contentious was that reformers wanted to expand the role of government to achieve it. Since government had never played a serious role in structuring how Bostonians interacted with their water supply, transferring responsibility for finding adequate water from the individual to the city seemed to some like a radical and potentially dangerous move. Instead, early experiments in municipal water like Boston's would prove to be the leading edge of a wave of change in municipal government. As the century progressed, cities would expand their power to fund large public works, often through borrowing, and they would pay the cost through general taxes rather than special assessments. Even the cost of smaller projects that did not require bond issues would increasingly be spread out among all residents of a city. Public water would encourage urban residents, in Boston and elsewhere, to expand their vision of the public good.

The reform position also reflected the desire to build a thoroughly different Boston, one that was cleaner, healthier, and guided by a stronger moral compass. Most Bostonians would have supported those goals, but those who threw their energies into reform causes had a more comprehensive vision of the city's future in mind. Edward Everett Hale remembered the period as a time of high expectations. "The rich men of Boston," he recalled years later, "really meant that here should be a model and ideal city."[54] Yet reformers, if optimistic about their ability to affect change, were not as unrealistic about the power of water as they might seem to modern eyes. They recognized that water alone could not create their city upon a hill. But they had faith that an abundant supply of clean water distributed to all parts of the city would enable Boston to take a giant step toward perfection.

"The Clamors of the Poor"

Although the opponents of public water in the 1830s and 1840s fought determinedly against the reformers and their ideas, they were not against health and morality—just expanded government and higher taxes. The most vocal opponents of public water were wealthy citizens trying to avoid tax increases. They were joined by a group of individuals and corporations that anticipated large financial losses from the construction of a municipal system. Holders of property that lay in the path of the proposed pipelines feared losing their lands; mill owners opposed any plan that would redirect the water powering their factories; and agents of the Middlesex Canal, which had been in financial trouble for years, claimed that an aqueduct would divert unacceptable amounts of water from their channel. The proprietors of the Boston Hydraulic Company and the Spot Pond Aqueduct Corporation also joined the fight. Incorporated in 1836 and 1843 to develop water through private investment, they saw little chance of building up their franchises if municipal water became a reality. But they had much less to lose than the Boston Aqueduct Corporation, which had already achieved profitability and was a regular critic of any plans for a public waterworks.[55]

These groups worked hard to portray the growing momentum for municipal water as an unjustified clamor of the poor against the rich. They frequently claimed to hear the voice of the mob in the popular referenda to which supporters of municipal water liked to resort. At a meeting in Faneuil Hall in August 1836, a committee formulated several nonbinding resolutions, one of which supported a water project undertaken at the city's expense. This resolution passed in a public vote six days later by a huge margin of 2,107 to 136. Although nonbinding, the adopted referendum was a powerful expression of the popular will. Proponents used the same tactic again in April 1838, this time securing support by 2,541 yeas to 1,621 nays.[56] "It never occurred to me," wrote an irritated Harrison Gray Otis to the City Council, "that popular impulses would be resorted to, in order to stimulate the action of the city authorities." Otis reminded the council members that the city charter had "disqualified the inhabitants from managing their municipal concerns except through the organ of a Representative Government."[57]

The "Selfish Taxpayer" agreed that the mob was strong-arming the city into building a public works. "The idea of coercing entire boards of council," he warned, "to act contrarily to their consciences, by the force of an *instructing* power, presumed to reside in an excited and multitudinous body, is the very maximum of jacobinical absurdity." "Selfish" claimed that the first impulse for water had come from Beacon Hill, where certain residents were unable to obtain water of adequate quality and quantity and so drafted the lower classes to their cause. "The rich," he claimed, "have called to their assistance the clamors of the poor."[58]

But those favoring public water insisted that their base of support cut across all social and economic classes. Their lawyers worked especially hard to convince legislators that many people of property supported municipal water. Attorney Richard Fletcher pointed out that the city's two richest wards had voted for municipal water through a referendum, and his co-counsel cautioned that there was no occasion "to raise a clamor of poor against rich or rich against poor. This was not the project of merchants alone, or mechanics alone, or of any class alone, but all had united on what they considered the common good of all."[59]

Both portraits of municipal water advocates contained some elements of the truth. The results of the referenda suggest that a large portion of the working classes endorsed a municipal plan. Also, those who signed petitions in support of public water tended to be much less well-off. In 1838, the city received four petitions for public water and four remonstrances against. City records show that the average real estate tax paid by the petitioners was only about a quarter of that paid by the remonstrants.[60] The battle over public water was not fought along simple class lines, but it was clear that many members of the working classes had a strong desire for cheap and pure water.

Much of the movement's leadership, however, came from reform-minded members of the middle and upper classes. The mayors who worked most strenuously to keep the water question in the public eye from the 1820s through the 1840s also tended to support many other reform causes as both city officials and private citizens. Josiah Quincy, the first mayor to advocate municipal water, had single-handedly transformed the way city government functioned. Theodore Lyman not only spoke strongly for a municipal water supply as mayor but also served as president of the Boston Farm School and founded the state reform school, endowing it with over seventy thousand dollars of his own money. Samuel Eliot lobbied for public water during his administration and also professionalized the police and fire departments and built several new schools, an insane asylum, and an addition to the House of Corrections. And Josiah Quincy, Jr., son of the first mayor and the official who would preside over the final construction of the waterworks, pushed for new primary and secondary school facilities and approved the construction of a new county jail. Several of the mayors who had shown less enthusiasm for municipal water while in office took correspondingly little interest in the reforms of the day.[61]

The city's physicians, many of them active in multiple reform movements, remained among the most vocal supporters of public water. They turned out in force to argue their case before legislative committees, and when the water debate—which blew hot and cold with the political winds—heated up once again in the summer of 1844, it was Walter Channing who sponsored a petition to hold another general meeting of the citizens at Faneuil Hall. Reform-minded individuals directed the campaign for water just as they led the temperance crusade and other antebellum movements, and they knew how to marshal mass support for a cause. In yet another nonbinding referendum in December 1844, Bostonians voted for municipal water by a large majority (6,260 yeas, 2,204 nays) and resoundingly rejected a proposal to charter a private water company (1,194 yeas, 7,144 nays).[62]

Nature Shapes the Debates

From the very beginning, the water debates had been influenced not only by competing social agendas but by the kinds of water resources that nature had provided to the Boston area. The most likely candidates for the main source of a new water supply included Spot Pond and Mystic Pond, about eight miles northwest of Boston; the upper Charles River, beyond the reach of the salt water tides; and Long Pond, about twenty miles west of the city. Spot Pond was the favorite source of private water interests. The pond contained good, clean water and was situated high enough above Boston that gravity alone could bring its water to the city. It was also already controlled by a group of entrepreneurs who were eager to develop it. But Spot Pond's capacity was so small that it would meet only present needs at best. Mystic Pond was just as close but would be a more expensive choice, since it would require a dam to keep back the salt water of the Mystic River and a pump to raise its water above the grade of the city. The water of the Charles River would also need to be pumped to a higher elevation, and it suffered from the additional liability of containing industrial waste released from nearby factories. The final option, Long Pond, was favored by supporters of municipal water. Its 659 acres contained more than enough water to meet present and future needs, and it was well above the elevation of the city. But private investors were reluctant to develop it themselves, since its great distance from the city would require a huge capital investment that might not pay dividends for years to come. The battle between public and private interests therefore did not play out on a blank environmental slate. Rather, the configuration of exist-

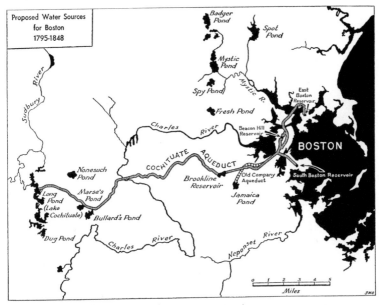

The area around Boston contained a number of possible sources for a water supply, each of which had a different set of advantages and limitations. The gray line indicates the route of the aqueduct as finally constructed. (Reproduced from Nelson Manfred Blake, *Water for the Cities: A History of the Urban Water Supply Problem in the United States,* 1956, courtesy of Syracuse University Press)

ing water resources contributed to the formation of a "Spot Pond" party that favored private development and a "Long Pond" contingent that supported a municipal system.[63]

After two decades of scrutinizing the area's water sources, scientists unexpectedly turned up a previously hidden characteristic of the local water that also began to shape the debate. In 1845, scientists found tiny animals and plants in Long Pond. The "animalcules," or microscopic life, were visible only with the assistance of a microscope, so most of the city's residents had neither seen nor heard of them. But the announcement of their existence created a great deal of concern about the fitness of such water for human consumption. Both supporters and opponents of municipal water quickly politicized the animalcules as they battled over the meaning of the small creatures.

The defenders of a city-built system rushed to placate the public's fears. Nathan Hale sat on a commission appointed by the city to resolve the water debate and argued that it would be impossible to find a source of water free of animalcules. He supported drawing water from Long Pond despite their presence and suggested that "the only remedy against them is, to avoid too curious a search by microscopic eyes." His advice was less than comforting. Channing, another advocate of Long Pond water, tried to disarm his adversaries by poking fun at those who feared that such small creatures "are about to devour, or to choke so many of our worthy burgesses." But both men found that public concern could not be so easily dismissed.[64]

Attempting to dispense with the matter, Channing secured the opinion of a local naturalist who claimed that the animalcules were not only harmless but beneficial. Dr. Augustus A. Gould explained that animalcules lived in all fresh and salt water and occasionally in well water. They were impossible to avoid. But Gould believed that, rather than having a negative impact on the water they inhabited, the animalcules actually enhanced its purity by consuming decayed and impure substances and then dying themselves. His argument sounded reasonable until he also claimed that animalcules had considerable nutritional value. Gould dubiously insisted that the human ability to survive on nothing but water for considerable periods proved his theory. He did, however, understand the human revulsion against the organisms and considered it a blessing that nature had made them so small that "we should neither be moved by sympathy at the wholesale murders we are obliged to commit, nor with disgust at their presence."[65]

Gould's final assessment of Long Pond water was as paradoxical as the other scientific arguments that infused the water debates. While praising animalcules for their nutritional value and ability to clean polluted water, he also cautioned that their presence indicated impurity and that one should not drink water that contained too many of them. Inconsistencies like this compounded the confusion of a public already beset by the dueling voices of competing experts. "The good people were never more entertained, if such things can amuse them," Channing reflected. "They were never so mystified, if council could possibly be darkened in such wise."[66]

The opponents of a municipal system latched onto the presence of animalcules to discredit Long Pond as a source. A supporter of tapping the privately-owned Spot Pond warned readers of the *Boston Daily Argus* that the animalcules would expand as they advanced through the proposed aqueduct and grow to the size of "gallinippers or dragon flies" by the time they reached the city.[67] Another advocate of private water distributed a broadside that contained a satirical cartoon showing a scientist explaining an image of Long Pond water magnified by a microscope. The enlarged view reveals water teeming with tiny creatures bearing horns, claws, tails, and multiple appendages. Most of those attending the scientist's presentation are recoiling from the image. One Irishman, playing off the common euphemism of whiskey as a "drop of the creature," calls the water "a dhrop of a thousand cratures," while another holds back a dog growling threateningly at the image. A woman comments that one could "make nothing of it but varmint broth," and another figure sighs: "Well if this is pure water I'm glad I never signed the Pledge." The most optimistic member of the crowd is a doctor who parodies Gould by predicting that the water will "appease both thirst and hunger" and thereby "prove a great blessing" to the poor.[68]

The tiny life forms had become a giant political football. Even John Wilkins, a local merchant who favored public water, used the animalcules to discredit Long Pond and promote his preferred source, the Charles River. He collected samples from both and claimed that Long Pond contained far more animalcules than the Charles. Wilkins concluded that running water was less likely to

A drop of Long pond water mag

In 1845, scientists discovered microscopic plants and animals in the water of Long Pond, the source preferred by public water advocates. Their opponents'

d by the Solar microscope.

response included this cartoon, which was designed to fuel the public's fear of drinking water with "creatures" in it. (Courtesy of the Massachusetts Historical Society)

contain animalcules than pond water, making it more fit to drink. Besides, he argued, people would never drink water if they knew that animals were swimming in it.[69]

Londoners had wrestled with the meaning of their own animalcules in 1828 and would again in 1849 when they began considering the merits of a public water system. Naturalists armed with microscopes searched the Thames River and other bodies of water for microscopic life and struggled to make sense of what they found. Some contemplated whether a causative link existed between certain animalcules and particular diseases, and others wondered if the presence of animalcules, rather than the animalcules themselves, suggested something important about the water's purity. But no study provided a definitive answer. In the end, all that the citizens of London could agree on was a common revulsion at the idea of imbibing the creatures. One observer regretted the way that such water filled people with "kicking things with horrid names, which you see in microscopes at the Polytechnic, and rush home and call for brandy —without the water."[70]

In Boston, the commission assigned to study the water problem finally put the matter to rest in 1845 by consulting outside experts. Professors from Yale College and West Point, presumed to have no interest in the outcome of the debate, assured the public that animalcules were not a health threat and were present in the potable water supplies of Philadelphia and New York City.[71]

The issue subsequently lost its political value and disappeared from public debate, but only after the lowly animalcules had significantly shaped efforts on both sides to construct a meaningful image of water. The private water advocates, who had argued that the minerals in the city's drinking water were harmless, were now attacking the presence of animalcules as dangerous and unhealthy. Public water advocates, for their part, had assailed mineral-laden water as dangerous and unhealthy, but they were now defending animalcules as harmless and perhaps even nutritious. Although neither side had the scientific evidence to back up its claims, each found itself compelled to define the meaning of these tiny plants and animals for the public before the opposition did it for them. The animalcules could not be ignored. Like other characteristics of the local water, from its hardness to its elevation to its proximity to the city, the animalcules helped to set the terms of debate.

Winning the Political Battle

Two decades of deliberation culminated in a final year of intensive political maneuvering that lasted from the spring of 1845 to the spring of 1846. Public water advocates established Water Unions on a ward level to organize support, while broadsides battled each other for the public's attention. The Spot Pond Aqueduct Corporation, desperate to prove its civic-mindedness, posted a broadside that offered to limit its profits to between six and ten percent if the city promised to stay out of the water business. But an opposing broadside derided the company as mercenary, duplicitous, and the servant of the upper classes.[72] Another claimed that a vote against public water would be sure to please those few "crusty, narrow, stingy, grumbling, rich men" who stood in the way of the project. "Is it not better, safer, more manly, more republican," the authors asked, "to help yourselves than to trust to the broken promises and doubtful generosity of private corporations?"[73]

Some still remained unconvinced that the city needed additional water sources at all. Lemuel Shattuck, a statistician who had just completed a comprehensive and groundbreaking census of the city's people, institutions, and resources, sided with the opponents of public water. Although Shattuck appreciated the health benefits of pure water, he publicly asserted his belief that certain groups were greatly exaggerating the need for new sources. Most of the complaints, he suggested, were coming from landlords and tenants who could not be bothered to keep their pumps in working order or to arrange to bring in water from existing mains in the street. "Such cases," he wrote, "should not be relied upon to prove a general want of water."[74] Yet his own statistics seemed to contradict this claim, since they showed that fifty-eight percent of the city's houses lacked convenient access to drinkable well water. The proportion shot up to seventy-three percent in the ward that included the immigrant neighborhoods of Broad Street.[75]

The tipping point came when nature itself seemed to endorse the movement for public water. The city had commissioned John Jervis, a nationally respected water expert, to assess the competing sources. Jervis had served as chief engineer on New York City's Croton works, completed just three years before in October 1842, and his professional opinion carried enormous weight. In November 1845, Jervis submitted a report advising that Long Pond—the preferred supply of many public water advocates—contained the purest water of the available sources. He also calculated that Long Pond alone among the several lakes that dotted Boston's hinterland contained sufficient quantity to adequately supply the city's growing needs. Long Pond's purity and size seemed to make it the only source worth developing, yet it was also the only source that private interests did not have the capital to develop themselves.[76]

A public system now seemed certain. Swept along by Jervis's recommendation and the growing support for a municipal system, the City Council petitioned the legislature for an act that would allow it to bring water from Long Pond to Boston. The legislation passed in March 1846, and a few weeks later Boston's citizens accepted the Water Act by an overwhelming margin of 4,637 to 348. The Boston Total Abstinence Society celebrated the victory on the following Fourth of July by hauling three thousand gallons of water from Long Pond to Boston Common and distributing what they called "Nature's beverage" to thirsty bystanders.[77]

Construction of the new public waterworks began just four months later. Mayor Josiah Quincy, Jr., turned over the first spade of dirt in a ceremony at Long Pond. His father, now seventy four years old, also took a turn with the shovel. "Hundreds of poor women," said the younger Quincy in his address, would no longer wait "with sleepless anxiety for the unlocking of the pump." During the ceremony, the Mayor convinced the City Council to restore what supposedly had been the pond's Indian name, "Cochituate." It was an Algonquin word meaning "swift water," but Bostonians translated it more creatively as "clear, beautiful water" to emphasize the lake's purity.[78]

As the celebrants took the train back to Boston, they passed a group of laborers who had already begun to excavate for the aqueduct. The city had chosen Jervis as its consulting engineer, and he wasted no time in starting the work. Jervis hired a number of contractors and 3,500 men, most of them Irish immigrants, to complete the job. Carpenters, blacksmiths, bricklayers, stonemasons, and countless laborers moved soil and rock to construct a brick, egg-shaped aqueduct five feet in width, over six feet in height, and fifteen miles long.[79] Miners worked around the clock in eight-hour shifts to carve two tunnels from solid rock so that the bed of the aqueduct could maintain its gentle fall of three and one-half inches per mile. "From the moment of its commencement," the mayor would later boast, "the work has been unintermitted, by day and by night, from noon to midnight, and from midnight to noon, the labors of the hammer and of the spade have been incessant."[80]

Progress was rapid, and in October 1848—just over two years after workers had first broken ground—the water reached Boston. From Lake Cochituate, it ran fifteen miles through the aqueduct to a hilltop reservoir in neighboring Brookline. The reservoir could hold up to one hundred million gallons of water, enough to supply the city for two weeks if difficulties interrupted service from the lake. The water took twelve hours to complete its journey from lake to reservoir, and from there it flowed another five miles through two pipes, one thirty and one thirty-six inches wide, to two smaller and as yet unfinished reservoirs within the city itself. The first, an imposing stone structure on Beacon Hill, would be able to hold over two and a half million gallons of water within its fifteen-foot-thick walls. The second, on Telegraph Hill in South Boston, would store about seven million gallons. From these reservoirs, the water would soon pour through over sixty miles of cast-iron pipes that workers had laid beneath every inhabited street in the city and shoot up from a new fountain in the center of Frog Pond. The current would convey not only water but also the many meanings of water that had made the new system possible.[81]

Interpreting the Victory

On October 25, 1848—the day set aside to celebrate the arrival of water in the city—heavy overnight rains gave way to a beautiful morning, and a discharge of artillery announced that the ceremony and parade would take place as scheduled. A crowd from the city and surrounding towns, reportedly nearing one hundred thousand people, assembled to partake in the festivities. "For miles," recorded one commentator, "nothing but compact masses of human beings were to be seen in our streets."[82] The ceremony on Boston Common consisted of speeches and songs, and the parade was on a scale never before seen in the city. Within the sea of elaborate floats sailed a fully rigged and manned ship, and seven black horses pulled sections of the large cast-iron water pipes used to construct the aqueduct. In each street, the parade crawled beneath white tablets strung from building to building that recorded the political history of the effort to bring water to Boston. Fourteen in all, the tablets traced the story from Mayor Josiah Quincy's call for water in 1825 to the groundbreaking at Lake Cochituate in 1846.[83]

The celebration proved large enough to support multiple interpretations of the new public water system. Jubilant temperance marchers recalled their central role in the water movement's success by filling an entire division of the parade by themselves. Fully eleven temperance organizations from various parts of the state marched with colorful flags proclaiming their love for pure water. Members of the Boston Temperance Society carried a white banner that read on the front, "O, that's the drink for me," and on the reverse, "The Second Declaration of Independence." The standard of the Washington Total Abstinence Society declared: "Goddess of Temperance, we bow to thee!" and a uniformed section of the Cadets of Temperance from nearby East Cambridge bore a banner with the words "Our Distillery" over a scene of Niagara Falls. Additional companies of temperance marchers came from all over New England to participate in the parade.[84]

Two temperance advocates composed new songs for the occasion, and the crowd received sheets with the lyrics set to popular tunes. William Bingham Tappan's song praised the better health and increased cleanliness that water promised, rejoicing that "Alcohol's conqueror merrily comes / To the shout of hurrahs and the music of drums." George Russell's contribution welcomed "nature's nectar" and celebrated the fact that all the city's residents would benefit from its powers.[85]

Another musical piece, composed by James Russell Lowell and performed by the city's school children, depicted water as a substance that contained mythological and Old Testament significance while also serving as the primary engine of industry. Lowell's work led the listener through some of water's many manifestations: as "Ceres' cupbearer," water rained down on the flowers, fruits, and fields of the earth; across the Atlantic, it filled "the fairies' acorn cups" of England; and everywhere it glowed in the rainbow that still shone as brightly today as it had for Noah. But as the song progressed, the rainbow transformed from a symbol of God's covenant to the machinery of a New England textile mill that sang of its talent for manufacturing: "I, too, can weave; the warp I set / Through which the sun his shuttle throws." Lowell's song went on to spend

An entire division of the water parade was composed of joyous temperance marchers. In this detail from a larger illustration, the marchers can be seen carrying a banner bearing the image of a fountain. (Courtesy of the Boston Athenaeum)

as many verses celebrating water's industrial uses as it did water's romanticized qualities. In that way, Lowell was as true to himself as to his class, for he was both a romantic poet and author and a member of the wealthy family that had helped to found the industrial city of Lowell.[86]

Yet another song, written by a local mechanic and disseminated informally during the parade, better reflected the working-class interpretation of the water's significance. The author, Benjamin Penhallow Shillaber, was both a printer and an accomplished poet. His contribution to the festivities, "A Song for the Merry-Making on Water Day," was one of the parade's highlights. Working on a mounted press pulled by four horses, his fellow printers struck off and handed out elaborately decorated lyric sheets as they road along. Shillaber's song set a festive tone as it described the trading of work for the most boisterous of celebrations. But rather than predicting water's contribution to sobriety or celebrating its romantic qualities and industrial applications, Shillaber's song interpreted Boston's new supply of water as a gift from God. Joyously declaring the "Advent Day of Water," the song attributed a "holy" influence to water as it completed its "blessed mission" to supply everyone in the city. The universal distribution of water lay at the heart of Shillaber's composition, which stressed water's importance to the working classes. Water came "to cheer the high and lowly," and "a gladsome shout from the mass goes out" to welcome its arrival. "Every tongue shall swell the song," Shillaber continued, "Whate'er its rank or station." If any doubt remained about the nature of water's new relationship with Boston's people, he spelled it out plainly:

> *Hail, hopeful stream! From thy bright gleam*
> *Our hearts reflect the omen,*
> *That water's want no more will haunt*
> *The thirsty man or woman.*

Temperance, romantic, and industrial imagery had no place in the poet printer's celebration. An abundance of water would cure the people's thirst, and that was enough.[87]

The parade's final destination was Boston Common, where banners celebrating the occasion festooned its gateways. "Streams shall run in our streets and play about our dwellings," promised one; "The springs of the hills have come unto us to refresh us," rejoiced another. Evergreens and flowers decorated many of the banners and reinforced the pastoral imagery evoked by the quotes. Each division of the parade completed its tour by passing through the Park Street gate onto Boston Common and taking its appointed position near a speaking platform built in the middle of Frog Pond. Mayor Quincy, whose address capped the festivities, cheered water's potential to improve "health and purity, temperance and safety."[88]

As the ceremonies concluded, and the sun sank over the Back Bay, the mayor asked the members of the crowd if they were ready to see the water in the new fountain. They expressed great enthusiasm, and the chief engineer ordered workers to open the fountain gate. All watched in wonder as a jet of water six inches at the base rose higher than the topmost branches of the Old Elm and fell in showers back into the pond. With the conclusion of the ceremony, the crowd dispersed to the streets where they watched fireworks and wandered among the thousands of lights illuminating the city's shops and private homes.[89]

Social Vision versus Social Reality

Once reformers had achieved their goal of constructing a public water system, water reform disappeared as an active movement. Yet, despite the jubilant tone of the celebration, the city's new relationship to water would not fulfill all of the expectations of its proponents. This was in part because working-class neighborhoods would not see water in the abundance that many had hoped. Although the city took the unusual step of offering to connect private buildings to the water mains at public expense, landlords remained unwilling to pay for plumbing in their tenements. As a result, many Bostonians who lived in rented apartments used the new public hydrants installed throughout the city. The quality of water dramatically improved, but the inconvenience of relying on distant street hydrants shared by many families placed practical limits on the use of the water. As late as 1868, only one hydrant serviced the seventy-two tenements and three hundred and fifty residents of Institute Avenue in the North End.[90] Such small and inconvenient supplies of water could not possibly create the well-scrubbed world that water advocates had imagined.

In fact, concern with the needs of workers and the poor, so prominent in the discussions that led to the new aqueduct, dissipated quickly once the system was completed. The new water commissioners rarely mentioned these groups in their reports. Instead, they focused attention on those who could afford to bring water directly into their homes. By 1868, the commissioners could boast that the buildings of Boston contained over one hundred thousand internal fixtures connected to the waterworks. Cochituate water washed Bostonians in 5,929 bathtubs and 759 shower baths, cleansed their cloths in 6,806 permanently installed washtubs, and flushed their waste in 17,654 water closets. It also played throughout the city in 21 public fountains.[91] George Templeton Strong's sensual experience with New York City's Croton water in 1843 suggested the aqueous joys that well-to-do Bostonians were coming to know. "I've led rather an amphibious life for the last week," he reported after installing a new bathroom, "paddling in the bathing tub every night and constantly making new discoveries in the art and mystery of ablution. Taking a shower bath upside down is the last novelty." Most working-class Bostonians, like their counterparts in other cities, would not enjoy such luxuries for decades to come.[92]

Even the image that came to represent the waterworks better reflected the concerns of the rich than the poor. Sheet music, guide-

The fountain on Boston Common came to symbolize the completed water works in a variety of publications, including this sheet music. But such images obscured the social and environmental concerns that had originally prompted the system's construction. (Courtesy of the Boston Athenaeum)

books, and histories of the city illustrated the new system with a rendering of the new fountain on Boston Common surrounded by well-dressed people at play. Such images did not evoke the joy that water brought to "the thirsty man or woman," as Benjamin Penhallow Shillaber might have had it, but instead directed the viewer away from many of the problems that had sparked the water debates in the first place.[93]

Working-class expectations were further disappointed just two years after the completion of the waterworks when city officials repudiated the idea of free water. As late as the water celebration, the mayor had indicated that the city might distribute water free of charge after paying off the construction debt.[94] But demand grew quickly and waste was endemic, leading the city's water commissioners to guard the supply jealously. The larger obstacle, however, proved to be a legal one. In 1850, a local charitable organization approached the city to provide water to it at no charge, but officials refused the request. They based their decision on an opinion provided by the city solicitor, who declared that the law viewed water as valuable property that the city held in trust for all its citizens. "If the City Council may give the water to one institution of this kind," explained the solicitor, "they may to all. If they may give it to a charitable institution, they may to an individual. If they may give it to a poor corporation, they may to a poor man."[95] City officials, concluded the solicitor, could no more give away water in such a haphazard fashion than they could give away the public lands.

Like the dreams of the city's laboring classes, the expectations of reformers remained partly unfulfilled as well. Few would have claimed that the new water system markedly improved the morality of the city's residents. In fact, arrests for drunkenness actually increased over the next few years.[96] Benefits to public health also could be difficult to detect. Although cleaner water undoubtedly improved individual health and reduced the number and severity of epidemics, tenement districts remained awash in sewage for decades. The relentless flood of immigrants and the ruthless pace of urbanization compounded these failures. Even if Boston's water had been as free and accessible as the most optimistic reformers had hoped, it still could not have begun to ameliorate the deep social and economic problems and the wretched environmental conditions that plagued the city.

Yet water would retain its romance for the city's poets, at least for a few years. The water in the new fountain rose and fell near the branches of the Old Elm, and local writers put this visual connection to poetic use by linking the purity of water with the purity of women. In 1849, the publisher James Fields wrote a short poem that portrayed the water of Lake Cochituate as a nymph, who like nature itself listened only to "the ripple of her own sweet song." When she matured, she heard duty's call and answered it by springing to the side of the Old Elm to become his "young enchanted bride." Fields' nymph simultaneously evokes a romanticized nature that awaits the shaping hand of humankind and a young woman of taste whose life has no purpose until marriage gives it meaning.[97]

Another poet, known only as "Eliza," picked up Fields's theme four years later and penned a much longer and more complex poem. In Eliza's rendition, the marriage is preceded by a lengthy courtship in which the Elm writes love letters on his leaves and sends them floating on the winds all the way to "Miss Cochituate." She eventually travels to the Common to marry the Elm. Throughout the poem, Eliza's Miss Cochituate embodies the best of water and woman: she is sweet, beautiful, graceful, refreshing, clear, bright, fresh, and—of course—pure.[98]

The two poems suggest how quickly some Bostonians had forgotten the reasons that the city had wanted water in the first place. Neither contains a single word of reference to the urban conditions or the reform ideas that had driven construction of the waterworks. Instead, in both poems the feminized water arrives on the Common without once dirtying her feet in the surrounding city or providing any service to the poor along the way. Fields's nymph simply springs from her country lake to the fountain on the Common, and Miss Cochituate's method of travel remains a mystery—it is simply "an impossible thing that has possible grown!"[99] By representing the story of how water came to Boston as an imagined marriage between two different aspects of nature, the poems left out the thirsty poor, the tax-averse rich, and the reformers who dreamed of a better city. All that remained was a lingering sentimentalism toward water and the vague notion that the coming of water had left the city better off than it was before.

For Bostonians, the unique properties of water, the geography of existing lakes and rivers, the mineral content of the groundwater supply, and even the presence of microscopic life in nearby lakes had become entwined with visions of pure water held by social romantics, public health experts, temperance advocates, members of the working classes, and promoters of private water corporations. What emerged from the debate was a radically new relationship with water and one of the fundamental building blocks of the modern metropolis: a water system that served the entire city. Boston's municipal water system differed significantly from the private alternative and represented a major victory against the culture of privatism. It provided a consistent and abundant supply of clean water and declared water to be the right of all citizens rather than the privilege of a few. It also expanded governmental control over the management of public health, a process that would culminate with the establishment in Boston of the nation's first comprehensive state board of public health in 1869. Even though the new water system had limitations, most Bostonians recognized it as a major civic accomplishment that had been constructed, in the words of Nathan Hale, "for the common benefit of a great people."[100]

Water had proven to be a powerful solvent, dissolving old ways of relating to the environment and outmoded understandings of government responsibilities. Over the next several decades, it would also work to melt municipal boundaries around the Boston area. As Irish immigrants fueled an industrial boom downtown, many middle and upper-class urbanites left for new homes in the rapidly developing towns that surrounded the city. But these largely rural areas lacked the water and other services that Bostonians enjoyed just across the municipal line. Their residents soon found themselves making difficult decisions about how urban they wanted their country towns to become. The result was a series of municipal civil wars that splintered some towns into multiple communities and saw others annexed to Boston to gain access to its services. This municipal reshuffling provides a revealing window into the creation of another new relationship between Bostonians and the natural world, a relationship embodied in the pastoral suburb.

3

Inventing the Suburbs

By the middle of the nineteenth century, with the nation's cities growing at an unprecedented pace, Americans found themselves struggling to resolve the dissonance between a rural past and an urbanizing present. Major literary and artistic figures joined the effort, including Boston author Nathaniel Hawthorne with his 1852 novel *The Blithedale Romance*. Hawthorne's inspiration was his stay in the small utopian community of Brook Farm, a transcendental city upon a hill located outside Boston in rural upper Roxbury. The story's protagonist, Miles Coverdale, leaves the comforts of the city to spend a summer in the rustic experimental community of Blithedale. Although at first Coverdale enjoys a sense of release from urban life, in time he finds Blithedale to be just as conventional as the society he has left. He ends an unhappy summer by returning to Boston, where his "taste for solitude and natural scenery" quickly yields to a renewed fascination with the bustle of the city. He revels in the din of voices in his hotel, the music of a marching band, and the clang of a fire company's bells. "All this was just as valuable, in its way," Coverdale decided, "as the sighing of the breeze among the birch-trees" at Blithedale.[1]

While Hawthorne used narrative to explore the tension between country and city, others were working with the natural environment itself. The small towns surrounding Boston were developing as rapidly as the city, and around 1840—just a few years before the conclusion of the water debates—their residents began creating a new kind of community in nature that fit into neither of the traditional categories of rural and urban. Known by historians as the "romantic" or "pastoral" suburb, it was a residential community situated in a rustic setting from which a family's breadwinner was expected to commute daily into the city for work. Romantic suburbs, at least in their idealized form, contained large homes on spacious lots and catered primarily to the domestic needs of well-off populations.[2]

The social and environmental relationships that characterized these new communities did not exist in America before the nineteenth century. They had to be invented. Inspired in part by a set of ideas that associated rural nature with health, morality, and domestic harmony, pastoral suburbs created a romanticized and leisure-oriented version of country life. Families could enjoy fresh air, scenic vistas, and rustic walks in a private setting, without the hard agricultural labor that had traditionally defined life in the countryside. The wealthiest urbanites had long enjoyed isolated country estates that functioned largely as summer retreats. But the idea of upper-class commuters living year-round in a rustic community, especially one designed specifically to secure the domestic and recreational benefits of nature, represented a new way of life. The semi-rural bedroom community had been born.

Boston's early growth gave the city a prominent role in shaping the romantic suburb, and municipal boundaries played an underappreciated part in the process. The crucial period in Boston's suburban development came between 1840 and 1880, when immigration increased dramatically and the city began to industrialize. New faces and new growth spilled into surrounding communities, many of which tried to stem the tide of change by redrawing their municipal boundaries to keep rural and urbanizing areas separate from each other. These border manipulations took place around the edges of cities across America and might seem like feeble attempts to stop the large historical forces at work. But the location of municipal boundaries had important social and environmental consequences, since they could be very effective barriers against the encroachment of unwanted people and institutions. By the end of the century, the strategic placement and defense of municipal lines had done much to sort metropolitan America in general, and the Boston area in particular, into distinct enclaves.[3]

Although scholars have paid considerable attention to how certain ideas about nature defined romantic suburbs, they have not looked as closely at the central irony on which such places were built: suburban residents could preserve their new, more "rural" environmental relationship only through the seemingly contradictory embrace of urban amenities like water and sewer systems. Nothing better illustrates this paradox than the stories of Roxbury and Brookline, country towns that bordered Boston and each other. Although the two began the century as similar communities set in comparable natural environments, their fates were very different. The larger part of Roxbury seceded from its urbanizing districts to pursue a suburban future. But its government's unwillingness to provide residents with the desired urban services led to its annexation to Boston and subsequent development along an urban grid. Brookline, on the other hand, provided exemplary services and managed to defend its municipal boundaries and develop as a pastoral suburb. In fact, the town was so successful that it gained a national reputation as a model suburb and helped to shift Boston's vision of the ideal community from a city upon a hill to a suburb upon a hill. Brookline had found the perfect suburban formula. The key was combining the pastoral suburb's new domestic and recreational relationship to rural life with just enough urban amenities to make the country comfortable.[4]

Rearranging the Countryside

Despite the Puritan pledge to create a "city" upon a hill, Americans had always thought more highly of the cultivated countryside. The nation's founders consistently praised agriculture as the ideal form of work and glorified farmers for their superior strength and morality. "Those who labor in the earth," Thomas Jefferson famously wrote, "are the chosen people of God," for in their breasts God had deposited "substantial and genuine virtue." He described cities, in comparison, as sores on the body politic. Even Benjamin Franklin, who lived most of his life in cities, saw the country as a crucible of wholesome values that were harder to find in cities. Farming, he concluded, was "the most honourable of all employments." Urban elites embraced this ideal from an early date by maintaining summer homes in the country. There, they lived as "gentleman farmers" and took leading roles in agricultural and horticultural societies, all to demonstrate their virtue and justify their right to lives of leadership and privilege. Rather than being restricted to elites, however, this "agrarian ideal" was universal. Before the first decades of the nineteenth century, virtually all Americans wished a rural future on their nation.[5]

But population growth and industrialization set America on an unexpected urban path, with unprecedented social and environmental consequences. Boston had already undergone substantial growth by mid-century, but its rate of development increased dramatically when a torrent of new immigrants began arriving just as the city was building its water system. In 1845, the population of Boston's small peninsula was about 100,000 people—a number that it could accommodate without severe overcrowding. But in the next ten years, close to a quarter of a million immigrants entered Boston, more than half of them Irish. Not all stayed, but their arrival exerted enormous pressure on the city's housing, helping to turn the North End and Fort Hill into Boston's first large slums. The newcomers also jumpstarted the city's industrialization by providing factories with labor that was far cheaper and more abundant than ever before. Boston's industrial growth had been stagnant in the prior decade, but the number of industrial employees doubled twice between 1845 and 1865. During those years, the city built or expanded clothing factories, sugar refineries, iron works, brass foundries, and shipyards, largely with Irish labor. The commercial city of Boston suddenly found itself the fourth largest manufacturing center in the nation.[6]

Across America, urban growth was accompanied by increases in pollution, noise, crime, and poverty, and native-born Americans often responded by blaming immigrants for urban troubles. Beginning in the 1840s, "nativist" organizations formed to oppose the continued influx of foreign Catholics. These organizations gave birth to anti-immigrant political parties, such as the American Party, that made important gains nationwide during the early 1850s. In 1854, the American Party swept the Massachusetts elections, winning the governorship, the House, and the Senate, and it also took control of three other New England states. The party's rapid rise, however, was matched by an equally spectacular fall as sectional rivalries tore the party apart just a few years before the Civil War. But the success of the American Party, though fleeting, reflected the depth of anti-immigration sentiment in American cities.[7]

Another common response to urban problems, especially among the middle and upper classes, was to flee to the countryside and build a new community organized around a modified version of the agrarian ideal. This new vision of country life retained the natural setting but replaced agricultural labor with genteel leisure and a focus on home life. Landscape gardeners, nature writers, domestic reformers, and other taste-makers popularized the image of well-off families enjoying comfortable houses on the picturesque borderlands of cities. Residents were just a short commute away from urban amenities, but far enough to be insulated from urban problems. Settlements of a purely residential nature began sprouting up on the edges of large cities like Philadelphia, Boston, and New York, as better-off Americans saw in country life the perfect antidote to the city. But this was not country life as Jefferson's generation had imagined it. Where the agrarian ideal encompassed people of all ranks and stations who earned their living from the land, the new "subur-

ban ideal" catered largely to wealthy urbanites who related to nature only through leisure and domesticity.[8]

Around Boston, the construction of new rural residences had to
take place in existing communities, since the city's countryside was
composed of small towns settled as much as two centuries earlier.
They were not quite as rustic as more outlying communities: their
farms were tied more closely to an urban market, they contained
numerous wealthy estates, and they often had small-scale industries
such as tanneries and chandlery works. But their open, largely agricultural environments evoked the country rather than the city, as
did their small populations. In 1830, only two of the towns nearest
Boston claimed more than six thousand residents. Roxbury contained just over five thousand people, and Brookline only one thousand. The sown fields, mown meadows, and thin settlement of the
urban fringe might have concealed distinctive economies that were
neither wholly rural nor urban, but contemporaries described them
as rural villages, and lovers of pastoral nature saw only their bucolic
charms.[9]

Despite this image of placid country life, Boston's urban fringe
was participating fully in the city's expansion and undergoing rapid,
uneven, and often divisive growth. Not surprisingly, the sections
nearest Boston tended to develop first. They attracted factories built
on inexpensive rural land, middle and upper-class commuters escaping the crowded urban center, and working-class urbanites seeking
employment as farm hands, domestic help, or factory workers. Distant districts tended to retain more consistently rural environments
made up of farms and estates. Problems between the two tended to
arise when their economic interests diverged. Citizens of urbanizing
sections wanted to spend tax dollars on services like water and sewer
systems, sidewalks, and poor relief that were less important to rural
areas. Farmers and country gentlemen balked at such expenses but
feared that their small numbers and great distance from Town Hall
left them at the mercy of their more urbanized neighbors. Disagree-

ments over tax rates and public spending mingled with worries about social and environmental change to produce an undercurrent of discontent beneath the country's peaceful facade.[10]

In the Boston area, dividing a town in two was an extreme but historically sanctioned way to resolve such disagreements, although early divisions had more to do with access to a place of worship than with urban development. The first Puritan settlers had organized themselves into a number of towns, each centered on a single meetinghouse. The boundaries of the towns were often quite expansive and ambiguously defined. Cambridge, just west of Boston, stretched some twenty miles inland to the Merrimack River; Dedham and Dorchester, to the city's south, extended all the way to what would become Rhode Island. Over the next two centuries, the spread of population beyond the first settlements produced new and distinct communities within the towns and made travel to the original meetinghouses difficult. Such communities often asked the General Court for permission to build their own meetinghouses and for legislation that would establish them as new towns. This process created many new municipalities from older ones, with Charlestown alone providing land for seven new towns and parts of nine others. Attempts to divide a town were not always successful and often produced considerable animosity between older and newer sections. But by giving priority to the meetinghouse over the municipality, the legislature made fragmentation an accepted part of development in Massachusetts.[11]

Beginning in the 1840s, the tradition of municipal fragmentation combined with increasing urban-rural tensions to produce a rash of town divisions. In just a dozen years, five rural communities in four towns around Boston determined that they could no longer live with their urbanizing neighbors and successfully petitioned the legislature to set them off as independent towns: Somerville separated from Charlestown in 1842, Revere from Chelsea in 1846, West Roxbury from Roxbury in 1851, and Swampscott and Nahant from Lynn in 1852 and 1853. Almost half of the municipal divisions between 1840 and the end of the century resulted from internal tensions between urban and rural areas. A growing social and environmental divide was rending old political affiliations, and astute observers like Henry David Thoreau recognized the conflict at its core. "It is evident," he wrote in 1854, "that there are, in this Commonwealth at least, two parties, becoming more and more distinct—the party of the city, and the party of the country." The conflict between these two "parties" was turning the centuries-old process of adjusting municipal boundaries into an important weapon in the battle for control over the American countryside.[12]

Roxbury Becomes a City

In the 1840s, the residents of Roxbury found themselves on the front lines of the fight. The town shared a common border with Boston at the neck of the Shawmut Peninsula and stood squarely in the path of the city's expansion. Roxbury was two miles wide and stretched for eight miles to the southwest, making it several times larger than its more urban neighbor. In fact, Roxbury was so large that it contained two distinct areas of settlement within its borders. The first, called "lower" Roxbury, was the easternmost section of the town and therefore the part closer to Boston. It was the part of town experiencing the most intense change and had become a mixture of country and city. The western part of lower Roxbury contained farmland and a series of highlands on which middle class and well-to-do urbanites were busy building country retreats. The hills had housed the scattered summer homes of wealthy Bostonians since the 1740s, and the start of hourly stagecoach service to Boston in 1826 and the growth of rail travel in the 1840s accelerated the pace of development. Near lower Roxbury's border with Boston, however, the highlands descended into low, marshy areas that attracted leather manufactories and other industries. Poor Irish immigrants built shanties in these flood-prone districts to be near their places of work. With farms and summer homes in some areas and factories and hovels in others, lower Roxbury had become two worlds.[13]

The other settled part of Roxbury—"upper" Roxbury—was the more westerly part of the town. It was larger than lower Roxbury and more consistently rural, containing a series of rolling hills and flat plains covered with farms, woods, and a smattering of country estates. The heart of the most developed area of upper Roxbury was the village of Jamaica Plain, which contained a large pond surrounded by expensive houses. At various points throughout the nineteenth century, a number of Boston luminaries had made Jamaica Plain their home. The rural atmosphere, proximity to Boston, and presence of Jamaica Pond attracted the physician Dr. John C. Warren, attorney and congressman Charles F. Sprague, historian Francis Parkman, merchant James Perkins, and exporter Benjamin Bussey, whose large estate would later become the Arnold Arboretum. Although upper Roxbury also had a brewery, tannery, other scattered industries, and an Irish population that provided much of the community's industrial and agricultural labor, its character remained predominantly rural.[14]

Before the 1850s, no one used the word "suburb" to describe either upper or lower Roxbury. "Suburb" had long been a derogatory term that identified areas on the urban fringe housing the poorest residents and the most noxious industries. Although some parts of Roxbury nearest Boston might have fit such a description, the middle- and upper-class urbanites moving from Boston to Roxbury thought of themselves as escaping to the country. For them, Roxbury was a "country town" characterized by agricultural pursuits and a rural landscape. It was a place where they could trade the problems of the city for the peacefulness of natural surroundings.[15]

By the middle of the century, however, Roxbury was one of the fastest growing towns adjacent to Boston. Between 1840 and 1850, its population swelled by 120 percent, twice Boston's rate. Urbanization was most apparent in lower Roxbury, but upper Roxbury was growing quickly as well. In the same ten-year period, the population of Jamaica Plain increased 170 percent, and the number of people engaged in agriculture declined precipitously. In 1840, two thirds of the men in Jamaica Plain found employment as farmers or agricultural laborers. By 1850, the fraction had dropped to a third. The remainder of the male working population fell largely into the middle and upper classes, although fully thirty percent of those heading households in Jamaica Plain were foreign born. For residents of the countryside, poor immigrants migrating from Boston provided potent evidence of urban expansion.[16]

The rapid conversion of country into city in lower Roxbury created a great deal of tension in the town and led to a number of attempts to divide it into separate municipalities. As early as 1817, and then again in the late 1830s and 1840s, wealthy farmers, estate owners, and other large landholders from Jamaica Plain organized petitions for separation. Worried that the town was using rural tax dollars to provide services to urbanizing areas, they resented the paved roads, streetlights, town watch, and other benefits enjoyed in lower Roxbury. The town's rural west and urbanizing east were growing apart, although the legislature repeatedly denied requests for division.[17]

Hoping to ease the town's sectional tensions, the residents of Roxbury successfully petitioned the legislature for a representative city government in 1846. Roxbury had begun to suffer from the same problem with its town meeting that Boston had encountered a generation before: although the voting population had grown quite large, only a small fraction attended meetings where decisions about the town's future were made. Proponents of the new form of government also hoped that it would address some of upper Roxbury's traditional complaints. A representative city council would eliminate the need for citizens to travel long distances to meetings, and the council would minimize the population advantages of the east by awarding extra seats to western wards. The move was also intended to preempt future efforts to divide Roxbury, since the legislature had sundered towns but never a city. Residents accepted their new urban status in the spring of 1846 by a majority of 836 yeas to 192 nays, with lower Roxbury's considerable advantage in population making the victory an easy one.[18]

To Be Rich and Rural in Roxbury

But a group of wealthy landholders from Jamaica Plain refused to accept an urban future for their community. They asked Arthur Austin, a successful lawyer and politician from Charlestown, to represent them in a new fight for division. Austin had just acquired a personal stake in the dispute by purchasing a large estate in upper Roxbury, where he planned to pursue a long-time recreational interest in horticulture. He accepted the case and listened as the Jamaica Plain gentlemen explained that they wanted to mold upper Roxbury's farms and fields into a wealthy residential enclave set in pastoral surroundings.[19]

This social and environmental vision was driven by economic and personal motives. As landowners, the gentlemen hoped to profit financially from the suburban ideal, and as residents of Jamaica Plain they hoped to live it. The group wanted a deliberate kind of low-density growth characterized by the construction of expensive country houses with a good deal of open space between them. It was just the sort of development that would attract well-off Bostonians looking for a rural experience, and it would both maximize the profits of landowners and restrict upper Roxbury to wealthy people like themselves. But the presence of urban government, claimed the members of the group, was inhibiting emigration from Boston, because people leaving the city wanted to move to a small country town, not from one city to another. One gentleman candidly told Austin that he faced financial ruin if he could not sell the large, unproductive lands he owned. The group believed that the kind of development they wanted would require separation from lower Roxbury and the return of a town government that would give them more direct control over environmental change.[20]

Austin suggested a legal strategy based on the simple idea of self-determination. He planned to argue that a majority of landholders in any community had the right to exercise authority over themselves and their property. If such landholders preferred to organize as a town, then they had the right to do so. "The true ground to put division on," Austin later recalled telling the group, "was that they had sufficient territory, sufficient population for a town, and that owning the soil they had an inherent right to manage their own affairs in their own way." Demonstrating popular support for separation was crucial to such argument, but easily accomplished. Supporters circulated a petition asking the legislature to divide the new city and grant the western district a town meeting. Sixty-five percent of upper Roxbury's registered voters affixed their signatures to it, suggesting that dividing the town would simply be democracy in action.[21]

But when Austin made his case before the Commonwealth's Committee on Towns in 1851, he added a powerful cultural argument to his legal one. Austin claimed that the environmental differences between country and city should play an important role in determining municipal lines. Accordingly, he devoted most of his opening argument to painting upper Roxbury as a place of wild beauty that could in no way be mistaken for a city. He described ageless and boundless forests stretching across its hills, broad meadows providing rest for migrating birds, and wild ravines punctuating romantic scenery. This was a place, claimed Austin, that could turn even politicians into poets. His sketch counted on both attraction toward the natural and dislike of the urban to work in his favor. "Is it such a territory as this," he demanded of the committee, "that you would condemn to the vices and miseries—the miseries and vices of a city government?"[22]

Austin's co-counsel, Rufus Choate, also emphasized the social and environmental differences between rural and urban communities. One of Boston's most prominent lawyers, Choate had recently served as a United States senator and had a national reputation for powerful oratory. In his remarks before the committee, Choate conceded that one could find mechanics, artisans, blacksmiths, and carpenters in rural upper Roxbury, since every town needed them. "But its general character is agricultural," he continued, "dotted here and there with a beautiful locality, standing out at last upon a plain farming land."[23] Choate contrasted this vision with the trade and commerce of lower Roxbury. "There are the artificial sidewalks, the gas-lighted stores, the artificial supply of water, the crowded and noisome population, the indestructible character of the town. And there it will be for ever." To claim, as did his opposing counsel, that country and city should be one was to argue against the natural and divine order. "God the first garden made," Choate reminded the committee, "And the first city Cain."[24]

Austin and Choate were not simply expressing a popular preference for the country. They were also helping to construct the image of a pastoral suburb as a community more attuned to rural than urban life. No well-defined middle category existed between "country" and "city," either in the physical environment or the public imagination. So Austin and Choate painted suburban life as synonymous with country life, framing their case as a question of what kind of government and level of services was most appropriate to each kind of society and environment. In their view, upper Roxbury and lower Roxbury were different worlds that should not be mixed. Noting that hundreds of robins routinely rested in the trees on his property, Austin asked: "Are these the denizens of a city? Is it necessary to have a police from Lower Roxbury, to protect or restrain them?"[25] His point was clear: urban services were unnecessary and unwelcome in upper Roxbury, and forcing the area to remain part of a city would be nothing less than a desecration of nature.

Although Austin and Choate highlighted the wild and natural

This 1854 painting of a spacious and affluent Roxbury neighborhood captures the suburban ideal as imagined by Arthur Austin and his contemporaries. The natural surroundings were supposed to fulfill only domestic and recreational needs, while the nearby city provided work. The horse-drawn omnibus, at center left, connected the two worlds. (J. W. A. Scott, *View of Roxbury,* 1854. Museum of Fine Arts, Boston. Gift of William B. Osgood in memory of John C. Kiley, 1999.535.)

beauties of upper Roxbury for rhetorical effect, they could not have done so without a firm basis in environmental reality. The rural parts of Roxbury were by all accounts charming and picturesque, with one guidebook calling particular attention to the area's "romantic beauties" and "crystal springs." Roxbury, the author wrote, "displays a great degree of agricultural taste and skill, and abounds in country-seats and pleasure grounds." He reserved the area around Jamaica Pond for special praise, calling it "exceedingly delightful." A local pastor took in the whole view and declared his parish to be "like one perfect garden, resembling the best cultivated villages near London." The rural charms of upper Roxbury's environment were quite real and well known, and they helped Austin and Choate to make their case.[26]

Choate tied together the two grand themes of the case—democracy and nature—by drawing an essential connection between town meetings and rural environments. He explained to the committee that only a town government would provide the conditions under which "the agricultural mind breathes freely and trains itself perfectly to the duties of citizenship." Choate thought representative government was fine for densely populated areas where "men become prompt in action," but he found the agricultural mind to be "slower" and "differently trained" than residents of the artificial city. Emerson would have agreed: he described the farmer as "a slow person, timed to nature, and not to city watches," and therefore inherently different from a city dweller. According to Choate, representative government had already proved a disaster for the rural residents of upper Roxbury. Without access to a town meeting, they were losing interest in public affairs. Representative government—the wrong government for an agricultural community—was promoting political apathy and ignorance.[27]

The presence of city government, according to Austin and Choate, was also deterring the construction of country homes in the more rural west. As proof, Choate called before the committee a series of landholders who testified that they had tried unsuccessfully to sell their property in upper Roxbury for development. They insisted that the issue of city government always killed the deal, because potential buyers wanted to live in the country. Although Choate admitted that concentrated populations made city government indispensable ("as war is indispensable"), he held that the question of whether this kind of government was inherently good or bad ultimately was irrelevant. Some people believed it was bad, and that was enough to check development. Bostonians looking for homes outside the city would not try to gather figs from thorns or grapes from thistles. Fortunately, the committee had the power to rectify this injustice by recommending division of the town to the legislature. "Make the change we ask for," Choate pleaded, "and Roxbury takes her place at once in the circle of prosperity that surrounds her. Capital and taste will add the beauties of art to the beauties of nature."[28]

The greater part of the committee embraced Austin and Choate's argument about municipal self-determination as well as their vision for a residential community in the countryside. Four of the seven members submitted a majority report to the state legislature recommending division of the town. "Here is an abundant territory for a large town, of a rural description," they concluded, "beautiful sites for country residences and farming, containing three thousand inhabitants, who nearly all desire a separation, who are entirely competent, and wish to govern themselves, their social feelings and sympathies being in another direction."[29] The committee recommended that such an area should be set free to develop as its residents saw fit. Their decision rested not only on a community's right to self-determination or its desire for direct democracy but also on the natural character of its environment. The fact that upper Roxbury had "beautiful sites for country residences and farming" mattered to the committee and figured prominently in their recommendation to the legislature.

The voting pattern of the committee members revealed the sharp divide between rural and urban points of view. The committee was composed of state representatives from seven different municipalities, four of them small country towns and three of them growing cities. Representatives from the towns of Ashby, Barnstable, Duxbury, and Russell voted for division, while their counterparts from the cities of Lowell, Worcester, and Roxbury voted against it. The rift must have been obvious to the members of the committee during the hearings, and it reinforced Austin's claim—echoed by Thoreau—that opposing interests and temper really did divide country and city.[30]

Dividing Roxbury and Escaping the Poor

The members of the committee who represented cities wrote a minority report that heavily criticized Austin's rationale for dividing Roxbury. "This formula," they charged, "stripped of its poetry, is, in substance, this: whenever a new town can be constructed out of an old one, leaving both towns respectable with the average of towns in numbers and area, then separation may very properly take place." They worried that this logic encouraged change for its own sake and set a precedent that could promote the endless subdivision of towns across the commonwealth. Choate had responded to this objection during the hearings by employing yet another rural metaphor. Division, he claimed, was like a field in which "two blades of grass grow where one grew before; and I call that pretty good farming, gentlemen, morally, politically, rurally."[31]

The minority committee members also accused Austin's clients of trying to avoid their public responsibility to support the poor. The statistics produced by the City of Roxbury's counsel had convinced all members of the committee that upper Roxbury was not only prospering under city government but was benefiting from *more* than its fair share of expenditures. Why, then, were its residents advocating so strongly for division? The minority recognized that the movement was about more than creating a community organized around a particular kind of relationship to nature. It was also an effort to create a new town that was largely unburdened by a poor population. Half of the residents in the sections of lower Roxbury closest to Boston were foreign-born, and most were poor. Their numbers had almost doubled in the prior five years alone, swelling the city's relief burden. Roxbury now supported more state paupers than the neighboring towns of Brookline, Cambridge, Charlestown, Chelsea, and Dorchester combined, and its total was second only to that of Boston. Feeding the suspicion of the minority members was the testimony of a wealthy petitioner who had stated the motivation for division more plainly than he might have intended. The people of Jamaica Plain, he said, "wish to get rid of the lower portion, on account of the pauper population. The pauper tax is a severe one and the apprehension is that it may be a great burden. This prevents rich men from coming out from Boston and settling among us."[32]

The residents of upper Roxbury undoubtedly feared the poor as much as they feared the poor tax, since in time the pauper population might find its way west into the rural neighborhoods. Roxbury's conversion of Brook Farm into an almshouse underscored the threat. In 1849, Roxbury officials purchased the buildings of that failed utopian community to shelter impoverished citizens who could no longer care for themselves. Although the new almshouse lay at the extreme western edge of upper Roxbury, far from the wealthy enclave of Jamaica Plain, its presence suggested that the problems of the city had arrived in the country. Hawthorne addressed the transformation of Brook Farm through his fictional Miles Coverdale, who regretted this betrayal of a place once filled with promise. "Where once we toiled with our whole hopeful hearts," he laments, "the town-paupers, aged, nerveless, and disconsolate, creep sluggishly a-field. Alas, what faith is requisite to bear up against such results of generous effort!"[33]

The desire to escape the poor reflected the dark side of the suburban ideal. Life on the urban borderland offered not only access to natural surroundings free from the dirt, noise, and congestion of the city, but also freedom from any obligation to assist with urban problems, especially support of the poor. In the idealized pastoral suburb, most of the population was wealthy, the taxes low, and public responsibilities minimal. Although we often associate the flight of affluent urbanites with the second half of the twentieth century, the process actually began a century before. It was an inherent part of the suburban ideal and was born with the residential suburb.

The irony was that the middle- and upper-class residents of such places spent their weekdays helping to create the urban conditions they were fleeing. They were the industrialists who built the factories, the real estate speculators who owned the slums, the bankers who financed new development, and sometimes the clerks who kept the whole system running. The residents of upper Roxbury included men like James W. Converse, who owned one of Boston's largest boot and leather manufactories and was president of the Mechanics' Bank of Boston, and Franklin Greene, Jr., a Boston merchant and insurance executive. Their professions contributed to Boston's growth, but their wealth enabled them to outrun the more undesirable consequences of their labors.

The minority members of the Committee on Towns criticized the wealthy petitioners for viewing the poor "simply in the light of dollars and cents." They insisted that the residents of rural upper Roxbury had a humanitarian and legal responsibility to feed, cloth, and educate the children of paupers. They also claimed that the relatively open and undeveloped character of upper Roxbury's environment argued for keeping the two halves of the city united, since the western districts would provide ample room for the expansion of the native population that was fleeing from the growing foreign presence. The native population could then help to support the burden of poor relief that lower Roxbury would otherwise struggle to carry alone.[34]

Choate had responded to similar allegations during the hearing by claiming that the potential to provide homes for the working classes in the pure air and delightful scenery of upper Roxbury was itself an argument for keeping the area rural. He admitted that access to the country was essential for everyone, especially poor urban families, and expressed hope that the railroad might encourage those of limited means to build cottages in the upper reaches of the community. He painted a picture of thrifty laborers enjoying the natural pleasures of an upper Roxbury cut loose from urbanizing areas. "I put it sir, as one great advantage," he concluded, "that we traverse this region of country to win it from the wild flower, the wild bird, the night breezes of the sea, and make it the pleasant abode of hundreds who would else seldom see any thing but dusty streets, and forests of masts at the wharfs." Choate must have realized, however, that economic realities would make it impossible for most members of the working class to participate in the lifestyle of the suburban commuter. They would never be able to afford the daily train fare back and forth to Boston for work, even if they could purchase a suburban house.[35]

The legislature, which was dominated by towns rather than cities, accepted the committee's majority recommendation and divided Roxbury. Lower Roxbury remained a city, while upper Roxbury became West Roxbury and regained a town government. On June 3, 1851, the citizens of the new municipality held their first town meeting in a local tavern and celebrated independence with cannons, bonfires on the hills, and fireworks in Jamaica Plain. Arthur Austin was well rewarded for his efforts. The citizens of West Roxbury elevated him to the status of town father, made him chair of the selectmen for the next eight years, and even renamed the main thoroughfare after him. His actions seemed to have earned the praise. Austin had done more than anyone to ensure that West Roxbury's slice of the country would remain rural rather than urban and upper-class rather than working-class.[36]

Under Austin's leadership, the selectmen kept the town's overall expenses low while spending considerable sums to construct new roads that would encourage residential development. To justify these expenditures to West Roxbury's tax-conscious citizens, Austin resorted once again to nature imagery. "Diversified by hill and plain," he wrote of the town's landscape, "by forest, meadow, grove and flowing waters—possessed of sites that command the ocean— of regions that must be forever rural—to render these accessible, belongs to our day and our generation—that abodes of elegance and refinement may spring up around us—that the stranger may re-joice within our borders." Of course, Austin limited his welcome to a particular class of strangers. He began working immediately to convince the legislature to remove the town paupers to the state fa-cility.[37]

The Allure of Urban Services

West Roxbury's leadership was committed to minimizing taxes by providing as few municipal services as possible. This would prove a risky strategy in the long run, however, because services were be-coming increasingly popular, even among those escaping to the country. Commuters wanted good roads and gas street lights, real estate investors wanted water and sewer systems that would in-crease the value of their undeveloped property, and the working classes welcomed any kind of large public work that created jobs. Each group might have found residential suburbs appealing for dif-ferent reasons, but they all stood to benefit from the kinds of ser-vices that were generally available only in cities and had never been common parts of rural life. Although pastoral suburbs were defined by their connections to the non-urban world, their newest residents had not forgotten the value of urban services. It was a time, as Mayor Frederick Prince of Boston would observe, when "municipal luxuries" were becoming "municipal necessaries."[38]

In many cases, such amenities were attractive simply because they made life more comfortable. William Dean Howells wrote in 1871 about the life that he and his wife were leading on Boston's ur-ban fringe with a maid who was unnerved by the lack of street lights. "We had not before this thought it a grave disadvantage that our street was unlighted," Howells confessed. "Our street was not drained nor graded; no municipal cart ever came to carry away our ashes; there was not a water-butt within half a mile to save us from fire, nor more than the one thousandth part of a policeman to pro-

tect us from theft."[39] Howells and his wife embraced the rural sim-
plicity of such a life, but their maid did not. She quit and moved to
Boston.

It was possible for the residents of growing towns to obtain such
services, but the price was high. They could rent them from a neighboring city, pay a private company to deliver them, or develop the
services themselves. Each option required substantial tax increases.
The only alternative was to sacrifice municipal independence by
convincing the legislature to annex the community to a city that already had the services.

Talk of annexing lower Roxbury to Boston had begun with the
debate over dividing the municipality in 1851. Annexation advocates
hoped that a union of the two would bring municipal water infrastructure, higher land values, and better streets and street lighting to
lower Roxbury, and they feared that the community might not be
able to control the proliferating shanties in the lowlands without assistance. With access to Boston's workhouses and hospitals, lower
Roxbury's poorest areas might avoid becoming as unmanageable
as Boston's Broad Street. Roxbury officials, however, opposed the
union. Their investigative committee concluded that opportunism
rather than an actual need for services was driving the movement,
particularly with regard to the supposed need for additional water
supplies. "Nothing was ever heard of the want of water," the committee claimed in its report, "until the annexation project was
started; . . . it was annexation that suggested this and other wants,
and not this and other wants, suggested annexation."[40]

When the residents of Roxbury considered—and rejected—annexing lower Roxbury to Boston, urban services were at the heart
of their deliberations. In 1851, a local merchant named Samuel Guild
authored a pamphlet entitled *A Word for Old Roxbury,* to which fifty
prominent citizens affixed their names. Guild first analyzed the need
for water, sewers, gas pipes, sidewalks, and street paving and concluded that the services sought by petitioners were either adequate

in Roxbury at present or could be added at no more expense than if Roxbury were part of Boston. Next, Guild revealed the many disadvantages that annexation might bring, like increased taxes and a more burdensome public debt, and decided that the benefits of joining Boston would not outweigh the costs. His pamphlet helped to convince the majority of lower Roxbury's citizens to reject union with their neighbor.[41]

Other growing communities that were considering annexation to Boston focused just as closely on environmental services and other traditionally urban amenities as Roxbury had. In 1856, the legislature received a petition for annexation from the City of Chelsea, located across the Mystic River from Boston. Hoping to secure water for their growing population, Chelsea's citizens voted in favor of the merger. But they brought little more than thirst to the union, and Bostonians rejected a marriage that would benefit only one of the parties. Two years earlier, a group of residents from the City of Charlestown had submitted their own annexation petition to the legislature. Charlestown wanted water, and Boston coveted its neighbor's extensive system of wharves. Both cities voted for annexation, but opponents challenged the constitutionality of the union in the courts and prevented the merger on technical grounds. All three communities—Roxbury, Chelsea, and Charlestown—had already experienced considerable urbanization and had traded their town meetings for city councils. They did not see their futures through the same rural lens as West Roxbury.[42]

Working against the desire to use annexation as a way to secure services was a widespread fear of giant cities that built on existing anti-urban sentiment. In 1860, faced with renewed efforts to annex Roxbury and Charlestown to Boston, a group of prominent residents from around the Boston area submitted a remonstrance to the legislature arguing against the mergers. Among the signers were former mayor Josiah Quincy, Sr., and future governor John Andrew. "The maxim of Mr. Jefferson," they declared, "that great cities are, in many respects, great sores on the body politic, is no longer a matter of prophesy or theory, but a fact." They held up New York City as an example of a failed large city, claiming that its government had proved incapable of protecting the lives, property, and welfare of its inhabitants. As cities grew beyond a moderate size, they argued, taxes, inefficiency, and corruption inevitably increased, and "the government accomplishes no more than a truce or absence of hostilities." Anticipating the draft riots that would consume New York just three years later, they expressed fear that the advent of hard economic times in a sprawling city might produce a level of violence that only military intervention could suppress. And they insisted that large cities would require endlessly higher taxes to pay for increasing obligations. The group concluded with a bleak vision of the future in which battling urban oligarchies, like the city-states of Italy, contended for commercial and political power.[43]

But others, like attorney John Clifford, associated a city's size with its national prominence and chided those who looked on Boston as a "great anaconda" to be feared. These were backward-looking people, he insisted, who wanted the city to return to "the days of its cow-paths and its cow pasture on Boston Common."[44] Clifford believed that Boston could no more live within its current borders than a man could wear the clothes of a boy. The city must grow in territory and population if it was to grow in commercial reputation. His positive vision of a city maturing and boldly reaching for its future contrasted sharply with Josiah Quincy's prediction of destructive competition and unmanageable chaos.

Despite such disagreements, and even though early attempts to unite lower Roxbury, Charlestown, and Chelsea with Boston had failed, cities across America would feed their growth throughout the century by annexing their rural neighbors. Annexation provided a way to recapture the wealth of former residents who had moved to surrounding communities, and it enabled cities to control areas that would someday house a portion of their populations. Some cities, like Detroit, nibbled slowly at their countrysides over many years. Others, like Chicago, Philadelphia, and New York, swallowed enormous areas with a single bite. But all large cities grew larger through annexation. The boundaries of St. Louis enclosed less than a thousand acres in 1841 but included 61 square miles in 1876. Philadelphia annexed its entire county in 1854, growing to 130 square miles, much of it agricultural. By the end of the century, annexations to New York City would make it more than twice that size. Municipal annexation, however, was not a uniquely American phenomenon but an international one: cities in Canada, England, France, and Germany all extended their boundaries by absorbing large swaths of the countryside.[45]

As cities began annexing their neighbors more aggressively, state legislatures across America strengthened the hands of rural residents. Legislatures had traditionally redrawn municipal boundaries without requiring a referendum in any of the communities involved. Massachusetts had been no exception. Transfers of land to Boston from surrounding towns had been small and infrequent but always enacted by legislative fiat. Without asking local residents of either municipality to vote on the matter, the legislature had granted parts of Dorchester to Boston in 1804 and 1855. As urban growth increased annexation pressure in cities nationwide, however, many states protected villages and towns from unwanted mergers by creating standard procedures and insisting on local self-determination. In Maryland, the state constitution of 1864 addressed the expansion of Baltimore by prohibiting counties from annexing districts outside their boundaries without the consent of the area's residents. In Illinois, the Annexation Act of 1889 likewise made mergers dependent on the approval of voters in both municipalities. Although the Massachusetts legislature never bound itself to the principle of local self-determination, after 1866 it regularly required voters in both communities to endorse annexation through a double referendum. Whether based in law or legislative custom, such practices gave residents of the urban fringe considerable power to determine the border between country and city.[46]

Annexing the Borderlands

Annexationists in the city of Roxbury continued to press their case into the 1860s with great determination but little success. They could take heart, however, from the fact that Boston's leadership had finally grown interested in extending the city's borders beyond its teeming peninsula. Before the Civil War, annexation schemes were hatched outside the city. But by the end of the war, crowding in Boston had reached a critical level. An even bigger problem was the flight of the middle and upper classes to the countryside, where their public responsibilities—especially their tax burdens—were considerably less. At an accelerating pace, lawyers, merchants, and bankers traded their urban houses for new ones in towns like Cambridge and Roxbury but continued to commute to their offices in the city on trains, omnibuses, and street railways. The result in some professions was striking: as early as 1851, only fifty percent of Boston's bankers still called Boston their home. The result of this demographic shift to the countryside was a steady erosion of the city's tax base. In response, Boston's leaders began to encourage annexations by setting up a bureaucratic mechanism through which interested towns could explore the benefits of union. For the first time, the city began actively courting its neighbors.[47]

Boston's new interest in expansion coincided with an 1867 decision by Roxbury's city government to pursue union with its sister city. The reasons were largely environmental. Fifteen years before, Roxbury officials had claimed that Boston's new water system was creating an artificial desire for annexation. But now a commission recognized the need and reported favorably on the merger. Roxbury still lacked environmental services that Boston could provide, like adequate water and sewer systems, and the creation of proper sanitary infrastructure for the developing areas that straddled both communities would require joint action on a large scale. In addition, massive land making on either side of Boston's neck had eliminated the geographical logic behind the historical border. "The boundary line between these cities," noted the committee members, "has ceased to be a natural one, and has become purely artificial in its character."[48] A parallel group of Boston commissioners also recommended union. So in 1868, seventeen years after annexation was first proposed, the citizens of Roxbury voted to join Boston by a strong majority of 1,832 yeas to 592 nays.[49] Boston's mainland territory doubled in area overnight.

The union of Roxbury and Boston created a powerful momentum for further consolidation that highlighted how deeply intertwined social and environmental agendas were with the process of annexation. Two years later, after a divisive debate, the residents of nearby Dorchester also voted to join the city, and three years after that, Senator J. S. Potter of Arlington submitted an ambitious bill recommending that the legislature annex fifteen more municipalities to Boston. One of his chief goals was to create a more centralized planning process to ensure that the countryside developed with broad and attractive thoroughfares and abundant parkland. But Potter also claimed that annexation would improve urban morality. He believed that density, rather than size, was producing the demoralization and crime that plagued the city, and that enlarging Boston's borders would ease congestion by encouraging the population to disperse across a wider area. Low-density development, he wrote, would eliminate the "shadows of narrow and crooked ways" that nurtured crime and replace them with wide-open, natural surroundings. "Wherever a family has a grape-vine, or owns and cultivates a flower-bed," claimed Potter, "there a voter is sure to be found who cannot be properly enumerated among those who belong to what are termed the 'dangerous classes.'" Although Potter wanted the towns around Boston to submit to urban control, he expected them—even counted on them—to retain semi-rural environments.

The legislature, however, preferred a more gradual annexation process and passed a bill that would join four of the suggested towns to Boston only if their citizens approved the measure. The towns were Brighton, Brookline, Charlestown, and Arthur Austin's rural idyll, West Roxbury.[50]

Twenty-two years of steady growth since its founding had dramatically changed parts of West Roxbury's built environment and heightened the pressure to merge with Boston. In just the five years that preceded the introduction of the annexation bill, population increases had compelled officials to construct a new town hall, a public high school, and a combined police station and courthouse. Yet many of the town's services remained primitive. It lacked water and sewer systems, its public grammar schools were second-rate, and its police and fire departments were ineffective.[51] By the early 1870s, upper Roxbury resembled lower Roxbury in the early 1850s: a rapidly growing area struggling to manage social and environmental change. Orchards, fields, and country lanes coexisted with rapid population growth, calls for improved services, and sharp conflict between native Protestants and Irish Catholics. Much of the town was still dotted with farms and estates, but to settlers in the more developed parts of West Roxbury, the romantic description of the town that Austin had given in 1851 seemed like ancient history. In 1870, annexationists read his words aloud to the Committee on Towns to demonstrate the stark differences between the "primeval town" of twenty years earlier and the modern West Roxbury that was now "almost a city."[52]

Anti-annexationists, fearing higher taxes and unwanted urban institutions, struggled to slow the drive for union with Boston. Some suggested that the town adopt a representative city government that could provide better services, and others pushed to divide the town once again, abandoning Jamaica Plain to the city and retaining independence for the most westerly part of the community. But the only plan they could agree on was to keep resisting annexation to Bos-

ton. The defenders of West Roxbury's independence defeated a call
for union in a town meeting in 1869 and another in the legislature in
1870. But momentum for annexation continued to grow. Two years
later, a vote showed that forty percent of West Roxbury's citizens
embraced the idea of union. Many supporters were real estate investors and business commuters who wanted urban services and
were willing to join Boston to get them.[53]

Annexationists could not win, however, without the support of
West Roxbury's growing working-class population. The town's laborers, many of them Irish immigrants, took great interest in the
changes overtaking the countryside. Their goal, however, was not
to enhance the value of local real estate or to influence debates
about the town's social and environmental future. They lobbied for
jobs and supported the municipal arrangement most likely to create
them. Boston always seemed to be in the midst of large-scale building projects, expanding its water system, constructing sewers, and
improving roads. West Roxbury officials, in contrast, had continued
Arthur Austin's policy of avoiding the large tax increases that such
projects required. To retain the infrastructure of a small country
town, they had sacrificed urban services for middle-class commuters and jobs for the immigrant working classes. As time passed it
became an increasingly perilous policy, since local laborers already
provided the needed votes in town meetings to pass street improvement projects and knew that union with Boston promised much
more substantial public works.[54]

Participants in the debate missed an opportunity to reexamine
the relationship between the Irish and the natural world. That relationship—as imagined by the group's detractors and as actually lived
by its members—was tightly intertwined with the prejudice that the
Irish endured. Anglo-Saxon natives considered the Irish to be an inferior race and a non-white people. Portrayed as ape-like in contemporary political cartoons, the Irish were seen as not only less civilized but less capable of becoming civilized. These racial theories

combined with religious intolerance to encourage the low wages, job discrimination, and housing segregation that forced the Irish into menial work and overcrowded quarters. But after being forced to live under such conditions, Irish immigrants were then criticized for their low social status and apparent lack of cleanliness and blamed for the epidemics that plagued cities. This self-reinforcing enmity became both cause and effect in structuring the environments in which many of the Irish would spend their lives. There was little interest at mid-century in breaking the cycle.[55]

Hostility toward the Irish and the rest of the urban poor made it difficult for better-off Bostonians to believe that the common man was even capable of appreciating the beauties of pastoral nature. Andrew Belknap, however, disagreed. Sixteen years after he had lobbied the city to preserve the flats at the foot of the Common, the aldermen were once again threatening to sell them, even though some private citizens were working to transform the flats into a public garden. In an 1850 editorial, Belknap appealed once more to the benefits that public green space brought to the poor. But he felt the need to convince his readers that the poor would actually desire such a place. "The love of nature," he claimed, "is not so unknown a sentiment to the mass of the people as some of the 'salt of the earth' seem to suppose. Even a poor man, notwithstanding his undoubted moral deficiencies, delights to look upon the face of Nature occasionally." Belknap went on to dwell at length on "the broken tea-pot with a bunch of primrose" and "the geranium in an old cracked jug" that appeared so frequently on the windowsills of packed tenement houses. They were proof enough, he argued, that the urban poor desired more access to nature.[56]

Whatever Belknap's contemporaries might have believed, America's Irish immigrants did not lack an affinity for the countryside. They wrapped their memories of rural Ireland in a nostalgia that was an important component of their ethnic identity. When speaking to the members of Boston's Charitable Irish Society, the organization's president evoked "the green hills that delighted the first visions of our infancy" and recalled a time when "we were as light-hearted and free as the lark that soared over our heads."[57] But such varnished memories obscured the harshness of agricultural life under British occupation and associated it with the past, which is where it belonged for most Irish immigrants. They may have been born in rural Ireland, but they would spend the rest of their lives in urban America. Even those who labored in the fields and gardens of the towns surrounding Boston had spread with the city and traced their family histories and social networks to Boston or New York. As the Irish became residents of the urbanizing countryside, however, they resolved to have a say in the future of the fields and gardens they tended. They began registering to vote in large numbers as the annexation referendum approached.[58]

On October 7, 1873, an unprecedented number of West Roxbury's voters turned out in the pouring rain to cast their ballots, and annexationists carried the day with fifty-four percent of the vote. Residents of Brighton and Charlestown also voted for union on the same day, and the three towns became part of Boston. Twenty-two years after drawing a new municipal line to keep out the city, West Roxbury's residents erased it. The result must have greatly disappointed Arthur Austin, who had lobbied against annexation and now watched the city consume the country town he had founded. A short time later, Austin fled Boston's newest ward for the outlying town of Milton, keeping one step ahead of the expanding city.[59]

Austin had recognized that the annexation of West Roxbury would mean the loss of local control over its development. In fact, it meant the absence of almost all public oversight, since Boston showed little interest in how the area developed over the next twenty years. Where Austin's Board of Selectmen had laid out new roads along carefully chosen routes and encouraged certain kinds of construction, Boston left the design of newly annexed sections of the city to the owners of streetcar lines and thousands of individual

BOSTON IN 1880.
SHOWING AREAS AND DATES OF ANNEXATIONS OF TERRITORY.

Boston expanded its boundaries considerably through annexation, with Roxbury becoming part of Boston in 1867 and West Roxbury joining the city in 1873. Brookline resisted, however, and remains to this day a town almost completely surrounded by a city. (From *Report on the Social Statistics of Cities*, compiled by George E. Waring, Jr., 1886, courtesy of the University of Texas Libraries, the University of Texas at Austin)

builders. Streetcar owners advanced their tracks into undeveloped areas, and real estate speculators bought up adjacent land and divided it into lots. Until Boston established a Board of Survey in 1891, the city did not involve itself in the layout of new streets at all. Rather, speculators laid out the streets themselves, almost always in an economically efficient grid that concealed the underlying topography, and the city subsequently provided the streets with utilities and accepted them for municipal maintenance. The speculators would then sell individual lots to builders, real estate dealers, and people looking to invest or build a home. Construction was piece-meal and progressed with no overarching plan.[60]

As a result of this informal and unregulated system, West Rox-bury's built environment began evolving in a radically different di-rection. After 1880, the area took part in a nation-wide residential building boom that left half of West Roxbury covered with houses by the end of the century. But these were not the kind of houses, or the kind of occupants, that Arthur Austin had envisioned. Although the structures were detached and rested on more land than their ur-ban counterparts, they were arranged along straight roads and sat close to each other and to the street. The arrangement owed more to the grid of streets and the presence of streetcar lines than a rural aesthetic or a sensitivity to local geography. The homes were both single and multi-family, and they housed middle- and lower-middle-class occupants who had been attracted to the countryside for the same reasons as their wealthy counterparts. But their experience of the country would be different from the typical upper-class sub-urban resident. "Each homeowner wanted to believe that his new house was in the country, or at least near it," explains historian Sam Bass Warner, Jr., of the newly annexed areas, "though in fact in ten to fifteen years his house and land would be lost in a great plain of new streets and new houses." Urban institutions were not far be-hind. Austin's former estate, with its landscaped ponds and orchards, became a home for impoverished women.[61]

But union with Boston also resulted in the preservation of a huge tract of land for public use that might otherwise have been devel-oped. Many Bostonians had been clamoring for a public park system since New York City opened Central Park to the public in 1859. Bos-ton permanently preserved the Public Garden as park land that same year, and together with the Common it provided an open area of about seventy acres. But that paled in comparison to Central Park's seven hundred acres, and Boston had no additional undeveloped space on its peninsula to devote to parkland. Annexation helped solve the problem. With access to large amounts of rural land within its municipal borders, the city hired Frederick Law Olmsted, the preeminent landscape architect of his day, to design a system of parks and parkways that looped around the most settled part of the city to form an "Emerald Necklace." When completed, it would be the first integrated system of public parks in America. In 1885, Olmsted finished the plan for the system's centerpiece: Franklin Park. A huge pastoral space of over five hundred acres, the park was designed to evoke the open countryside and rested squarely in the middle of West Roxbury. Had Arthur Austin's rural community developed as he had hoped, it would not have needed a public park on this scale, since many homes would have been situated in their own private park-like settings. But a large and crowded city did need such a public space, and it was only by becoming part of Boston that West Roxbury gained the crown jewel in the Boston Park System. The city, it seemed, could paint with a green brush of its own.[62]

"Beautiful Brookline"

Of the four towns compelled by the legislature to vote on annexation in 1873, only Brookline rejected union with Boston. Just west of Roxbury and West Roxbury, Brookline stretched southwest from the Charles River and shared a long municipal boundary with its two neighbors. The town was about seven square miles in area and had been part of Boston until 1705, when the state's tradition of municipal division helped Brookline to achieve independence. Since then, it had grown into a farming community serving the urban market and had acquired more than its share of wealthy residents. As early as the 1780s, some of the biggest names in Boston society began to build summer homes in the town. The Cabots, Lowells, Perkins, Amorys, Sargents, Codmans, and other prominent families all settled in Brookline, which came to house an even larger concen-

After annexing West Roxbury, Boston chose a 500-acre site in the former town to become Franklin Park, the crown jewel of the city's new Olmsted-designed park system. Had West Roxbury not become part of the city, it is unlikely that the site would have been preserved as open space. (Courtesy of the Library of Congress)

tration of Brahmins than West Roxbury and perhaps any other town in the region. By the end of the century, Brookline's residents would describe their community as "the richest town in the world."[63]

Until the 1870s, Brookline's development largely paralleled that of West Roxbury. An omnibus in the 1830s, a railroad stop in 1848, and a street railway in 1858 facilitated migration to the town and enabled new residents to commute to work in the city. In the twenty years between 1840 and 1860, the population of the town increased by almost four hundred percent. Most of the growth was in northern Brookline, the section closest to Boston, and many of the new residents were Irish immigrants who congregated in the low areas surrounding the Muddy River. By 1850, a quarter of the town's population haled from Ireland. Change was everywhere, even in south-

ern Brookline where farms were rapidly being converted into country estates. As in the other towns close to Boston, the rattle of
horsecars, pounding of hammers, and lilt of Irish accents grew
louder with each passing year.[64]

But the residents of Brookline embraced an evolutionary step in
the suburban ideal that developed after upper Roxbury had won its
independence and committed to a future with few urban services.
In the mid-1850s, architects and horticulturalists redeemed the word
"suburb" and used it to describe not only a residential community
that celebrated the country and rejected the city but one that combined the best of both. In 1871, Olmsted provided a concise description of suburbs as communities of "detached dwellings with sylvan
surroundings yet supplied with a considerable share of urban conve-
nience." This definition suggested a different set of relationships
than one would find in a traditional rural setting, one that had the
potential to provide more than a mere escape from the city. Suburbs
could be true middle landscapes, where it was possible to have a
country setting and water and sewer service, too. This revision of
the suburban ideal suggested a way to resolve the tension between
country and city that was so central to the annexation debates. West
Roxbury's leadership had failed to embrace it, but the residents of
Brookline valued urban services as highly as their political autonomy and rural environment.[65]

Perhaps more than any other residents of Boston's periphery, the
citizens of Brookline derived their identity as a community from the
romantic natural environment in which they lived. "We were so ac-
customed to hearing our town called 'beautiful Brookline,'" recalled
one resident, "that we almost fancied the adjective to be a part of its
real name." Visitors seemed to agree that there was, in fact, something special about Brookline. Poets Henry Wordsworth Longfellow and William B. Tappan praised the town's natural charm, with
Tappan likening it to "Eden in its primal beauty." Father Edward
Taylor also chose a biblical metaphor to describe Brookline. A North

End minister who spent his days caring for Boston's sailors, Taylor tempered his language—but not his candor—when invited to preach in a local church. "You people of Brookline ought to be good if you're not," he scolded the congregation. "You live in Paradise already!"[66]

The town even captivated the great landscape architect Andrew Jackson Downing, one of the century's great tastemakers. A resident of the picturesque Hudson River valley and a tireless advocate of country life, Downing founded an influential magazine called *The Horticulturalist* and wrote several immensely popular books on landscape and cottage design. Brookline perfectly illustrated his rural aesthetic. "The whole of this neighborhood of Brookline is a kind of landscape garden," he wrote in 1841, "and there is nothing in America, of the sort, so inexpressibly charming as the lanes which lead from one cottage, or villa, to another." He appreciated that the landscape combined a certain degree of environmental order—the town did not permit animals to run loose—with "an Arcadian air of rural freedom and enjoyment." To Downing, Brookline was the country improved.[67]

Control of the town government by upper-class families ensured that development did not compromise the rural landscape. Every real estate developer needed the town to build sewers, assume responsibility for maintaining streets, and construct roads that gave access to their new neighborhoods. If the town refused to provide these services, a fledgling development could fail. So savvy builders divided their land into generous lots and sold them with restrictive covenants that required large setbacks and residential use. Such plans quickly won approval. In contrast, one builder who insisted on producing cheaper housing on smaller lots was denied services by the town, and his development scheme failed. The town also used financial incentives to encourage the preservation of the great estates, which contributed much to the town's rural character. Assessors routinely undervalued large land holdings, thereby limiting

Brookline's town seal was adopted in 1848 and reflected the community's identity as a "country town" distinct from the city. A series of rural symbols in the foreground represent Brookline, and a vast space traversed only by a train separates the town from a distant Boston. (Author's collection)

taxes on them and making it possible to leave extensive areas undeveloped and unproductive. Control of the town government ensured control of its environment, and a pastoral environment supported the community's claim to social status and a suburban identity.[68]

Residential developments in Brookline that attempted to preserve a rural ambience dated as far back as the 1840s. In 1848, David Sears began to develop his land as the subdivision of Longwood. The new neighborhood was designed by a civil engineer who had been involved in laying out Mount Auburn Cemetery, and it included a number of small parks that provided views of greenery to many of the expensive homes that sprang up on the property. A year later, another landowner laid out the Fairmount or Lakeside neighborhood in a manner that complemented rather than competed with its hillside setting. Both estate owners lived on the land they were developing and intended to continue doing so. Rather than mere speculators looking to make a profit before moving on, they were residents of the town and made a personal commitment to the pastoral neighborhoods they created.[69]

At the same time that the residents of Brookline were grooming their rural environment, they were also building urban services that were far superior to those in neighboring suburbs. By the 1850s, Brookline had one of the best school systems and public libraries outside of Boston, and gaslights illuminated the streets of its most settled areas. This was unusual given how rural much of the town was: more than a third of its adult male workforce was still employed as farmers or farm laborers. But such traditionally urban amenities were made more affordable by Brookline's incredible wealth. Although the town housed a sizeable working-class population to serve the needs of the wealthy, and had a small middle class, a full thirty-six percent of the town's residents were wealthy enough to employ live-in domestic servants.[70]

By 1870, Brookline's growth and Boston's desire for expansion led to talk of union. Leadership of the annexation movement came from families that had lived in Brookline for generations and looked forward to the day when they could sell their land at a large profit. Farmers and property owners in rapidly growing areas near Boston joined them, as did others who would benefit from more intensive development. All hoped that merging with Boston would produce higher real estate prices. Although most annexationists did not intend the complete destruction of the town's country charm, they saw development as progress, and for many it was profit as well. So advocates of annexation looked forward to trading the town's "narrow country roads" for "broad avenues, well-graded and drained."[71]

But opponents of annexation liked the narrow country roads as they were—that was the point of living there. This group included people who had arrived in the town more recently, such as wealthy Brahmin families and middle- and upper-class commuters. These new residents had forged a stronger connection between their personal social status and their environment: they had moved to Brookline not only for the low taxes of the country but for the cultural cachet of a suburban setting, and they were not about to see their country town transformed into a city. Most were not against growth, but they preferred low-density residential development, and they trusted the town to control it. The editor of the aptly named *Brookline Independent* feared that annexation would destroy the town's wealth, natural beauty, and social order. "Will she end all this," he asked, "to become the smallest, most insignificant, outlying suburban-ward of a commercial, money-worshiping metropolis?" A former town selectman worried that developers "would cut down the hills, remove the groves, and lay out streets everywhere like gridirons across the territory." Echoing many of the environmentally-based arguments made before him, the selectman claimed that Brookline's rural qualities should preclude any attempt to attach it to the city. "No suburb should be annexed," he insisted, "until it becomes a city in character."[72]

To preserve their town's independence, Brookline's leaders had to succeed where West Roxbury had failed: they had to embrace the urban by making the town's services competitive with Boston's, but without compromising the non-urban character of Brookline's physical setting. They were well on their way in the 1850s, and by the end of the 1870s had achieved that goal. The town had established a full-time police force, built two public playgrounds, completed its own water works, and begun a large-scale system of sewers. It even enjoyed limited telephone service.[73] Yet much of Brookline retained its country charm. Even twenty-five years later, residents could still claim that the town was "celebrated for its rural beauty."[74] Faced with an appealing balance of abundant municipal services and a green environment, annexationists found it increasingly difficult to find compelling arguments for union with Boston.

Yet agitation for annexation remained strong through the 1870s. For most of the decade, the town entrusted its defense to a young lawyer and Brookline native named Alfred Chandler, who repeatedly led the town to victory over residents who favored annexation. In 1872, Brookline's citizens rejected annexation by a margin of four to one. In 1873, they resoundingly rejected it again, in part because plans to build a public water works—which promised jobs in the midst of a severe economic downturn—had helped secure the working-class vote. But the subject of annexation resurfaced in a town meeting just three weeks later. In response, the town authorized a special committee to oppose annexation that would draw on the town treasury. When opponents secured a court injunction against using town money to preserve Brookline's existence, private donations poured in to finance the work of the committee, which defeated legislative attempts to annex the town in 1875 and again in 1876. In January 1880, sixty percent of Brookline's voters turned out to defeat annexation one last time by a majority of two to one. Given the popular opposition to union, the legislature's Committee on Towns advised against it, and annexationists finally gave up the fight.[75]

After 1880, the owners of large properties in Brookline continued to develop the town as an exclusive pastoral suburb. While the areas closer to Boston experienced denser development, much of Brookline was divided into spacious new subdivisions. The town benefited from the design talents of Olmsted, who created plans for a number of new neighborhoods. The two that were eventually executed reflected the design principles that he helped to pioneer: elegant single-family homes sat on large lots far back from the streets, which curved with the site's topography. Other developments employed the same methods, and Brookline's environment evolved into a series of looping thoroughfares and low-density neighborhoods. These characteristics stand out in sharp relief on modern maps, where little more than a thinly drawn municipal line separates Brookline's loose coil of roads from West Roxbury's tight grid of streets.[76]

To local architect F. Manton Wakefield, Brookline proved that development did not have to mean the "sacrifice of charm in the home or its environment." He cited the neighborhood of Aberdeen near Chestnut Hill as a perfect example. "Here amongst the trees, ledges and boulders," he wrote, "are built the houses, combining easily with the picturesqueness about them, with here and there bits of smooth green and gardens, the bright color contrasting and offsetting the ruggedness." Wakefield used West Roxbury as a counterpoint to emphasize not just what Brookline had accomplished, but what it had avoided. Brookline, he wrote, "has no suggestion of being crowded—each place has a character of its own, and seems not to elbow its neighbor, as do the houses in some of the other newly peopled districts, where we see them standing awkwardly shoulder to shoulder, like so many children in a spelling match." Wakefield's critique of West Roxbury's new neighborhoods was justified from the perspective of the suburban ideal. But like so many other advocates of the pastoral suburb, Wakefield ignored the fact that the vast majority of Bostonians could not afford the price of admission to the kind of community in nature that he favored.[77]

Brookline's success demonstrated that the synthesis of the rural and urban—in environment, society, and services—was both possible and highly marketable. Even the great Olmsted himself succumbed to Brookline's allure. By the late 1870s, he was involved in a number of projects near Boston and frequently stayed in Brookline to be close to his work. In the winter of 1881, while spending a few days at the home of the noted architect H. H. Richardson, who was a close friend and resident of the town, Olmsted awoke one morning to find the landscape blanketed in snow. The scenery must have been beautiful, but Olmsted's attention was drawn instead to the site of a snowplow already at work clearing the street. "This is a civilized community," he said to Richardson. "I'm going to live here." He began renting a house that summer and purchased his own two years later. Olmsted lived in Brookline for the rest of his life.[78]

But Brookline was not yet done helping urban elites to invent new ways of relating to the countryside. In 1882, a group of Boston Brahmins created a new and unique American institution—the country club—on one hundred rural acres in the town. Called simply The Country Club, the organization promoted "rural" activities like horse racing and lawn tennis and rapidly attracted a large membership composed of the best families in Boston. Despite the club's English pretensions, there were no comparable institutions across the Atlantic. English elites tended to engage in rural activities on their ancestral estates, where they spent much of the year, and organized athletic clubs around particular rural pursuits, like hunting. Wealthy Bostonians, however, were an urban upper class, not a rural one. So creating social networks that evoked country life required a new kind of organization that emphasized rural activities in a rustic setting close to the city. Defining what it meant to be upper class, rather than participating in shared recreational interests, was the driving force behind the organization. It quickly inspired other country clubs around the nation, marking Brookline's innovation as a singular act of creation that produced one of the defining social and environmental institutions of the affluent American suburb for the next century.[79]

The Country Club would eventually grow to over two hundred acres, far larger than the public parks constructed and maintained by the town. That meant that Brookline's single largest green space was private rather than public and restricted by class rather than open to a broad cross section of people. The Country Club was a private natural retreat set among smaller residential retreats, all catering to the needs and tastes of those who had competed most successfully in the race for private gain. Yet for all its beautiful private spaces, Brookline had no great public space comparable to Franklin

Park in West Roxbury. One of the ironies embedded in the landscapes of these two communities is that Brookline developed with
substantial oversight by its town government but has no great public park, while West Roxbury developed with little public oversight
and contains the grand public space of Franklin Park.

Making the Pastoral Suburb Permanent

Despite its success, Brookline had one last obstacle to overcome if it
was to permanently retain its independence. It had to adapt the
town meeting form of government to the realities of a growing
population. Brookline avoided a crisis until November 1899, when
more citizens showed up for a meeting at the town hall than the
structure could accommodate. Over eight hundred voters crowded
the building, while more waited outside, unable to participate and
effectively disenfranchised. Within days, nearly two hundred citizens had signed a petition asking to replace the traditional town
meeting. But others feared that representative government held a
special danger for Brookline. Becoming a city would constitute an
admission of urban character that might reopen the annexation
question and render the line between city and suburb too obscure to
defend.[80]

Many residents of Brookline also retained a strong cultural attachment to their town meeting that had everything to do with the
community's pastoral environment. Simply put, one of the great
advantages of having a town meeting was that it implied the rural
rather than the urban. Even though Brookline had a population of
approximately twenty thousand by the end of the century, most of
its citizens still thought of themselves as residing in a country town.
In the New England imagination, such a place was characterized by
both its environment and its social and political world. Meadows
and woods framed a supposedly distinctive kind of life in which
neighbors knew each other and made decisions collectively in town
meetings where everyone, no matter their wealth or station, had a

voice. It was essentially the same connection between politics and environment that Rufus Choate had made a generation earlier when arguing for the creation of an independent West Roxbury: a town meeting was the right form of government for a rural area.[81]

The development of a racially informed view of municipal government further strengthened the connection between town meeting and rural environment. Herbert Baxter Adams, one of the most influential historians of his generation, argued in 1882 that a connection existed between New England town government and Anglo-Saxon precedents. Adams traced the region's institutions first to England and then to the villages of ancient Germany, where farmers had lived close to one another and shared common fields. Although little evidence actually supported Adams's theory, it lent historical significance to the town meeting and racialized the roots of democracy during a period of intense anxiety over immigration. It also planted the origins of the town meeting squarely in a past that was both rural and Anglo-Saxon.[82]

Alfred Chandler applied this argument directly to suburban Brookline. Like Arthur Austin before him, Chandler's defense of his community had won him the chairmanship of the Board of Selectmen and made him a local hero. From that platform, he argued that the direct democracy of the town meeting had been born of the freedom-loving Anglo-Saxon mind, while representative city government concentrated power in a way that smacked of continental monarchy and papism. The implication was that pastoral suburbs were the natural place for Protestants and native-born Americans, while cities catered best to Catholics and foreigners. For Chandler, who did not make a secret of his anti-immigrant views, the battle for Brookline's independence was therefore part of a larger struggle to protect the Anglo-Saxon race and its pastoral roots.[83]

Chandler himself eventually solved the problem of the town meeting by developing a hybrid form of municipal government: the representative town meeting. His plan divided the town into five wards and required citizens to choose sixty town meeting representatives from each. Only the representatives would have the power to vote in town meetings, although all citizens could attend and speak on issues that concerned them. In essence, Chandler's plan proposed a representative government but made the deliberative body larger so that it functioned more democratically. The plan drew on ideas developed seventy-five years before, when Boston had debated the future of its own town meeting, but it also incorporated the desire of progressive reformers to make government more democratic. Progressives were turning to tools like the initiative and referendum to increase the power of voters and to curb corruption, and they compared such tools directly to the New England town meeting. Brookline, encouraged by necessity and the national movement to enhance democratic access to lawmaking, endorsed a version of Chandler's plan in 1915 and became the first town in the state to adopt the representative town meeting. Dozens of Massachusetts towns followed its example, and the new form of government spread throughout the region.[84]

Brookline's residents had less success resolving an important question about public responsibility raised by the town's independence: what did suburbanites owe the city? With its large commuter population, Brookline benefited greatly from Boston's economy and cultural institutions but did nothing to support the city's finances. Thoughtful residents pondered this ethical dilemma, and some even proposed solutions in the first and only issue of *Brookline Magazine*. Howard Bridgman, a minister and editor, hoped that suburban residents might act as conduits through which rural values could flow to cities. The problem, Bridgman believed, was that "our ideal Suburbanite has not yet evolved. He is in the process. When he emerges, he will blend the best traits of the pure city man and the pure countryman." The influence of both country and city would produce a suburbanite who was "broad, symmetrical, responsive to life on all sides and alive to all life's obligations." The suburban environment was the essential crucible—the smell of a rosebush snaking up the veranda of a home, and the feel of sunshine dappling a path fortified the suburbanite for the daily challenges of the city. Bridgman believed that the suburbanite might bring this purifying influence to the city and thereby repay his debt through morals if not money.[85]

An anonymous editorial, entitled "The Suburbanite's Opportunity," offered a similarly nebulous solution that drew on suburban environment and society for inspiration. The author suggested three ways in which the suburbanite might contribute to public service and the city. The first was by simply allowing the town's gardens and trees to shape his moral development. "Green grass," he assured his readers, "plays a large part in molding character." Secondly, the suburbanite might construct a community that would serve as a model for urbanites. Non-partisan government, a happy family, and the influence of church, school, and home on character—in short, the life of the country town—could provide a shining example to the city. Finally, the suburbanite could help the city more directly. "If a man makes his money in the city," the author believed, "it is at least courtesy that he should pay for that privilege by helping the city carry some of its burdens." The suburbanite might pay back some of the money, suggested the author, or he could lend "the earnestness of his best self" to the city. But there he abruptly ended, never moving beyond generalities that were of little practical use.[86]

Entries in a symposium called "The Advantages and Obligations of Residence in Brookline" were even more telling. The ten authors who contributed short reflections had no difficulties listing the advantages: references to Brookline's beautiful pastoral environment, its town government, and its superior services were ubiquitous. But not one of the contributors ever got around to discussing the obligations of residence in a suburb, despite the title of the symposium. Perhaps they believed, as Alfred Chandler did, that the mere presence of a pastoral suburb was gift enough to a bordering city. Brookline, claimed Chandler, "instead of being a drag upon its powerful neighbor, is an inspiration."[87]

Although no one realized it at the time, Brookline's rejection of annexation signaled the beginning of a national movement away from urban consolidation. Boston's appetite for expansion space was temporarily sated, and by the time interest in annexation revived among its leaders, many suburbs had followed Brookline's example and improved their services. Union with the city lost its appeal, and suburbs fought to retain their independence. The pattern would repeat itself across the country. In the early twentieth century, East Cleveland and Lakewood rejected Cleveland; Cicero, Evanston, and Oak Park rebuffed Chicago; and Beverly Hills refused union with Los Angeles. Boston annexed its last suburb, Hyde Park, in 1912. Some cities continued to expand, but most, particularly in the Northeast and Midwest, found themselves powerless to annex anything but troubled communities unable to govern themselves.[88]

One additional environmental innovation sealed the boundaries of Boston forever: the creation of metropolitan districts to manage environmental services for the entire region. Population growth in the suburbs was increasing the need for water and sewer systems, but since environmental resources were scattered unevenly among the many municipalities, towns found it difficult to build them without extensive cooperation from their neighbors. Regional systems had become necessary. In 1889, the legislature created the Metropolitan Sewerage Commission, a semi-autonomous body charged with developing and managing a regional drainage system for Boston and its immediate suburbs. It was the first effort of its kind in the nation and reflected the realization that the management of some environmental relationships required the transcending of political boundaries. A Metropolitan Water Board followed in 1895, and together they made it possible for suburbs as far as ten miles into the countryside to secure key urban services without having to resort to annexation. Boston officials would submit annexation petitions to the legislature into the 1920s, but to no avail. The physical expansion of Boston had ended.[89]

The independent pastoral suburb was more than just a new kind of place. It represented a new set of relationships between people and nature. By gathering the most desirable characteristics of a rural past and an urbanizing present, the residents of edge communities like Brookline invented a suburban future. Their social and environmental middle ground combined the spacious natural settings and rural governmental institutions of the countryside with the comfort and convenience of urban technologies. This suburban blend is such a central part of American life today that it might be tempting to see the rise of the suburb as inevitable or even "natural." But that was not the case. Pastoral suburbs remained largely unknown outside of England and America until well into the twentieth century. Seemingly overnight, however, they became fundamental components of the American metropolis, together with the deeply appealing relationship to the natural world that they embodied.

The impact of the independent pastoral suburb on Boston, and on urban America more broadly, was dramatic. It set a standard to which many other suburbs aspired, encouraged further suburban development, and became America's new model of the ideal community. Although elite Bostonians still spoke of building a city upon a hill, they were moving to the suburbs in droves, and many other residents dreamed of doing the same. The new suburbanites would reenact the founding of Boston again and again, driven by the fear that the original had lost its promise and attracted by a new vision of community. But they would find the suburbs just as carefully petitioned by class as the city and even more dedicated to the culture of privatism, and they would leave behind a city struggling to manage a landscape of industry and poverty without help from many of its best minds and deepest pockets. In just a few decades, the social and environmental world of greater Boston was transformed as the shifting line between city and country became a permanent line between city and suburb.

The ideas about nature and society that inspired the pastoral suburb had also helped to create other new lines that partitioned the metropolitan area into discreet political, environmental, and social enclaves. The lines ran between town meetings and representative governments, between rural and urban, between rich and poor, and between native-born Protestants and foreign-born Catholics. Although porous and moveable, such lines have continued to define Boston into the present day. But they were not the only lines that Bostonians were drawing at the time. During the same decades, they were also debating the proper line between land and water as they dumped ever increasing amounts of fill into Boston Harbor to expand their small peninsula. The outcome of those debates would help to revolutionize the relationship between the city and its harbor.

4

Making the Harbor

A s important as annexation was to the growth of Boston, the city's residents had found a way to acquire new land long before they began absorbing neighboring towns: they made it. This ability relied on a distinctive feature of the city's geography. Thousands of acres of gently sloping tidal flats extended from the shoreline into the harbor, and thousands more stretched from the banks of the Charles and Mystic rivers to the edges of their channels. Most flats were hidden at high tide by shallow water but visible when the ocean receded, revealing bountiful growths of sea grass. Building up these areas with dirt, gravel, ashes, and other material proved an easy and inexpensive way for owners of waterfront property to expand their real estate, especially since the process was largely unregulated. In fact, into the middle of the century, the relationship between Bostonians and their harbor could best be characterized as haphazard and oriented toward private needs.[1]

But as early as the 1830s, when Boston's landward and seaward expansions were beginning to accelerate, a concern developed that this relationship might be damaging the harbor. Competent observers claimed that the ship channels were shoaling, and the merchants, ship captains, and engineers who knew the harbor firsthand embraced a scientific theory that blamed landmaking for the deterioration. According to the theory, Boston Harbor existed in a fragile equilibrium of natural forces that excessive landmaking could disrupt. If thrown out of balance, the huge and complex harbor might prove impossible to repair.[2]

In response, Bostonians gradually traded their haphazard and

This detail from a 1780 map shows the extensive tidal flats that surrounded Boston. They sloped gently away from the higher ground and could easily be filled to the level of dry land. (Courtesy of the Norman B. Leventhal Map Center at the Boston Public Library)

privately-oriented way of relating to Boston Harbor for one that was scientific and more mindful of the public good. The drive for change came from the maritime community and concerned citizens who rallied city, state, and federal governments to their cause. Over the opposition of real estate developers, railroad corporations, and pro-growth legislators, the defenders of Boston Harbor convinced these various levels of government to use the scientific theory as a guide in regulating landmaking and directing the construction of harbor improvements into the twentieth century. Their cautious and controlled approach to the harbor—guided by science and managed by government—gave Boston's coastline the shape it has today.

Like any other scientific model, the theory represented a set of ideas about nature intended to make sense of the natural world. In that way, it was akin to the other ideas about nature that shaped nineteenth-century Boston, such as the ideas that linked pure water with improved morality or pastoral settings with harmonious communities. Such a claim might seem odd to anyone who equates scientific ideas with "reality." But science does not describe reality. Instead, in the words of environmental historian Carolyn Merchant, "Science is an ongoing negotiation with nonhuman nature for what counts as reality." Our scientific observations of the natural world are made through cultural lenses that human beings cannot avoid. Even when employing the scientific method, we can never know the non-human directly, unmediated through culture. In many cases, perhaps most, the best that science can do is to give us an approximation of the principles that inform the natural world. Despite the rigor and care that go into the construction of these theories, they remain human ideas about how nature works, and as such are always imperfect.[3]

As a result, scientific theories can turn out to be just as wrong as other forms of human knowledge, as Bostonians would eventually discover. In the early years of the twentieth century, a new understanding of Boston Harbor's hydraulics emerged that showed the older theory to have been entirely incorrect. Landmaking, it turned out, had done little if anything to harm the harbor. But the fact that the theory had not accurately represented the harbor's hydraulics had not lessened its power as a force for change. Several generations of Bostonians had used this set of mistaken ideas to rethink how they approached the harbor and to guide their deliberations about landmaking, dredging, and seawall construction. The resulting decisions would transform the harbor and help to structure the new relationship between Bostonians and the sea.[4]

The Nature of Boston Harbor

In the nineteenth-century, the voyage of a large ship westward into Boston Harbor was a journey through deep-water channels that meandered through a maze of steep headlands and hilly islands. Travelers approaching the main ship channel, the deepest of three, first encountered the scattered and windswept Outer Islands where Bostonians had erected the first lighthouse in North America. They then entered the outer harbor through two headlands that lay seven miles apart. Point Allerton appeared close by on the left, while its partner, Point Shirley, remained hidden behind more islands to the right. Ships followed the main channel up to Nantasket Roads anchorage and tacked northwest through the Narrows, a tight passage between the pastures of Lovell's Island on one side and the farm and fort of Gallup's Island and George's Island on the other. They then turned west again and sailed into President Roads anchorage, passing between the tips of Deer Island and Long Island, the largest in the harbor. To the south lay another dozen or so islands, and beyond them the harbors of Dorchester, Quincy, and Hingham.[5]

Ships continuing on to Boston moved from the outer harbor to the inner harbor by turning northwest again and passing between the forts on Governor's and Castle islands. By this point in the journey, a ship would have traveled some twelve miles since first encoun-

Boston Harbor, shown here in a bird's-eye view from 1870, contained forty-eight square miles of land and water. The main ship channel wound its way through the harbor's many islands and connected the city with the open sea. (Courtesy of the Norman B. Leventhal Map Center at the Boston Public Library)

tering the Outer Islands, but it still had at least three to go. Anyone on deck would begin to see the scores of busy wharves that lined the shores of Boston proper, East Boston, South Boston, and Charlestown, and if the tide was low, they could see hundreds of acres of mud flats extending into the harbor. Finally, their eyes might climb the rising mound of roofs and spires on Boston's peninsula until they rested on the dome of the State House. Yet, by the time the ship was nestled into its berth, the passengers would have seen only part of the forty-eight square miles of water and land that composed Boston Harbor. Residents of the city liked to brag that their harbor was big enough to hold all the nation's shipping at once.[6]

Boston Harbor was not only a place of natural beauty and human activity, but also a complex convergence of land and sea. The Outer Islands, together with the headlands of points Allerton and Shirley and the islands strung between them, sheltered the harbor from the large waves, relentless winds, and fierce storms of the open ocean. The remaining islands divided the outer harbor into tranquil basins, creating almost seven square miles of anchorage deep enough for large ships and calm enough for frailer vessels. The main ship channel—an underwater trench that snaked between the islands and linked the anchorage grounds—provided deep water for large ships. Without its island buffers, the harbor would have suffered from the worst of wind and wave and provided a much less friendly environment for commerce. Without deep-water channels through its shallow bed, the harbor would have lacked the highways that enabled goods from all over the world to reach Boston.[7]

The harbor was also part of a larger hydraulic system that extended far inland. Twice each day, flood tides rolled in and raised the water level around the city's wharves between eight and eleven feet, depending on the point in the monthly tidal cycle. Seawater filled the large tidal reservoirs of the South Bay, Back Bay, and Mill Pond and pushed several miles upstream into the freshwater of the

Charles and Mystic rivers. These flood tides alternated with ebb tides that, twice each day, dragged water back out of the reservoirs and rivers, through the harbor, and toward the open sea. The estuary functioned like a great liquid lung that breathed ocean water in and out. In the process, it blurred the lines between seemingly distinct natural categories like freshwater and saltwater, river and ocean, land and sea.[8]

Boston Harbor was one of many excellent natural harbors along America's eastern seaboard, and each had its own environmental peculiarities. Portland's harbor was relatively easy to enter, since the distance from the sea to the docks was only three and a half miles and the ship channel ran unusually straight. Baltimore's harbor, in contrast, lay a full 152 miles inland from the sea and was approachable only by a winding channel that was difficult to follow. New York's harbor had more immediate access to the ocean, but a broad sandbar stretched across the harbor's entrance from Sandy Hook to Coney Island. All, however, had sufficient depth and shelter to accommodate any ship seeking entrance in the first half of the nineteenth century, and all were part of complicated hydraulic systems that were essential to the cities they served.[9]

Yet good natural harbors were not present on every shore. Boston was fortunate to have one, and doubly fortunate to have one of the finest. The harbor was, in fact, the golden goose that supplied the city's wealth. It made Boston's commercial prosperity possible by extending the city's hinterland to the distant corners of the world, and it underpinned Boston's identity as a seagoing city. No single totem better reflected the city's reliance on the ocean than the large wooden codfish that hung prominently in the chambers of the state's House of Representatives. It reminded lawmakers every day that the ultimate source of the community's wealth was its connection to the sea. That made Boston Harbor the city's most indispensable natural asset.[10]

"The Destruction of Boston Harbor"

The maritime community, then, was understandably concerned when it began to notice some unsettling changes around the harbor in the 1830s. The most obvious problem was that the islands and headlands were visibly deteriorating. Deer Island, one of the princi-

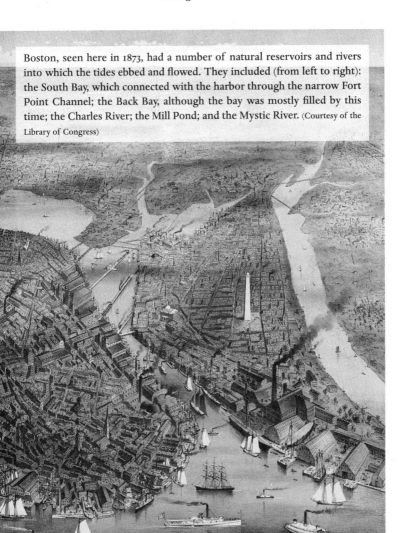

Boston, seen here in 1873, had a number of natural reservoirs and rivers into which the tides ebbed and flowed. They included (from left to right): the South Bay, which connected with the harbor through the narrow Fort Point Channel; the Back Bay, although the bay was mostly filled by this time; the Charles River; the Mill Pond; and the Mystic River. (Courtesy of the Library of Congress)

pal buffers between the ocean and the harbor, had lost an astonishing sixty acres in the prior century, and a high point on George's Island large enough to contain an earthen fortification during the Revolutionary War had crumbled into the sea. Some of the smaller islands had disappeared entirely. Nix's Mate contained about twelve acres in 1636, but half of that had washed away by 1769. Further erosion had reduced it to a mere two acres by 1805, when concerned members of the maritime community saved it from complete destruction by constructing a seawall around what was left of it. Bird Island was not so fortunate. Although large enough in 1650 that locals went through the trouble of harvesting its hay, by the nineteenth century the island had wasted to little more than a shoal visible at half tide. By the middle of the century, all of the islands had suffered from considerable wear and loss of acreage.[11]

The natural evolution of the islands had always produced some shifting of material, but resource extraction increased the rate of erosion. When the first English settlers arrived, trees had covered many of the islands and anchored the soil against weathering. Writing in the 1630s, William Wood noted that the islands "abound with woods" and suggested that ship crews would find more than enough timber on them to replace masts and repair weathered boards.[12] The owners of the islands harvested the trees more systematically. In 1700, for example, the owners of lots on the Brewster Islands agreed to clear the woods on their individual properties within eight years, with any remaining uncut woods becoming common property after that date. Such incentives accelerated the deforestation of the harbor islands and serve as a reminder that clearing their trees was part of the larger effort to harvest the forests of the Boston area. Both progressed with remarkable speed.[13]

The owners of the islands and headlands also encouraged erosion on their beaches by removing the stone and gravel that served as natural barriers against the constant pounding of the waves. Rocks of all sizes could be sold as ballast, and ships sailing out of Boston Harbor required more than the usual load. Since Boston imported far more than it exported, many ships that entered the harbor fully laden left it empty, forcing captains to stabilize their ships for the next part of the journey by purchasing ballast. Owners of the harbor islands and headlands met the demand by selling the rocks and gravel that protected their beaches, and sometimes ship crews simply helped themselves to the material. By the 1840s, the islands and headlands were losing a staggering 150,000 tons of rock and gravel each year, exposing the loose sand directly to the wearing action of the waves. Ballast became Boston's de facto bulk export, producing an unanticipated and destructive link between economy and environment.[14]

Even more than the islands and headlands were at risk. The eroded material often found its way into the channels of the outer harbor, or impeded navigation by creating dangerous shoals. The Narrows had filled by several feet in places as the islands that bordered it bled into the channel, and material from Great Brewster Island formed a treacherous spit that stretched for over a mile and lay hidden beneath the waves at high tide. Erosion also threatened the harbor's anchorage grounds—those calm and protected areas where waiting ships could safely drop anchor. The wearing away of Deer Island risked exposing President Roads anchorage to the full force of ocean storms. In short, the erosion of the islands and headlands was causing a massive migration of rocks, soil, and sand from where it would preserve the harbor to where it would cause the most harm.[15]

Many observers insisted that the inner harbor, the part closest to the city, was filling as well. Winslow Lewis had been sailing in and out of Boston since 1783 and claimed that the main ship channel off Governor's Island had shoaled four feet in the thirty-five years between 1814 and 1849. Samuel Sewall, agent for the Cunard steamship line, complained that the slips between the line's wharves had required dredging twice in just nine years. All around the harbor, wharf owners complained of similar maintenance burdens. Comparisons of old charts with more recent ones supported some of these claims, although the charts were of varying degrees of sophistication and reliability, and a few dated to before the Revolution. Still, the evidence suggested that the inner harbor might be deterio-

Sailors routinely removed rocks from islands in the harbor for use as ship ballast, and some owners of coastal property made a business of it. Over time, the practice contributed to the erosion of material into the harbor. (Reproduced from *Ballou's Pictorial Drawing-Room Companion*, December 27, 1856, courtesy of the Boston Public Library, Print Department)

rating as fast as the outer harbor. The title of an 1852 pamphlet expressed a common fear: "The Destruction of Boston Harbor."[16]

Observations of physical decay in the harbor were difficult to separate from widespread anxiety about the weakening of Boston's commerce. The completion of the Erie Canal in 1825 had catapulted New York City's growth well beyond its rivals and made much of the West its hinterland. Although Boston remained one of America's busiest ports, its relative decline wounded the city's pride and

prompted a search for causes and solutions. Some Bostonians blamed shoaling in the inner harbor for the port's commercial problems, and many others interpreted the harbor's deterioration as a physical manifestation of the port's economic erosion. Both the economic and environmental problems required specific solutions. To energize their faltering commerce, Bostonians turned to railroad building, with mixed success. To repair their decaying harbor, however, they turned to science.[17]

The Theory of Tidal Scour

Merchants, ship captains, marine insurers, engineers, and other close watchers of the harbor interpreted the shoaling observed in the inner harbor through a scientific paradigm they called the "theory of tidal scour." Drawing on observation of the harbor and analogy with other estuaries, the theory described Boston Harbor as a series of channels created and maintained by the scouring force of water moving in and out of the rivers and tidal reservoirs. A trio of engineers wrote as early as 1837 that "the harbor of Boston is not an open broad bay, surrounded on all sides by the sea shore, where the tides simply flow and ebb with a gentle and almost imperceptible current." Rather, they explained, the harbor "is wholly made and continued as channels, through which the tides ascend into immense basins and rivers . . . and from which the tides descend again to the ocean, and in their progress scour out the channel." The idea of tidal scour was also applied to many other navigable waterways, from the Saco River in Maine to the Thames in London, where engineers believed that increasing the speed of the outgoing water would deepen the channels. Any decrease in the speed was thought to encourage shoaling instead.[18]

Although the application of the theory to Boston Harbor represented the best science of its day, the field of hydraulics was still in its infancy. Engineers expressed considerable uncertainty over how water and land behaved when they met. As late as 1874, Thomas Stevenson, a British authority on harbor design and maritime engineering, acknowledged that many seemingly basic questions about how scouring forces worked awaited definitive answers. Some engineers, for example, believed that only freshwater had scouring power, while others insisted that saltwater did most of the work. Such disagreements arose from the incredible complexity that inhered in any large estuary. The volume and velocity of water and the width and depth of channels constantly fluctuated, and the materials that composed the beds of rivers and harbors existed in endless combinations. Stevenson confessed that the number of variables at work presented "an almost hopeless complexity for the mind to grapple with, or for even elaborate observations to unravel." As Heraclitus might have said, no one can step twice into the same harbor.[19]

Boston Harbor not only seemed too complicated to understand fully, but it also appeared to be in peril. Many longtime observers felt sure that the harbor had existed for uncounted years in a happy equilibrium that some force had recently disrupted. This sense of lost stability made the harbor seem fragile and encouraged the fear that making land in the wrong area, or letting a key island erode too far, might disrupt the balance of natural forces even further. How such a destructive mechanism might operate remained unclear. "No one," wrote a concerned ship captain in 1872, "however learned and skilful as an engineer, can predict the consequences which will result from any considerable change in the character or direction of the forces which nature has provided for keeping the channels open."[20] Similarly, no one knew whether engineers would be able to repair whatever damage might occur. The harbor's hydraulic secrets, still only partly understood today, remained largely hidden in the nineteenth century. The result was a potent combination of anxiety over the harbor's condition and uncertainty about how the harbor actually worked. This led many to argue that the city should break with past practice and approach future development with caution.

The theory of tidal scour provided an attractive model for understanding the harbor, in part because it made intuitive sense, given the city's geography. It also gained additional credibility by suggesting a plausible cause of shoaling in the harbor's channels: landmaking. According to the theory, filling the flats diminished the amount of water entering and leaving the harbor, less water meant a weaker scour, and a weaker scour could not maintain the ship channels at the needed depth. Some observers even believed that landmaking in the inner harbor was so disruptive that it was contributing to the filling of the Narrows in the outer harbor ten miles away.[21] Such long-distance connections were difficult to prove, but the notion that filling flats was upsetting the harbor's natural equilibrium and diminishing the scour seemed logical and even likely. In the cloudy context of inscrutable natural forces and an uncertain commercial future, the theory of tidal scour seemed to clarify the harbor's origins and pinpoint the source of its problems. It also armed efforts to curb landmaking with the authority of science.

To Fill, or Not to Fill

There was no question that the city's residents had created an enormous amount of land by filling flats. The first settlers began the process by building solid wharves to accommodate their ships. Over time, many wharf owners expanded their properties by extending their wharves outward or filling the docks between them, a process called "wharfing out." With the exception of a few large projects, the filling of flats progressed gradually in the seventeenth and eighteenth centuries. By the beginning of the nineteenth century, however, the acceleration of urban growth was dramatically increasing the need for more land and the desire to create it. In 1803, the Mount Vernon Proprietors began to develop their new neighborhood north of Beacon Street by excavating material from Mount Vernon and dumping it along the shore of the Charles River. In 1807, a private corporation that planned to build housing for local mechanics began filling the Mill Pond between the North and West Ends with material from Beacon Hill and other sites. Countless other projects also moved forward, many of them by dumping the peninsula's hills into its coves.[22]

In the 1830s, the new railroad corporations also began to contribute heavily to landmaking. Boston was at the forefront of America's railroad boom. As early as 1835, it had three rail lines radiating into the countryside, making it the nation's first rail hub. The railroads needed to build downtown depots and connect their tracks with the city's wharves, but there was little open space along the congested waterfront. So the railroad corporations threw themselves into land-making, and Boston's first three railroads opened facilities built on newly filled flats. Eager to encourage railroad development, the city had begun the trend by selling an area of flats on the Charles River to the Boston & Lowell. The company also purchased nearby Pemberton Hill, removed the top sixty-five feet, and hauled it to the flats where workers covered eight acres with fourteen feet of gravel. The former flats became the site of a new depot. At about the same time, the Boston & Providence built a depot on made land in the Back Bay, and the following year the Boston & Worcester settled on newly filled flats in the South Cove. Other railroad lines followed their example throughout the century, adding dozens of acres to the city at a time as they expanded.[23]

The heavily polluted state of many flats created an additional incentive to make new land. Countless drains carrying storm runoff and industrial and domestic wastewater emptied onto the flats surrounding the city. Many flats also received seepage from leaking privies and provided convenient spots for discarding trash, dead animals, and anything else that was unwanted. As a result, some of the largest early landmaking projects, such as the creation of Quincy Market and the filling of the Mill Pond and the Back Bay, had pollution control as major goals. Converting water into land was a way for the city to manage an environmental problem and create more building space at the same time.[24]

Overall, the city's relationship with the harbor and its flats during the first decades of the nineteenth century was largely unregulated, guided by individual whim and the assumption that large-scale harm to the harbor was impossible. There was no master plan for development, no restriction on the kinds of material that could be used as fill, and no standing city or state board charged with overseeing individual projects. The harbor was large, the need for land was great, and individual landowners pushed the boundaries of their properties into the harbor as they saw fit.

Much of the fill that Bostonians used to make new land came from the Shawmut Peninsula's hills. In this lithograph, which was based on a drawing from 1811, workers are reducing the top of Beacon Hill behind the State House by about sixty feet. (Courtesy of the Massachusetts Historical Society)

Landmaking in Boston was also aided by an unusual colonial-era property law. In the Ordinance of 1641–1647, the Massachusetts General Court extended the property rights of riparian owners to the line of *low* tide, up to a maximum distance of one hundred rods—about a third of a mile—from the line of high tide. English common law, in contrast, drew the line of private property at the line of *high* tide, and most other colonies would do the same. This large concession of the public domain seems to have been an effort to stimulate commerce by encouraging wharf construction. But it also enabled riparian owners in Massachusetts to build and fill to the very edge of the state's natural shoreline. In Boston, where development pressure was most intense, this law underlay the ability of waterfront property owners to convert enormous amounts of water into land at will.[25]

Despite the impact of this peculiar law, Boston was just one of many nineteenth-century cities extending their shores into the lakes, rivers, and bays they bordered. Chicago filled land along Lake Michigan, New York built into the Hudson and East rivers, and San Francisco reclaimed parts of its bay. Charleston, New Orleans, Seattle, Washington, D.C., and many other cities made more or less land depending on local desire and local geography. It was a worldwide phenomenon: urbanizing places from Toronto to Tokyo that wanted more space and bordered on shallow water made a great deal of land and continued to do so into the twentieth century.[26]

But by mid-century, members of Boston's maritime community were insisting that the city's rapid commercial growth and a dramatic increase in the size of ships indicated a need for more water rather than more land. Despite the port's commercial decline relative to New York, the value of imported goods entering Boston through the harbor had tripled in the twenty years between 1830 and 1850. Many in the business community expected exports to increase as well with the completion of railroad links to the west.[27] At the same time, advances in shipbuilding technologies were revolution-

BOSTON, 1630 TO 1675.

The Original Topography and Early Settlement together with the present Shore Line.

THE FAINTER LINES SHOW STREETS OF 1880.

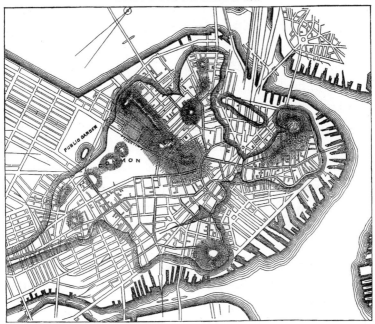

By the end of the nineteenth century, Bostonians had made an enormous amount of new land along the coast by filling tidal flats. This image shows the Shawmut Peninsula's original topography laid over a map of Boston from 1880. (From *Report on the Social Statistics of Cities,* compiled by George E. Waring, Jr., 1886, courtesy of the University of Texas Libraries, the University of Texas at Austin)

izing the size of ships. As late as 1833, the largest Boston ships could carry only 300 tons. Just seven years later, thirty-four ships had capacities between 500 and 800 tons; and by the end of the nineteenth century, ships twenty times larger would seek access to the port.[28] Expanded commerce required more space in the harbor, and larger ships needed deeper water. One commission that studied the harbor's problems put the consequences of choosing land over water this way: "It may be some inconvenience to the merchant to reside out of the city,—but it would be a greater one to have his vessel compelled to anchor out of the harbor."[29]

Although the theory of tidal scour encouraged its adherents to view any changes to the harbor with suspicion, the group did not oppose all development. Merchants, ship captains, and marine insurers had tremendous financial incentives to expand port facilities, and the business of civil engineers was to harness the power of nature for human use. These groups insisted, however, that any changes to the harbor safeguard its natural hydraulics. They conceded that the future needs of a growing commerce might require filling certain carefully chosen flats to supply additional wharf space and other harbor infrastructure. But they were more likely to advise that, if the city's flats must be changed, they should be dredged rather than filled. Dredging would expand and deepen the harbor's anchorage so it could accommodate more and larger ships, and the greater volume of water entering and leaving the harbor would enhance the scour and keep the channels clear. London and Liverpool provided models, since these cities created docks by excavating their riverbanks rather than building out from shore. The guiding principle of those concerned with the harbor's protection was that the state should not permit any development that decreased the total volume of water in the harbor. That set them firmly against the centuries-old tradition of landmaking.[30]

In contrast to the harbor's defenders, those who favored land over water—like powerful railroad and real estate interests—tended to see landmaking as indispensable in a city with Boston's geography. They argued that economic and population growth required more land, much of it on or accessible to the waterfront, and that the only way to get such land on Boston's narrow peninsula was to fill flats. Although they recognized the harbor's complexity and supported efforts to save the islands from erosion, they denied that the harbor was fragile or difficult to repair. Placing their faith in technology and the ability of humans to manipulate nature, this group insisted that any problems caused by landmaking would be reversible. Accordingly, they criticized preservationists for following a "let-everything-be-as-it-is" policy that they believed favored established economic interests and inhibited the city's growth.[31] But their formula for development resisted change as well, for they clung to a now fading relationship with the harbor characterized by individual and uncoordinated expansion into a natural system presumed to be infinitely malleable.

Preservation Begins

Among the most vocal opponents of unregulated landmaking was the influential Boston Marine Society. Founded in 1742 as the Fellowship Club, the society was a social, professional, and charitable group composed of several hundred local ship captains as well as merchants who previously had commanded vessels. No other organization embodied the collective knowledge of the harbor shared by the society's members, and few could match their willingness to speak out on issues of concern. They frequently petitioned the state for additional lighthouses and other improvements, created a standing committee to monitor the harbor's growing problems, and complained as early as 1816 about the negative effects of removing ballast from Governor's Island. In 1846, when the debate over a municipal water supply consumed Bostonians, the members of the Marine Society reminded their fellow citizens that the city had other water problems as well. "While the city government is contemplating the expenditure of millions for the admission of *fresh* water for the use of the inhabitants," they warned, "let it not be blind to the necessity of keeping up the necessary supply of *salt* water in the main channels."[32]

Any kind of large-scale preservation effort would require governmental oversight and funding, and the federal government had the authority—and at least for a time the motivation—to take a leading role. The United States military viewed Boston as a key link in the nation's system of coastal defenses, and it already managed an extensive navy yard in Charlestown. As early as 1825, the Army Corps of Engineers began building seawalls to preserve some of the islands, and in 1833 it began constructing forts to defend the harbor. To ensure the preservation of the Narrows, the federal government purchased George's and Lovell's islands outright, while the city bought Gallup's Island in 1860, bringing all three of the islands that bordered the Narrows under public control. But partisan wrangling in Congress over the wisdom of internal improvements led to chronic underfunding. By 1854, most federal work in Boston Harbor had come to a stop regardless of its state of completion.[33]

The city of Boston also had an obvious stake in defending the harbor, but unlike the federal government, the mayor and City Council had to balance competing demands on the flats. As a result, the city sometimes pursued inconsistent policies that worried the harbor's defenders. Although it created a standing committee to monitor the harbor's problems and energetically lobbied the state and federal governments to take action, the city also began a massive landmaking project in 1845 that required filling sixty-seven acres of city-owned flats in the South Bay. Acting against the advice of several state commissions, the city hoped to create a residential neighborhood for native Bostonians who might otherwise be tempted to escape foreign immigrants by fleeing to the suburbs. From the perspective of city leaders, the deterioration of the harbor was no more pressing a problem than the deterioration of the city's tax base and the threat that immigrants might take over the reigns of government. But such a policy seemed hypocritical to the harbor's defenders, who questioned the city's commitment to their cause and resisted its efforts to gain control over state-owned flats.[34]

The state held even more control over landmaking than either the federal or city governments. It exercised the rights of a property owner, since it owned many of the flats surrounding the city, and it had the power to restrict the building of structures over privately owned riparian areas if they impeded navigation.[35] But more importantly, the state could take selective actions to protect the harbor by using its "police power." This was a vaguely defined right that allowed governments to exercise control over private property, without compensating the owners, if it determined that the health and welfare of its citizens were at stake. Such actions were always controversial. In 1845, under the authority of its police power, the state passed legislation that forbade the extraction of stone, gravel, or sand from certain parts of the harbor. The state repealed part of it, however, under pressure from interested parties. Then, in 1856, the state enacted a new, more comprehensive law that prohibited the removal of such materials from all harbor islands or headlands without a permit from the city. This time the legislature stood firm, and anyone who had sold ballast from a sensitive area of the harbor found himself out of business.[36]

The state also used its police power to protect the channels of the inner harbor by drawing "harbor lines" around the city's waterfront areas. First adopted for parts of the peninsula in 1837 and later supplemented and adjusted, the lines set boundaries beyond which no property owner could fill, even if the owner held title to flats that extended past the line. The purpose was to protect the harbor from encroachments that might block navigation or reduce the volume of water available to scour the channels.[37] Harbor lines were a cutting-edge tool for managing environmental change. New York City, for example, would not follow suit for another twenty years. But the state legislature was committed to the lines and defended them aggressively against unlawful encroachment. In 1846, it sued twenty-three wharf owners who had extended their wharves over public flats to reach the lines or expanded them beyond the lines without permission from the state.[38] Although subsequently altered on various occasions, the harbor lines—and the theory of scour that informed them—determined the shape of the city's coastline.

Like the city government, however, the legislature did as much to facilitate development of the flats surrounding the city as it did to preserve the harbor. Petitions for permission to fill various public flats streamed into the legislature, which readily authorized the extension of wharves or the creation of new land to the established harbor lines. But the state's generosity did not end there. The legislature also granted permission to fill flats in areas of the city around which harbor lines had not yet been drawn, even when such projects were controversial. In the 1850s, it authorized the Mystic River Corporation to build a massive wharf on flats off Charlestown despite strong opposition from the maritime community, and it permitted the Boston Wharf Company to extend its wharf far into the South Boston flats. In several cases, the legislature went so far as to grant permission to fill beyond existing harbor lines, since the state—unlike private individuals and corporations—was not legally bound to observe them. Although the harbor lines did much to constrain ad hoc development, they did not end it.[39]

In the 1840s, growing interest in filling the immense basin of the Back Bay encouraged further public discussion about the future of the flats surrounding the city. As its name suggested, the Back Bay was an inlet of the Charles River on the west, or back, of Boston's peninsula. About eight hundred acres of tidal water covered it until 1820, when entrepreneurs completed a series of dams that cut off the bay from both river and ocean and divided it into two basins. The "full basin" received water from the flood tide and then drained into the lower "empty basin," with the falling water intended to power a series of factories. The project was an early experiment in industrialization, but a failed one. The owners built only a few factories, and over the next twenty-five years the empty basin became a noxious cesspool. Filling it would not only eliminate a nuisance but also provide building space within the city for native-born Bostonians. By the time the filling and development of the Back Bay began in earnest in the 1850s, the bay had not provided a beneficial scour to the harbor for many years, and few supporters of harbor preservation objected to the project. But the discussions highlighted the fact that the state lacked a clear policy for managing the thousands of acres of flats under its control.[40]

With no guiding principles in place, the state continued to act in a piecemeal fashion that sometimes pitted different branches of government against one another. A particularly rancorous confrontation occurred in 1851, when the legislature approved the construction of a solid roadway across the South Boston flats, and Governor George Boutwell vetoed the bill. A veto was a rare thing in Massachusetts politics: no governor had vetoed a bill in the previous twenty-five years, and the last one to do so had cited constitutional grounds for his reason. But Boutwell believed that the proposed roadway failed to give due regard to "the rights of individuals, the rights of the Commonwealth, and above all, to the safety of the harbor." The road would connect Boston's peninsula with South Boston and enclose thirty-eight acres of flats. Although drawbridges and sluiceways would give the tide access to the flats, Boutwell feared that the area would become another Back Bay, largely cut off from the sea and eventually so filthy that the state would have to fill it. His decision drew considerable fire from those who believed that the project would not harm the harbor, but he successfully killed the plan. The idea that the harbor was a complex and fragile system governed by the theory of tidal scour, and the belief that harbor preservation was the greatest public good, were slowly shaping the course of the harbor's development.[41]

Distinguishing Public and Private Interests

But determining whether harbor preservation, landmaking, continued resource extraction, or other activities served the public good or catered to private interests was not always easy to do. Were railroads important enough to the public interest to justify the filling of some flats to create room for new depots? Was conservation of the harbor worth increasing the density of living quarters on the peninsula even further? Did preserving the harbor excuse the financial damage done to those who made their living by removing ballast? What was the real balancing point between public and private interests?

In the first half of the nineteenth century, state courts began giving the authority to decide such questions to city governments and state legislatures by strengthening their existing police power. The courts upheld the ability of New Orleans to ban hospitals from the city limits for reasons of public health, even if the institutions were privately owned and operated. They also found for New York City when it sought to tame its chaotic harbor by regulating the docking of ships at private wharves. Urban environments were evolving rapidly, and in case after case courts were reinforcing the police power of cities and states so that they could guide and manage growth.[42]

Boston Harbor played a central role in the development of this new legal relationship between governments and privately-owned natural resources. Of particular importance was a case that challenged the Massachusetts legislature's power to create and enforce its new harbor lines. In the late 1840s, a wharf owner named Cyrus Alger extended his wharf on South Bay. The wharf covered only flats that Alger owned and did not impede navigation, but it did extend beyond the harbor lines. The matter ended up before the state's Supreme Judicial Court, which ruled for the state. "All property in this commonwealth . . . is derived directly or indirectly from the government," wrote Chief Justice Lemuel Shaw in the court's decision, "and held subject to those general regulations, which are necessary to the common good and general welfare." The decision strengthened the power of government to regulate private property and became a landmark ruling in the evolution of police power and coastal management.[43]

An earlier case had tested the state's ability to protect the crucial headlands that guarded the harbor. William Tewksbury owned a beach and flats on Point Shirley. Like the owners of neighboring beaches, and like his father before him, Tewksbury collected rocks, gravel, and sand from his property and sold them for ballast and other purposes. By the 1840s, Point Shirley provided a total of 25,000 tons of ballast each year.[44] When Tewksbury flouted the 1845 law forbidding removal of material from his property, the courts ordered him to halt his activities. He appealed, claiming that the law violated the constitutional prohibition on taking private property without compensation, but lost the case. The higher court ruled that the law was a legitimate exercise of the state's police power, suggesting that the headlands were too important to the public interest to risk their destruction at the hands of private individuals.[45]

The matter might have ended there, as it would in the later Alger case, but this was new legal ground and Tewksbury still believed that justice had not been served. So he continued to pursue his cause outside the courtroom by appealing to the legislature. Switching from a legal to an environmental argument, Tewksbury claimed that the material he wanted to remove from Point Shirley had not originated from that site but had washed there from Winthrop Head, a rapidly deteriorating hill to the north. At least two engineers agreed that the material did not contribute to the stabilization of the headland and that removing it would do nothing to encourage erosion. Tewksbury convinced the legislature, which passed a special exemption that excluded the beaches owned by Tewksbury and his neighbors from the requirements of the 1845 act. It also paid him five hundred dollars for his losses. For the next ten years, Tewksbury legally removed material from his beaches and flats over the protests of the Boston Marine Society and the town of Winthrop. Pushed by the legislature, the pendulum had swung back and vindicated the rights of the private landowner.[46]

When the legislature passed the 1856 law protecting all islands and headlands within the harbor, Tewksbury's exemption ended and the state once again subordinated his private rights to the public interest. But he obtained another indemnity payment from the legislature for the losses he incurred from the new act, this time for twelve hundred dollars. He also tried to secure an exemption from the new law, pledging only to remove material that the tide routinely threw onto the beach and then reclaimed. The Committee on the Judiciary agreed that such limited action was unlikely to do much harm, but its members were reluctant to risk the harbor's safety in the absence of further scientific study of the site, and they denied the petition. The pendulum had swung once more toward the interests of the public, but its movement had been slow. By the time the committee reported its decision, the case had been going on for seventeen years and Tewksbury had died, leaving the now unprofitable beaches to his children. The length and intricacies of the Tewksbury case illustrate how difficult it was for Bostonians to navigate the line between public and private in a period when environmental relationships and the laws governing them were evolving so rapidly.[47]

The precise nature of the state's public responsibilities in the administration of its *own* flats could be just as murky. Some claimed that, although the state held title to many of the flats, it held the property "in trust for the benefit and security of commerce."[48] In other words, the state owned the seafloor but had no authority to sell it, because all citizens had an inalienable right of passage through the water above it. Like the advocates of grazing rights in Boston Common a generation earlier, this group insisted that even a governmental entity sometimes lacked the authority to alter the traditional uses of a particular natural resource in the public domain. Others believed that the state must use its flats solely for the benefit of the harbor. It could sell them for development, but only if the project would improve the harbor or its accommodations. Still others claimed that the flats were property like any other, and the state had the power to sell or use them for whatever purposes it desired. Although the last interpretation prevailed among jurists, the maritime community continued to insist that the state had a moral if not legal responsibility to do what was right for the harbor to protect the commerce of the city. A duty to the public good demanded it.[49]

The harbor's friends argued that the state should favor commerce when dealing with its flats because commerce best represented the interests of the public. A committee of harbor commissioners explained in 1848 that "the demand for land is, in a great degree, an individual demand,—the demand of companies engaged in speculations." The demand for water, however, was "a demand of the public,—a demand of commerce,—in which the State and nation have a deep and vital interest."[50] Although they agreed that no law limited the state's power to determine the future of its flats, the commissioners still maintained that the state had an obligation to the public to use the flats to benefit the harbor. "We regard this interest in the flats," they wrote, "as a sort of marine investment for the benefit of the State, which should be managed with a sole reference to the commercial prosperity of the whole people." Boston's real estate developers and railroad executives would undoubtedly have disagreed with this interpretation of the public interest.[51]

Calling in the Troops

Despite the combined efforts of city, state, and federal governments, the inner harbor continued to lose water to landmaking and the outer harbor continued to lose land to erosion. The islands showed the clearest signs of deterioration. Although the Army Corps of Engineers had built sturdy seawalls around some of them, the federal government's sporadic work proved insufficient to halt the tide of destruction. In the thirteen years between 1847 and 1860, Great Brewster Island lost another five acres. Nathaniel Hooper, the resident lighthouse keeper, complained that half his pasture had fallen away and that he now had to import hay for his cows. Much of the material washing from the island settled on the long spit that trailed westward into the harbor. Hooper paid close attention to its growth and calculated that the spit had expanded by eighty-five feet in just over three years and was encroaching on the Narrows. Gallup's Island, Deer Island, and others told similar stories of wasting. By 1860, efforts to preserve the harbor had not yet outpaced the forces destroying it.[52]

Mayor Frederick Lincoln began looking for ways to involve the federal government more closely in the harbor's management. He suspected that Congress would make a greater commitment if advised to do so by its own impartial experts, so in 1859 Lincoln asked three federal engineers to form a commission to study the problem. After receiving their consent, he petitioned their superiors to reassign them. Lincoln sweetened the deal with the offer of city funds to support their work, and the federal government formed the officers into the United States Harbor Commissioners on Boston Harbor. It was a distinguished group, composed of General Joseph G. Totten, Chief Engineer of the United States; Professor Alexander D. Bache, Superintendent of the United States Coast Survey; and Captain Charles H. Davis, Superintendent of the United States Naval Academy. They were impartial, however, only with regard to local political and economic interests. Their professional training gave them a decided preference for water over land.[53]

For the next seven years, including the period of the Civil War, the U.S. Commissioners studied the harbor closely. They reviewed old charts and coordinated a series of detailed new studies to clarify the harbor's condition, while other federal engineers completed the harbor's forts to defend against Confederate attacks that never materialized. Within a few years, the U.S. Commissioners had completed a meticulous survey of the inner harbor, a hydrographic survey of the main ship channel, and a topographical survey of the shores and islands of the outer harbor. They also took detailed measurements of the currents in the Charles and Mystic rivers and answered queries about projects all over eastern Massachusetts, from Mystic Pond in Medford to Cape Cod. Between 1860 and 1866, they published their findings and recommendations on the harbor in a series of ten reports.[54]

Based on their studies, the U.S. Commissioners advocated a cautious approach to the harbor. They endorsed the theory of tidal scour, opposed most landmaking, and insisted that the harbor's survival required the restoration and strengthening of existing natural systems. They also confirmed that the depth and width of the main channel in the inner harbor depended on the scour produced by the flow of the Charles and Mystic rivers and the tidal waters that entered and exited the rivers and bays. Although the U.S. Commissioners admitted that the river currents were feeble compared to those in other harbors, they believed that any river current, no matter how small, helped to sweep sediment out to sea by producing stronger ebb tides than flood tides. Further shrinking of the harbor's reservoirs and rivers through landmaking would therefore ruin the harbor, especially since preliminary data already showed substantial shoaling. With no intended exaggeration, they concluded that the inner harbor "cannot, in our opinion, afford to lose another cubic yard of tide water."[55]

Like past observers, the U.S. Commissioners were using information gathered from the harbor to construct their ideas about how its hydraulics worked. That gave the harbor a big role to play in its own future. Every day, the harbor produced a never-ending stream of observable phenomena, such as the rise and fall of tides, the erosion of beaches, the shifting of material on the seafloor, and the mingling of fresh and saltwater. Scientists reduced these phenomena to data that they used to reshape their understanding of how the harbor worked, and they then used their modified ideas to make recommendations about how to reshape the harbor. There was a constant feedback loop between physical nature, in the form of the harbor's natural hydraulics, and cultural nature, in the form of scientific theories that pointed toward particular courses of action.

After interpreting the data they collected, the U.S. Commissioners organized their specific recommendations around the principles of "preservation" and "improvement." Their first goal was "to preserve the great physical features in their ancient order, and to hold on to the old landmarks."[56] Accordingly, they recommended a renewal of efforts to protect the key harbor islands and headlands by building seawalls. They also advised against the continued filling of South Bay and Fort Point Channel, which some Bostonians believed must inevitably disappear to form a land bridge between South Boston and the main part of the city. The bay was essential to commerce, argued the U.S. Commissioners, and both were too important to the scour to tolerate continued encroachment. In general, they strongly advised against haphazard landmaking schemes that did not consider the needs of the harbor.[57]

They also recommended a series of improvements to the harbor that would offset prior damage and increase its commercial potential. To enhance the natural scour, they proposed a seawall around the South Boston flats that would concentrate and accelerate the tidewater passing into the main channel, and they suggested converting the lower Mystic Pond into a tidal reservoir. Gates would hold freshwater back in the pond to allow more tidal water into the river, and then during ebb tide they would open to release the surplus water down the Mystic River toward the harbor. Both projects reflected the Army Corps of Engineers' preference for large engineering works. Finally, the U.S. Commissioners recommended a radical restructuring of the network of bridges that crossed the Charles River into Boston, since their piles did not align with the current and interfered with the river's flow. With the "great physical features" of the harbor preserved, and some of their natural functions augmented through engineering, they claimed that the harbor's scour would function even better than it had before.[58]

The U.S. Commissioners self-consciously modeled their approach to engineering on nature and even considered their methodology and its underlying science to be in some sense "natural." In an early report, they noted that the primary principle informing their work "consists in the improvement of the natural and existing state of things; making it the object to assist nature, and to use the laws of nature derived from study and observation." They believed in using "the means which nature herself supplies." The U.S. Commissioners deepened their point by paraphrasing a line from Shakespeare's *A Winter's Tale,* claiming as the character Polixenes did that "above that art which adds to nature is an art that nature makes." Polixenes was defending the selective breeding and hybridization of flowers by arguing that, since such activities employed means that nature itself had developed, there is something natural about them. This is a rather profound philosophical reflection to find in an otherwise business-like engineering report, and it gives us an unexpected window into the thought that informed the U.S. Commissioners' work. Rather than merely using culture to act on nature, they saw themselves as improving the non-human world through a process that was itself natural.[59]

Nothing highlighted the U.S. Commissioners' commitment to working with natural principles like their proposed system of "compensation in kind." They were not blind to the pressure for land-making, and they acknowledged that developers could fill some of the state's flats with little damage to the harbor. But they were adamant that the volume of tidal water not be further reduced and proposed that no flats be filled without creating an equal volume of water elsewhere through dredging. If the state selected the site to be dredged carefully, "a new receptacle of tide water may perhaps be chosen possessing all the advantages of position of the natural one, or even more."[60] The state alone should perform the work to ensure its proper execution, although developers would pick up the cost by paying a fixed amount into a "compensation fund" for every cubic yard of tidewater they displaced.

Compensation in kind was a form of water mitigation that anticipated by more than a century the land mitigation so popular today. Where the former would compensate for displaced water by dredging in another area, the latter compensates for the loss of wetlands and farmland by enhancing, restoring, or creating new wetlands and by using conservation easements to protect equivalent areas of farmland elsewhere. All manage the environmental costs of development by exchanging one resource for another and placing the financial burden on developers. The idea of a resource exchange might be older still, since compensation in kind was not a new idea even in the 1860s.

The proposals made by the U.S. Commissioners, as ambitious as they were, must have seemed conservative when compared to those of a local merchant. In 1865, Thomas Lamb, a distinguished member of the Boston Marine Society, proposed the construction of a series of dams that would create two enormous basins within the inner harbor, one on the East Boston flats and one on the South Boston flats. Gates in the dams would allow the basins to fill as the tide came in. Then the gates would shut as the tide receded and the water would exit through different openings that concentrated the scouring power on the main channel. The proposed basin on the East Boston flats was particularly impressive. It called for linking East Boston, Governor's Island, Apple Island, and the town of Winthrop with over two miles of dam. The resulting basin, 1,230 acres in area and holding almost twenty million cubic yards of water, would empty above the city through Chelsea Creek and supplement the scour of the Mystic River.[61]

To increase the scour in the outer harbor, Lamb suggested a dam linking Point Shirley and Deer Island on the north, and two more connecting the Quincy shore, Moon Island, and Long Island on the south. The narrow passage between Deer and Long islands through which the main ship channel passed would be the only remaining entrance to the inner harbor, and the full power of the tides would scour the channel at this point as it rushed in and out of the narrow passage twice each day. Although the plan resonated with the U.S. Commissioners' preference for supplementing existing natural processes, it was complicated and expensive and generated little enthusiasm.[62]

In contrast, support for the recommendations of the U.S. Commissioners was strong and extended well beyond the maritime and engineering communities. In 1863, the noted astronomer Benjamin Apthorp Gould threw his considerable reputation as a scientist behind the U.S. Commissioners' efforts. In a series of six articles in the *Boston Daily Advertiser,* Gould translated their technical findings for a popular audience. He explained how the harbor's hydraulic systems functioned, where and why the system was breaking down, the extent of damage caused by erosion, and what actions the U.S. Commissioners recommended. Although Gould considered himself a disinterested party, he did not hesitate to assign blame. He claimed that "the hand of man has recklessly destroyed natural agencies on which the harbor depended for protection," and he pointed an accusing finger at private interests intent on making land at any cost. The city council and board of aldermen liked Gould's newspaper pieces so much that they assembled them into a pamphlet and ordered five hundred copies printed.[63]

Five years later, Charles Francis Adams, Jr., promoted the plans of the U.S. Commissioners in a now classic essay on Boston's transportation problems. On his way to becoming one of the nation's foremost authorities on railroads, Adams brought his exceptional rhetorical powers to the harbor's story by penning a brief and damning history of the damage caused to its rivers, bays, and channels by development. "This tidal way created Boston," he claimed, "and the whole history of Boston has been one long record of short-sighted abuse of this first gift of Nature." But Adams reassured his readers that hope existed. "Scientific men," he wrote, had "sought out at once the cause and the remedy of the evil" and showed how the harbor could be saved. Adams explained that, through the application of scientific principles to the construction of seawalls and artificial reservoirs, the harbor could not only be restored but made better than it was before. His simple but powerful story of environmental decline and scientific redemption cast the U.S. Commission-

ers in the role of saviors and suggested that only science could rescue the harbor.[64]

In 1866, the U.S. Commissioners issued their final report, which
criticized the role that private interests had played in damaging the
harbor. They believed that the sources of Boston Harbor's injuries—
excessive landmaking, careless bridge design, and reckless resource
extraction—were rooted in a quest for profit in which individuals
posted the gains and society paid the cost. Rather than being unique
to Boston, however, difficulty navigating the line between private
rights and public good seemed to adhere to the city building process
itself. "In our own experience in the study of many different harbors," they wrote, "we have found everywhere the traces of injuries
inflicted by individual interests."[65]

So encouraged was the legislature by the work of the U.S. Commissioners that in 1866 it finally acted on the past recommendations
of several ad hoc harbor commissions and established a permanent
Board of Harbor Commissioners. The board had the power to rec-
ommend new harbor lines and to reject or force alterations in any
plans for development that involved filling flats or building structures in or over tidewater, no matter who owned the underlying
land. The work of the U.S. Commissioners had shaped the debate
over the harbor's future so deeply that the legislature wrote the concept of compensation into the statute that created the board. From
that point on, when developers displaced tidewater in Boston Harbor, the Harbor Commissioners were to make them restore the volume through dredging in a carefully selected site, or compel them
to pay into a compensation fund so that the board could do the work
itself. The state appointed two of the most vocal friends of the harbor to the five-member board: Samuel Sewall, for many years the
agent for the Cunard steamship line, and former mayor Frederick
Lincoln, who had organized the U.S. Commissioners. The powerful
new board represented a major shift in the city's relationship to the
harbor.[66]

The Theory under Attack

That same year, the U.S. Commissioners ended their six-year study of the harbor, leaving only one analytical task unfinished. When completed by other federal engineers two years later, however, the analysis threatened to unravel all of their previous recommendations. The U.S. Commissioners had begun to compare soundings they took of the inner harbor in 1861 with a similar survey performed in 1835. They expected the results to give a picture of the inner harbor's deterioration over that period. But when finished after their departure, the data revealed that the volume of water below the line of low tide had not changed significantly in thirty-six years. The massive shoaling described by close observers and the U.S. Commissioners themselves had never taken place.[67]

Instead, the data showed that the changes many had sensed over the years represented a much less threatening shift of material from one place to another rather than a generalized process of accretion. The constricting of the river mouths through filling and their obstruction by bridge piles had increased the velocity of water traveling through them. As a result, the water's enhanced force had excavated half a million cubic yards of material and distributed it unevenly around the harbor floor. The new data explained years of anecdotal evidence for shoaling and suggested that massive landmaking over the last third of a century had done little if any harm. Boston Harbor's enigmatic hydraulics had dealt its friends a powerful blow.[68]

Those who favored land over water used the new findings to assail the harbor's defenders. In 1868 and 1870, two legislative committees reported on the practicability of filling various flats around the city, including the massive tract off of South Boston. Francis W. Bird, a paper manufacturer and state legislator with a passion for polemic, chaired the committees. He also wrote both reports, which sharply attacked "the received doctrine of those who claimed to be the special protectors of Boston Harbor."[69]

Bird complained that all of the opposition to filling in South Boston rested on an attachment to the idea of compensation in kind, which he resolved to discredit. He reviewed the U.S. Commissioners' writings on compensation and concluded that true compensation could take place only in the tidal reservoirs and rivers that drained into the harbor. The U.S. Commissioners themselves, however, had eliminated South Bay as a site for dredging, and the new data eliminated the Charles and Mystic rivers since their rapid flow was already moving material around the harbor floor. If anything, Bird claimed, the tidal reservoirs were already too big. So by his reasoning, compensation, which "never had any scientific basis or fair and thorough practical test," was unnecessary and maybe even counterproductive.[70] "Compensation in kind," he concluded, "may be consigned to the receptacle of things lost upon earth."[71]

But Bird did not stop there. He also used the new data to argue that landmaking itself did not hurt the harbor. The doomsayers, he lamented, had done their work so well that their prophecies had gained the status of common knowledge. To believe a fraction of their predictions, however, would be to conclude that in barely a generation or two the city's residents would see "a vast mud-hole, or at best, a larger-sized frog pond" where their harbor used to be.[72] Bird claimed that the evidence showed something different. The city had made over 1,300 acres of new land since 1835, an amount that looked alarming "when read by the light of a theory." In the light of hard data, however, "it is readily seen that there has been much more fear than danger."[73] Even cutting off the huge Back Bay from the tides and later filling it seemed to have had no effect on the harbor, leading Bird to view the project as a model for future action.

As a result, Bird's committee proposed a radical amount of landmaking, advising the state to fill South Bay, Fort Point Channel, and parts of the Charles and Mystic rivers. It also suggested that the state cut off the Charles River to navigation, since the drawbridges inconvenienced the railroad corporations, and looked forward to a day when the Charles would become a narrow, two-way canal covered with a continuous bridge from East Boston to Brookline, a distance of about three miles. Bird and his committee concluded that Boston's greatest need was land, and that as long as the state preserved the ship channel and sufficient anchorage, it could fill flats with no worries about injuring the harbor. If damage did occur, the state could simply repair it.[74]

But Bird's reports failed to shake the legislature's confidence in the theory of tidal scour. To the harbor's defenders, the new data actually confirmed their suspicions that development was in fact affecting the harbor floor in negative ways. The harbor might not have suffered in the precise way that they had feared, but the damage was worrisome and continuing to take place. Most importantly, the new data failed to suggest an alternative theory for how the harbor's hydraulics functioned. The theory of tidal scour still seemed to provide the only explanation, and until a better one came along, landmaking would continue to seem like a threat.[75]

Using Science to Reshape the Harbor

Undeterred by their critics, the Board of Harbor Commissioners began reshaping the harbor with the theory of tidal scour as a guide. One of its first challenges concerned the South Boston flats, some nine hundred acres of land that stretched from shore to ship channel at low tide but lay beneath ten feet of water at high tide. A state commission had advised as early as 1847 that building a seawall along the flats would improve the scour by training the water from South Bay directly into the channel. The U.S. Commissioners had recommended a similar plan, and the state decided to build the wall and pay for it by filling the flats behind it, since engineers believed that the shallow water flowing over the flats contributed little to the scour. The project took decades to complete and is easy to mistake for just another landmaking scheme. But the Harbor Commissioners and legislature consistently viewed the project as a harbor im-

provement. The creation of new land was of secondary importance.[76]

The South Boston project was the first harbor improvement to
contemplate the replacement of a natural scour with a mechanical
one. Since filling the flats would remove a sizeable volume of water
from the harbor, the city planned to compensate by dredging along
the new seawall to a depth of twenty-three feet at low water. Workers would then dump the dredged material over the wall to fill the
flats. The federal engineers who had finished the analysis begun by
the U.S. Commissioners supported the plan and insisted that it did
not contradict the principle of compensation. "The object of compensation is the maintenance of the scour," they explained. "Under
this plan, the scouring force is the dredging machine instead of the
current of water."[77] From this point forward, the reliance on dredges
rather than water to shape the harbor would only grow.

The Harbor Commissioners regulated other development around
the harbor just as closely. When approached, for example, with a
proposal to fill several hundred feet into the Charles River from
Cambridge to build housing and parks, the Harbor Commissioners
refused to approve the plan. The commissioners explained that they
did not sanction lightly the replacing of natural scour by dredging,
since natural forces were cheaper and required no human supervi-
sion. Only developments that required access to water, like commercial facilities, warranted such a change. Since the developers
could build houses anywhere, they should build them elsewhere.[78]

There were cases, however, when the Harbor Commissioners
thought filling was appropriate. In 1874, they approved a proposal to
fill about fifty-five acres of flats on the Cambridge side of the Charles
River for a commercial development. Although the filling would dis-
place eight hundred thousand cubic yards of tidewater, the Harbor
Commissioners decided that the flats did not contribute to the scour
and that the developers could compensate for the filling by dredging
in the channel of the river. Two years later, they also allowed Charle-

stown to fill an area of flats, again with compensation. The Harbor Commissioners decided each petition on its individual merits, always with a preference for development that expanded maritime facilities and an eye to maintaining or improving the scour.[79]

When the Harbor Commissioners did allow developers to make land, they zealously collected compensation money from them. In 1870, after the city filled a sizeable area to create Atlantic Avenue, the Harbor Commissioners sent the city government a whopping bill for $61,663.46 payable to the compensation fund. The city appealed the bill to the legislature and even tried to escape payment by adopting Francis Bird's argument that the theory of compensation had been discredited. But the Harbor Commissioners refused to reduce the amount.[80] They faithfully collected 37.5 cents per cubic yard of tidewater displaced from everyone who made land, and by 1878 the compensation fund contained over $130,000. The commissioners used the interest to make improvements around the harbor.[81]

Neither did they hesitate to use their power to force changes from the railroad companies. In 1869, when the legislature required the railroads to widen drawbridges crossing the Charles and Miller's rivers, the Harbor Commissioners used their regulatory powers to force additional improvements. They offered to accept the proposed designs only if the railroads improved some of the bridges as well by realigning the piers and draws with the current.[82] They also used legal proceedings to prevent the Boston & Lowell from filling flats without authorization.[83] Moving with scientific certainty and legal authority, the Harbor Commissioners halted abuse, compelled improvements, and became the most powerful guardians the harbor had ever known.

By the 1870s, Bostonians had committed themselves to a very different relationship to the harbor and its development. They had largely abandoned the old unthinking and piecemeal approach to landmaking that assumed an indestructible harbor and favored the wants of private landowners. In its place was a more cautious and heavily regulated approach that assumed a fragile harbor and gave more emphasis to the public good. This transformation reflected the evolution of local and state governments across the country from weak bodies reluctant to interfere with business interests to strong institutions more willing to guide the process of environmental transformation. But it was not just the government that had transformed its approach to the harbor. Every individual or business involved even remotely with development along the coastline was compelled to interact with the harbor differently than they had before.

Paradigm Shift

Bostonians could not have known at the time that they were already planting the seeds of another transformation. Two factors proved particularly important in producing it. The first was the physical alterations that the Army Corps of Engineers began making to the harbor. Shortly after the Harbor Commissioners' initial appointment in 1866, they successfully petitioned Congress for funds to build seawalls and remove obstructions from the main ship channel. Between 1867 and 1879, Congress spent 1.25 million dollars to blast dangerous rocks from the channels, widen the Narrows, and build granite seawalls to shield the islands and headlands.[84] The latter work was especially important. Federal engineers estimated that, in the hundred years before 1870, enough material had eroded into the area around the main ship channel from Point Allerton alone to cover Boston Common to a depth of sixty-four feet.[85] Although appropriations were inadequate and work often stopped halfway through the season for lack of funds, the major projects were substantially completed by the end of the century.

More dramatic were efforts to deepen and widen the harbor's channels. In response to seemingly endless increases in the size of ships, and beginning with the South Boston project, the Corps of

Engineers began an aggressive regimen of dredging. Before this work, parts of the main ship channel had been only eighteen feet deep and one hundred feet wide at low tide. By the end of the century, federal dredging had left the channel as much as twenty-seven feet deep and one thousand feet wide. At the urging of the maritime community, federal engineers also began to dredge Broad Sound Channel—which had been even shallower than the main ship channel—to a depth of thirty feet and a width of twelve hundred feet. By the end of the century, Broad Sound was so deep and wide that it became the harbor's new main channel.[86]

In a strikingly short time, dredging had not only altered the harbor itself but reshaped how people thought about such massive environmental transformations. In 1864, Benjamin Gould had looked at the forty-eight square miles of Boston Harbor and claimed that humans "cannot long maintain the unequal struggle with nature."[87] But within a generation, dredging had gone from a tool for selectively enhancing natural processes to a replacement for them. Once reliant on natural scour to keep existing channels open, Bostonians were now constructing entirely new channels. Such feats were in evidence all over urban America and enhanced the belief that humans could engineer any natural system to their own needs. Technological change and faith in the human ability to transform nature were evolving together.

Dredging soon became an essential component of port cities around the world. The application of steam engines and other technological advances to the process made it much cheaper and more easily available than it had been earlier in the century. As the Corps worked in the waters off Boston, it was also deepening and widening the harbors of New York, San Francisco, Baltimore, New Orleans, Galveston, and other coastal cities. Engineers performed similar work in Great Britain, especially in the Rivers Tyne and Clyde, which emptied near the important port cities of Newcastle and Glasgow. By the end of the nineteenth century, dredging had become a powerful tool that enabled harbors to grow with their cities.[88]

The second factor encouraging a further transformation in the city's relationship to its harbor was cultural rather than physical. Building on the expansion of mass leisure and the new appreciation for the recreational potential of waterfronts, Bostonians reinvented their harbor as a leisure-time playground. Inexpensive steamboat excursions soared in popularity, and seaside resorts sprang up on Hull and Nantasket to cater to better-off crowds. Publishers rushed to take advantage of the surging interest in the harbor by producing illustrated guidebooks that discussed its natural and historical features. "The perfection of physical comfort is enjoyed," one book trumpeted, "when, on a warm day of summer, one leaves the hot and crowded streets and many cares of the city, and passes down Boston Harbor." Although use of the harbor for recreation dated to the earliest years of settlement, changing patterns of consumer culture in America made Boston Harbor a more active site for leisure activities than ever before.[89]

The growth in recreation eventually brought park advocates into conflict with the defenders of the harbor. The public wanted more recreational space along the waterfront, and the banks of the Charles River, on both the Cambridge and Boston sides, seemed ideally situated. But the Charles was heavily polluted. Boston's Board of Health reported that the most offensive areas of the river produced a stench "so strong as to arouse the sleeping, terrify the weak, and nauseate and exasperate nearly everybody."[90] Public health officials faced a sanitary nightmare, but collaboration with park advocates pointed toward a solution. In 1894, a joint board composed of the Board of Health and the new Metropolitan Park Commission proposed that the state dam the Charles River for sanitary and recreational purposes. A high, stable water level would not only permanently cover the offensive areas along the river's banks, but also encourage recreational boating and park construction. A major obstacle to the plan, however, was that the Harbor Commissioners considered the Charles to be an important source of scour for the harbor channels.

The joint board used the findings of Frederick P. Stearns, a well-respected engineer, to challenge the Harbor Commissioners' understanding of the harbor's hydraulics. After reviewing the available data, Stearns determined that the Charles River carried little silt and that its current was too weak to produce a significant scour. He therefore concluded that damming the river was unlikely to cause any damage to the harbor, and he even claimed that the last thirty years of landmaking had done no harm. Stearns's position echoed the stance taken by Francis Bird a quarter of a century before. But such a conclusion, coming from an engineer, was unprecedented and reflected how difficult it had become to fit new data from the harbor into the established theory of its origins and function. This was an important moment, because it was the first time that someone trained in the engineering sciences had contradicted the dominant ideas about the harbor's hydraulics in such a high-stakes fight.[91]

The Harbor Commissioners, heavily invested in both their policies and its underlying theory, objected to the plan and defended the river's role in maintaining the harbor. They believed that years of managed development had restored the harbor's natural hydraulics to a state of equilibrium, and that damming the Charles River would represent a giant step backward. The existing science still backed their position: in the thirty years since the U.S. Commissioners had written their reports, every federal engineer who studied the harbor had agreed that scour maintained it and that the rivers made important contributions to that process. The Harbor Commissioners recognized that large amounts of dredging in the harbor made new studies necessary, but saw no reason "to adopt the theory of novel impression." Nor were they about to relinquish their attachment to the idea of a naturally scouring harbor. "Although the dredging machine is resorted to frequently," they admitted, "we are not yet ready to welcome it wholly as a substitute for natural forces." Their opposition played a major role in the proposal's defeat.[92]

Advocates of a dam tried again a few years later, but this time the legislature hired John R. Freeman to study the problem. Freeman was the most influential hydraulic engineer of his day. A tireless worker, he supervised a biologist, geologist, chemist, medical doctor, and two engineers who prepared a wide variety of reports. Freeman himself contributed a number of additional studies on topics ranging from the velocity of harbor currents to air temperatures in the Charles River basin. In 1903, he summarized the collective findings in a report still admired for the rigor of its analysis. Freeman noted in the report that his team had "found itself face to face with a long-accepted theory of the maintenance of Boston harbor, which, in the end, it has felt obliged to reject."[93]

Freeman concluded that the theory of tidal scour that had dominated thinking about the harbor since the 1830s did not apply to Boston Harbor. With the aid of far more sensitive and reliable equipment than previously available, Freeman determined that the inner harbor had experienced no substantial shoaling in the past seventy years, despite an enormous amount of landmaking. He also found that the rivers did not carry enough silt to threaten the harbor floor and that their currents were too feeble to perform any meaningful scour. In short, no large source of silt confronted the channels, and they required no scour to maintain them. Boston Harbor was not a naturally scouring harbor and never had been.[94]

Freeman proposed a radical new explanation for the origins of the harbor that amounted to a paradigm shift in how scientists understood its formation and hydraulics. Drawing on advances made in the science of geology, particularly glacial theory, Freeman explained that the Charles and Mystic rivers had not dug the channels of Boston Harbor because they had not existed at the time of the channels' creation. When the Ice Age glaciers were retreating from the Boston area some 14,000 years before, they had melted into giant rivers that carved the channels from the blue clay now forming the bed of the harbor. The present rivers, much reduced in size and force, could not possibly have moved such large quantities of material. Since that time, the entire Boston area had sunk relative to the sea, and the old river channels had become harbor channels. "In other words," concluded Freeman, "the harbor channels are strictly what may be called a series of drowned valleys." With a single stroke, the new paradigm brushed aside the theory of tidal scour that had dominated the development of Boston Harbor for much of the nineteenth century.[95]

The defenders of the harbor must have been equally surprised to hear Freeman declare that their naturally scouring harbor was in reality artificial. Freeman believed that the harbor was still a natural one when the U.S. Commissioners had studied it in the 1860s. But since that time, "the natural conditions have been so altered by dredging that such equilibrium of forces as maintained the original channels has been entirely destroyed." Natural forces like tides, rivers, and winds were still important to the harbor, but they could not sustain the new depth of the channels without human help. Besides, Freeman noted, modern dredging and blasting were so inexpensive and efficient that even the severe level of shoaling feared a generation before could be removed without excessive cost. "For the future," he concluded, "Boston harbor will be an artificial one."[96]

Just as shocking was Freeman's assertion that the city had been subsiding for thousands of years and was still settling slowly into the ocean. Modern scientists attribute this effect to rising sea levels, but Freeman suggested that the land itself was sinking. His claim seemed to defy almost three centuries of lived experience on the peninsula and required residents to reimagine the natural foundation on which the city had been built. One of Freeman's associates, however, believed that residents of the city upon a hill would wrestle less with the geological science that supported the new theory and more with its psychological implications. "It contradicts all notions that Bostonians have of their own city," he wrote to Freeman, "and I fear that even your scientific report will not convince them that their tendency is downward rather than upward."[97] The incredulity felt by Bostonians was mirrored in the *New York Times,* which called the claim "astounding." Its editors accepted the new theory based on Freeman's reputation, however, and lightheartedly predicted a time when Boston, which "would never be happy in the thought of a commonplace ending," would "take its place in tradition and romance beside Atlantis."[98]

The legislature also embraced Freeman's ideas about the harbor and used them to justify dam construction and additional landmaking into the twentieth century. In 1909, six years after Freeman's report, the state completed a dam across the upper Mystic River. One year later, a new dam across the Charles turned the river into a lake and made parks along its banks possible. Where damming the two rivers that fed the inner harbor had seemed like madness only a few years before, it now appeared logical in the context of a new scientific paradigm. That new explanation of the harbor's origins and hydraulics also made later landmaking projects, such as the construction of a massive airport on the East Boston flats, seem much less threatening to the harbor. A different reading of scientific data had led to a different set of ideas that would allow Bostonians to alter the nature of their harbor more confidently and aggressively than ever before.

After seventy years or more as a dominant scientific paradigm, and half of that period as the foundation for official state and federal policy, the theory of tidal scour as wielded by the harbor's defenders had left Boston and its harbor transformed. The harbor lines drawn early in the century to protect the scour defined the city's shape.

Landmaking projects had lived and died at the pleasure of the Harbor Commissioners, who accepted, denied, or modified proposals based on how the developers' plans might affect the scour. South Boston, the city's largest landmaking project before the twentieth-century construction of its airport, began as a harbor improvement intended to train the tide and increase its force. Narrow Fort Point Channel still exists today because nineteenth-century engineers thought its current was necessary to preserve the main ship channel. The construction of the Charles River Dam was delayed by a decade because the Harbor Commissioners opposed it. Even the islands and headlands of the harbor, although not directly implicated by the theory, benefited from the energies of those who treated the harbor as an integrated whole. Only when these effects on Boston's development are considered together does it become clear how deeply the city was shaped by the harbor's complex and inscrutable natural system and the scientific ideas used to explain its mysteries.

Those who used the theory of tidal scour to defend Boston Harbor have since been largely forgotten. One of the few historians even to mention their efforts discounts all of the research and thought behind their ideas and dismisses them as "traditionalist maritime alarmists."[99] But they were more than reactionaries panicked by the prospect of change. In fact, the members of this group actually accomplished some good by preventing the indiscriminate expansion of the city's shoreline. Using government to temper the culture of privatism, they convinced the federal government to bring the erosion of the harbor islands and headlands under control, and they persuaded the state legislature to create a permanent board to manage the harbor. They also avoided some of the more radical efforts to reshape Boston's estuary, like Thomas Lamb's suggestion for a network of massive dams and Francis Bird's vision of a Charles River reduced to a narrow channel and covered with a bridge three miles wide. Working toward what they sincerely believed to be the greatest public good, the harbor's defenders used the best science of their day to encourage growth while safeguarding one of the key natural systems that supported the city's economy.

If that description makes them sound like Progressive Era conservationists, it is because the two groups had much in common. Anticipating the conservation movement by decades, the defenders of Boston Harbor embraced a scientific, government driven, future-oriented, and public-spirited relationship with the natural resource they were trying to manage. In 1872, the mariner and author Captain John Sleeper had railed against short-sighted approaches to the harbor in which "the past seems to be forgotten, the present only is regarded as of importance, and a veil is drawn over the future."[100] His words would apply just as well to later efforts to preserve wilderness and conserve forests.

In fact, the preservation and conservation movements would have their own impact on the building of Boston. Toward the end of the century, forest advocates began turning their attention to the city's suburbs, where the last remnants of wild forest in the metropolitan region were threatened by development. Although arguments for preservation and conservation were born of a national concern about deforestation, they echoed loudly among the stony peaks that encircled the city. That echo, however, had a distinctly Bostonian resonance, for the weight of the Puritan past lay as heavily on these rugged suburban areas as the rocks and trees that clothed their untamed hills.

5

Recreating the Wilderness

Since the very founding of Boston, the relationship between its inhabitants and the built and natural environments had contained a sense of the temporary or provisional about it. Bostonians lived in a new country dedicated to progress, and like other Americans, they believed that the nation's growth required ongoing alterations to familiar scenes. Buildings came and went, open space awaited development, and land-use regulations like zoning were as yet undreamed of. Constant and unplanned change was simply the nature of things. That was the message that the Reverend Samuel Lothrop conveyed to his Brahmin parishioners in 1871 as they prepared to trade their colonial-era Brattle Square Church for a new building in the Back Bay. "Change," he assured them, "is the order of Divine Providence; nothing is permanent or enduring upon earth but truth and duty."[1]

But this way of relating to the environment was more human than divine, and the culture of change was itself beginning to transform. In the last third of the nineteenth century, the pace at which Bostonians were altering their environment reached such unsettling heights that many began to embrace the virtues of permanence. No place was changing more dramatically than the suburbs, where private development was preceding at an ever quickening pace. In response, conservation and wilderness protection movements—usually associated with the forests of the West—emerged around greater Boston to defend local landscapes. Advocates applied contemporary thought about forest preservation to the urban fringe, warning that the wholesale felling of suburban woodlands would threaten future timber supplies and degrade the American spirit. The push for increased environmental stability found abundant support around the region, and over the next generation Bostonians would lead the nation in promoting the idea that some places should stay just the way they are.

For Boston's Brahmins, relentless urban and suburban growth represented a threat not only to nature but also to history. The New England landscape held tremendous cultural meaning for them. In particular, the notable homes and family farms that dated to the colonial period both reinforced the group's identity and helped to justify its leadership. The rapid disappearance of such places around Boston therefore seemed like a direct assault on the Brahmin past. This physical threat to history was compounded by the continued growth and expansion of the Irish population. For many Brahmins, such as the poet James Russell Lowell, Irish ignorance of the American past seemed just as powerful a threat to Anglo-Saxon history as development. While out walking one day in the 1880s, Lowell noticed two Irishmen contemplating the equestrian statue of George Washington in the Public Garden. Lowell bent his ear toward their conversation and learned that the men had no idea who Washington was. "I had been brought up among the still living traditions of Lexington, Concord, Bunker's Hill, and the siege of Boston," Lowell remembered. "To these men Ireland was still their country, and America a place to get their daily bread." The Brahmins were loath to leave what was left of Boston's past in such unreliable hands.[2]

Besieged on multiple fronts, many Brahmins entered the last decades of the nineteenth century convinced that their city's best days were behind it. Their mood was somber, reflective, and thoroughly uncharacteristic of a group raised to believe that they were building a city upon a hill. The Boston they had known seemed to be fading away, and many Brahmins expected to fade with it. "We Yankees are as much things of the past as any race can be," wrote Harvard professor Barrett Wendell in 1893. "I feel a certain regret that I had not the fortune to be born fifty years earlier."[3] Other Brahmins, however, were not content to sit quietly and wait for the end. Instead, they threw themselves into causes that pushed back against the tides of change through an ethic of preservation. They provided important leadership both locally and nationally in park development, forest conservation, wilderness protection, historic preservation, and the colonial revival movement.[4]

These seemingly disparate causes, and the ideas about nature and history on which they drew, found common ground in two rocky, wooded, and largely undeveloped areas in suburban Boston. The Middlesex Fells and Blue Hills sprawled for thousands of acres north and south of the city and still exuded a sense of wildness at the end of the century. "Each of these scenes," wrote landscape architect Charles Eliot in 1890, "is, in its way, characteristic of the primitive wilderness of New England, of which, indeed, they are surviving fragments."[5] In other words, these forests were left over bits of the wild landscape that the Brahmins' ancestors had encountered centuries before—or at least they could be imagined as such. Eager to preserve areas that held both natural and historical value, Eliot and other upper-class Bostonians worked to make the Fells and Blue Hills the anchors of the nation's first metropolitan public park system. This expansive collection of suburban parks and parkways simultaneously protected thousands of acres of forest and created a living monument to Boston's first settlers. Other cities soon followed Boston's example, taking a major step away from the culture of change and toward a relationship with natural places that recognized the value of permanence.[6]

The Geography of Wilderness

The Middlesex Fells and Blue Hills seemed destined to retain their wildness a bit longer than other places near Boston. Although each lies less than eleven miles north and south of Boston's City Hall, that short distance traces a dramatic change in topography. The

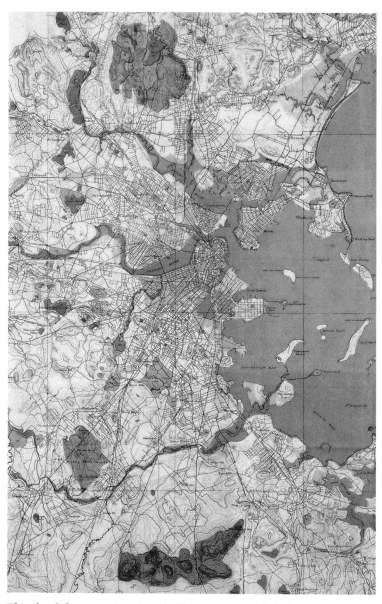

This detail from an 1893 map highlights the areas that planners wanted to preserve as the Middlesex Fells and Blue Hills reservations (the large dark areas lying north and south of Boston, respectively). The reservations would ultimately take slightly different shapes, with the Blue Hills growing even larger than the area pictured. (Courtesy of the Francis Loeb Library, Harvard Graduate School of Design)

coastal city lies in a depression surrounded by a horseshoe of hills. The Fells and Blue Hills form part of the northern and southern edges of this rugged rim, while the Belmont Hills and Newton Highlands complete the loop in the west. Although many of the western hills proved easy to develop, the hills of the Fells rise to over three hundred feet, and the Blue Hills to twice that height. Great Blue Hill is the most elevated point on the eastern seaboard of North America from Maine to Mexico, and on a clear day its summit extends the horizon to a distance of over sixty miles. Both regions presented formidable challenges to nineteenth-century suburban developers.[7]

The first English settlers had found the Fells even more intimidating. Upon reaching its four thousand acres in the 1630s, an exploring party sent out from Boston turned back after deciding that their settlement would never extend "beyond the mountainous and rocky country."[8] Although the party underestimated the speed at which their population would spread, they correctly identified the Fells' stony elevations as its most forbidding quality. Its vast forests, on the other hand, were a logger's dream: pine, hemlock, beech, and oak clothed the hills and bordered the meadows, while maples, birches, and cedars filled the low areas. These two dominant natural features—rocky hills and thick forests—defined the Fells not only physically but in the public mind as well: early colonists referred to the area simply as the Rocks, and nineteenth-century Bostonians knew it as the Five Mile Wood.[9]

The Blue Hills are especially mountainous and stretch from east to west in a chain five miles long and a mile wide. They contain about a dozen major summits and shelter a small lake on the south. Pine and hemlock dominated the pre-settlement forests, and the rolling topography inspired the Indian name for the area: Massachusetts, meaning "the place of the great hills." The early settlers adopted that name for their new colony.[10]

Despite the fact that the rugged terrain of the Fells and Blue Hills left them largely undeveloped throughout the nineteenth century, they experienced enough human interaction to make them curious choices for parks that preserved "wild" nature. Little is known of the uses made of the Fells by the Pawtucket Indians, who inhabited much of the region north of Boston, but the earliest settlers treated it as common land where they gathered fire wood, pastured cattle, and hunted feral hogs. The settlers began dividing the commons as early as 1658, and the construction of several sawmills suggests that the area saw heavy logging. A number of local industries made specific demands on the woods and contributed to rapid deforestation. A factory in Woburn converted the Fells' canoe birches into shoe pegs; shipbuilders in Medford fashioned its pine trees into ocean-going vessels; and artisans in Stoneham transformed its cedars into posts, shingles, and clapboards. By the time residents of metropolitan Boston were considering the area for a park, loggers had cut it several times, and a new growth of pine, hemlock, and oak wrapped the rocks once again.[11]

Rich in stone, water, and timber, the Fells contributed to the Boston area's rush to industrialize in the middle of the nineteenth century. Quarries employing dozens of men operated near Pine Hill from the 1830s to the late 1870s, producing a dark building stone called Medford Granite and a reddish gravel used on the paths of Boston Common and the Public Garden. Frederic Tudor, who founded the nation's ice industry, extracted ice from Spot Pond, which had figured so prominently in earlier debates about bringing water to Boston. A competitor, hoping to vie with the ice king, built an artificial pond to the south. Logging continued as well, but Spot Pond Brook made possible some of the largest changes to the area by powering factories that produced snuff, dyes, spices, and brass. By the 1860s, the Hayward Rubber Company was operating an eleven-acre complex that employed about forty men and women and supported a small community called Haywardville. Throughout the century, almost every acre of the sparsely-settled Fells, in-

Rocky hills and forested slopes defined the Middlesex Fells, seen here in 1896. Note the advance of residential development on the left. (Courtesy of the Massachusetts Department of Conservation and Recreation Archives)

cluding the ponds, supported some kind of extractive or productive industry.[12]

Agriculture was a more difficult enterprise in the area's thin and rocky soil, which provided abundant pastureland in the first two centuries after settlement but only a few sites suitable for raising crops. Small-scale farms had clustered north and west of Spot Pond, and a few persisted into the late nineteenth century. But besides these small homesteads, the community in Haywardville, and the few country estates built on the east side of Spot Pond, the Fells remained largely unpopulated.[13]

A crowd of tourists arrived in the summer, however, when city dwellers flocked to the country. Entrepreneurs turned one summer home into the Langwood Hotel, which overlooked Spot Pond from the east and became a popular resort for well-to-do urbanites. Less than half a mile to the north on the same shore, an open-air dance hall located among pines and cedars catered to the city's immigrant working classes, as did pleasure grounds known as Tudor's Grove and Green Mountain Grove to the south. Spiritualists frequented a small campground east of the pond, and an island at the pond's center was the favored sight for clandestine (and illegal) boxing matches. The green and secluded Fells appealed to a wide variety of groups engaged in a broad array of recreational activities.[14]

Although the Blue Hills were a bit farther from Boston and never attracted the level of industrial or recreational use experienced by the Fells, they did share a similar history of logging and scattered agriculture. The woods supplied timber for shipbuilding from the earliest times, and settlement followed the cleared areas into the valleys and up the hills. Colonial farms were small and unprofitable, however, and their owners eventually abandoned them. Until the end of the nineteenth century, the Blue Hills remained little more than a frequently cropped source of firewood ravaged by severe conflagrations about once every ten years. As a result, many areas were "covered with a dense thicket of brush, a crop of scrubby sticks or a forest of poles," as one late-century observer put it, while others had regained a more mature growth of trees.[15]

Of little economic value despite these uses, most of the land in the Fells and Blue Hills escaped large-scale development and continued to seem wild. New trees sprouted in the wake of logging expeditions, wetlands sustained large flocks of waterfowl, and small mountains of stone seemed unchanged by the centuries. As late as 1865, a resident of Winchester living at the edge of the Fells snared a wild hog weighing over four hundred pounds.[16] The resilience of nature was evident everywhere, and the right cultural filter could mask environmental change even further. At least one observer dismissed over two centuries of human history in the Blue Hills with a single stroke by claiming that if one of Boston's Indians returned from the past he would have no trouble recognizing the area as his home.[17] Whether experienced through the physical nature of a giant hog or

The Blue Hills in 1893. Views such as this one sometimes left visitors with the impression that they were standing in a primeval forest. (Courtesy of the Frances Loeb Library, Harvard Graduate School of Design)

the cultural nature of a romanticized wilderness aesthetic, the Fells and Blue Hills seemed like islands of ancient greenery that had survived the first gray surges of the coming urban tidal wave.

Forest Conservation and the End of History

In the 1870s, however, when advocates first began lobbying in earnest for the preservation of these forested areas, their interest stemmed less from a fear of losing the past than from a fear of losing the future. In 1864, George Perkins Marsh published one of the founding texts of the conservation movement, *Man and Nature; or, Physical Geography as Modified by Human Action,* which prodded Americans to begin linking the nation's destiny to that of its forests. Marsh insisted that the great civilizations of the past had perished because they destroyed their environments through deforestation. The aggressive removal of trees had increased the number of droughts and floods and accelerated erosion. In time, environmental degradation had destroyed agricultural land, which in turn led to the deterioration of social and economic conditions. Marsh feared the same fate for America, where lumber barons were clear-cutting forests in pursuit of quick profits. Too much uncontrolled change was happening too quickly. Although his vision of environmental apocalypse did not halt the subjugation of the American wilderness, it would later inspire the creation of state and national forests and continues to inform conservationist thought today.[18]

Marsh's ideas also provided a context for interpreting environmental change in the area around Boston, where development was destroying forests at a rapid rate. Although outlying towns tended to be largely agricultural, the rocky hills and poor soil that characterized so much of the region ensured that large wooded areas remained in many towns. As late as 1872, an advocate of forest preservation who lived in Cambridge noted that "we cannot pass over five miles of any road in New England without meeting with large fragments of wild wood, and assemblages of trees in some places of sufficient extent to be called forests."[19] But suburban construction was overrunning these remnant stands at an astounding pace. In the decade between 1880 and 1890 alone, the population of the towns in which the Fells and Blue Hills were situated grew between twenty-five and ninety percent. When Marsh spoke of deforestation, he had envisioned the large-scale clearing of forests by lumber companies or settlers as they advanced along the rural frontier. But the urban frontier was wreaking similar havoc in the suburbs.[20]

In some cases, urbanization had actually led to the preservation rather than destruction of forests. Like Boston a few decades before, rapidly developing suburban towns found themselves searching for new sources of water. They often turned first to ponds within their own municipal limits, and since water supplies were only as clean as their watersheds, towns often seized not just the ponds but some surrounding land as well. Beginning in 1870, the city of Lynn acquired several upland water sources. That same year, the towns of Medford, Malden, and Melrose jointly developed Spot Pond in the Fells as a reservoir. In 1873 Winchester created a water supply in the northern part of the Fells by damming the outlets of a swamp. All three of the projects preserved considerable areas of surrounding land to protect their watersheds and anticipated by more than a decade the vast Adirondack Forest Preserve that would later safeguard the up-state water supply of New York City.[21]

The social reformer Elizur Wright hoped to expand these existing municipal holdings by preserving the remainder of the Middlesex Fells for public use. A professor of mathematics and a prominent abolitionist in the 1830s and 1840s, Wright later worked with various life insurance companies and served as the state's commissioner of life insurance for nine years. In time, he combined his skill with numbers and interest in social change by fighting for insurance reform. Wright introduced mathematical innovations into the compilation of actuarial tables and lobbied successfully for state laws that protected policyholders. His impact on the industry was so large that historians consider Wright to be the father of modern life insurance.[22]

In 1864, Wright moved to the base of Pine Hill in the Fells and quickly fell in love with the area. Time spent twenty years before among the parks of London had convinced him that urban green spaces were necessary in America as well, and he was undoubtedly familiar with the park movement that arose after New York announced the design of its Central Park in 1857. But there was nothing central about the Fells, which were miles from downtown Boston and outside the city's political boundaries. Its rocky forest was also quite different from the open and pastoral grounds that park advocates seemed to prefer. As a result, Wright's effort to convince Boston's Common Council to purchase the Fells as a municipal park landed on deaf ears. Local lawyer George Hillard summed up the city's response when he said, "you might as well try to persuade the

Common Council to buy land in the moon as in the Fells." Undeterred, Wright began buying up property himself and publicizing the area's virtues to a wider audience.[23]

Although Wright began as a park advocate, the ideas that he would soon bring to the Fells were also influenced by a growing conservation movement sparked by Marsh's work. In 1874, the American Association for the Advancement of Science pushed Congress to fund research into the state of the nation's timber reserves. Two years later, a group of concerned botanists and horticulturalists founded the American Forestry Association. The year after that, wilderness activist John Muir published one of his first pieces in defense of nature: "God's First Temples: How Shall We Preserve Our Forests?" Some forest advocates were inspired by the desire to safeguard future timber supplies, while others like Muir sought to preserve a wilderness that seemed to reflect the divine. Both motivations proved popular with a public that was growing increasingly aware of the threat to the nation's woodlands. As a result, the effort to temper America's relationship to its forests with a new ethic of permanence entered the next decade with considerable momentum.[24]

By the late 1870s, Wright's ideas about forests were evolving in new and visionary directions. He wanted not only to preserve trees, but to manage them as a sustainable resource, and to do so in the suburbs of cities rather than the mountains of the West. In 1880, a decade before the conservation movement began to emphasize scientific forestry, Wright suggested that the state administer the Fells as both a working forest and a wilderness park. He lamented what he saw as centuries of resource mismanagement in the area and suggested a program of scientific logging. Wright advised selectively harvesting the "interest"—mature trees—on three thousand acres while safeguarding the "capital" of the larger natural system.[25] The remaining one thousand acres, an area larger than Central Park, would provide ample space for recreation. Under this plan, the Fells would become a highly managed and profitable suburban forest that simultaneously served the leisure needs of the city. Although some feared the economic consequences of removing such a large area from the tax rolls, and others believed that logging and recreation were mutually exclusive activities, Wright found encouraging support wherever he went. He repeatedly reminded his audiences that preserving the Fells was "everybody's axe, and if everybody grinds it, it will be dull for the generations to come. The wood-choppers are sure to grind theirs while a tree is left."[26]

To Wright's mind, more than trees were at risk. He believed that the destruction of the nation's forests to feed the needs of its cities would ultimately lead to the death of the cities themselves, including Boston. Wright recognized that the coal and petroleum burned in urban factories and homes produced enormous amounts of carbon dioxide, and that plants cleaned the air by absorbing carbon dioxide and emitting oxygen. Although convinced that the world's fossil fuel reserves were finite and would someday run out, he worried more about the deterioration of urban air supplies in the meantime, particularly if the nation lost its forests.[27] "In the neighborhood of great and overcrowded cities," he claimed, "groves and forests become of great sanitary importance. Perhaps no vigorously-growing tree can be destroyed within ten miles of Boston without shortening some human life."[28] He warned that heavily landscaped parks, like Boston's five hundred-acre Franklin Park, could not do the environmental work of forests. Echoing Marsh, he claimed that deforestation had ruined the Assyrian Empire, despite the construction of Babylon's hanging gardens.[29] Babylon's decline had shown that parks and gardens would not be enough. "Forests alone," Wright insisted, "can save great cities."[30]

Wright believed that the stakes were too high to leave Boston's large suburban forests in private hands any longer. An individual proprietor was much more likely to clear-cut a forest, "forgetful of the fact that, though he owns the trees, he does not own the air which the trees purify."[31] The atmosphere, Wright claimed, was a public common, and since trees maintained the atmosphere, the public had an interest in maintaining the trees. Besides, he argued, only the state could maximize a forest's economic potential. Drawing on his actuarial experience, Write suggested that individuals could not responsibly manage such resources for the long-term benefit of society. "Individual life is too short for the average farmer to have the care of woodlands," he explained. "The state, which does not die, can manage the woodlands so as to get, in a hundred years, four times the annual income from them."[32] Since society relied on pure air and the wise management of resources for its very existence, the public interest demanded public ownership of forests. Only public ownership would lead to permanence.

Wright's thought drew from a number of intellectual streams that seem more discreet from a present-day perspective than they did to contemporaries. Public health advocates would have recognized his efforts to reduce the effects of urban pollution by maintaining large green spaces near cities. Wilderness advocates would have respected his love for areas that were, or at least seemed, untouched by human hands. Conservationists would have sympathized with his desire to preserve the nation's timber resources. Park advocates would have recognized the leisure potential embedded in such a large natural reservation. Although each movement had its own agenda, their intellectual borders overlapped, and advocates for one often became advocates for another. Each represented an attempt to manage the environmental transformations and changing human relationships to the natural world of which city building was such a central part. The very nature of the Fells—a wild and undeveloped tract of land on the urban fringe—was perfectly suited to attract the wide variety of approaches to the natural world embedded in these diverse movements.

Like so much nineteenth-century thought about nature and cities, Wright's ideas also emerged in part from a fear of the urban poor. Land in the Fells was cheap, and over time it had fragmented into some 130 parcels, many of them quite small. Wright worried that the presence of so many inexpensive lots might eventually attract "the least desirable population for dwelling places."[33] He warned that the towns holding parts of the Fells within their borders had to reckon with this potential future and decide now what they wanted the area to be for all time: a series of sylvan valleys and hills, or a collection of bare and rocky slopes "adorned with wretched shanties and tethered goats."[34] Such comments were rare in Wright's work and seem uncharacteristic of a man who spent much of his life as an abolitionist and social reformer defending groups unable to defend themselves. But he knew how to tailor his message to specific audiences, and his warning must have rung clear in the ears of those most likely to favor wilderness and fear immigrants.

Publicizing the Need for Permanent Forests

Early on, Wright's plan for preserving the Fells coexisted with one that used yet another lens for viewing nature: natural science. The noted naturalist and nature writer Wilson Flagg began advocating as early as 1856 for the preservation of the Fells as a forest conservatory. Flagg believed that the Fells' natural wonders carried more importance for botanists and students of natural history than for foresters and pleasure seekers. He wanted to exclude embellishments to the landscape, forbid the disturbance of plants and animals except for study, and plant only those vegetables that would encourage desired species of birds. Public access would be by foot, although those managing the area might provide and operate carriages at no cost to users. "Rational recreation" would replace the usual picnics and pleasure parties. Flagg's plan for the Fells was part of his larger proposal to preserve forests in every state so that Americans did not thoughtlessly "render this earth uninhabitable by man."[35]

Flagg envisioned his conservatory as a gendered space, but not one that used rugged nature to breed rugged men. Instead, he believed that the primary beneficiaries of his plan would be women. "It would be a paradise for thousands of cultured women," he claimed, "and indeed for those of but little culture who have sensibility and a love of the beauties of nature." In the Fells, women could "ramble, as it were in the primitive forest," with a special police force protecting unescorted visitors. Flagg even specified that the clerical force should be composed of women. His conservatory drew on the widely accepted idea that women enjoyed a special relationship with nature, and it sought to create a space that, if not reserved for women alone, catered to their perceived needs and interests.[36]

Although Flagg's plan found some support, he lacked the leadership qualities needed to make it a reality, and Wright assumed command of the fledgling movement. Years of fighting against slavery had taught Wright the value of organizations in building support for a cause, so in 1880 he formed the Middlesex Fells Association. Wright, Flagg, and the naturalist and writer John Owen—all elderly by this time—were its heart. The author Thomas Wentworth Higginson remembered the three huddled in conversation, their white hair and flowing beards close together, working like a "council of old Greek wood gods, displaced and belated, not yet quite convinced that Pan was dead, and planning together to save the last remnant of the forest they loved." The organization never exceeded twenty members, however, and Wright did most of the work himself.[37]

Yet Wright's voice reached well beyond this small group and began to arouse some real interest in his cause. Tireless even at the age of seventy-six, he wrote letters, delivered lectures, offered tours, drew the first detailed map of the Fells, and hosted an annual forest festival. He even convinced the National Forestry Congress to meet in Boston. To participants in his festivals, Wright read original poetry on historical themes, and to the members of the Woman's Club of East Boston, he talked of "mother earth" and concern for "the rosy little cherubs that are yet to be born." He also began to organize Public Domain Clubs in the municipalities containing the Fells. In just a short time, the Medford Public Domain Club alone claimed two hundred members.[38]

By the early 1880s, the Appalachian Mountain Club was also taking an interest in the Fells and Blue Hills. Formed in 1876 by academics and wealthy gentlemen from Boston, the club met monthly in a home on the corner of Park and Beacon Streets that overlooked Boston Common. Its members were interested in conservation issues and mountain exploration, and since most members lived in or around Boston, the Fells and Blue Hills provided an opportunity to explore wild areas that were just a carriage drive away. The club publicized the forests through its journal *Appalachia* and paid for the construction of a wooden observatory on Bear Hill in the Fells. Although Elizur Wright belonged to the club and spoke to fellow members about the importance of forests to urban air quality, the chance to immerse themselves in a wild landscape was probably a bigger draw for the organization's members. Unlike "the ordinary garden-park with fountains, flower-beds, and gravel-walks," wrote the club's secretary, the Fells offered visitors a green space "after Nature's own heart."[39]

Wright finally convinced the legislature to pass a conservation law that would enable municipalities to preserve and manage the Fells and other wooded areas. The Forest Law of 1882 authorized any town or city to take or purchase land within its limits for the maintenance of working forests or the preservation of water supplies. The title of the land would vest in the state, and the state Board of Agriculture would use income from the land to manage it. The municipalities in which the land was located would receive any profits collected from the forests. Wright worked hard to publicize the law, which was even featured in *The American Journal of Forestry*. But the idea of purchasing large amounts of land just to give it to the state without reimbursement was unpopular among municipalities already struggling with the cost of population growth. The law was seldom if ever used and saved few trees.[40]

Wright's ideas nevertheless formed an intellectual cornerstone for the later creation of the metropolitan park system, although he did not live to see the Fells permanently preserved. The aged leaders of the movement died in quick succession: Owen and Flagg passed on first, and then Wright died from a stroke in 1885 while working at his desk. A group of citizens in nearby Lynn, however, had shared Wright's vision and was trying to apply it to a different stretch of forest. Just a few years after his death, they put his ideas into practice by creating the Lynn Woods, which remains today one of the nation's largest municipally-owned forest preserves.[41]

Conserving the Lynn Woods

The Lynn Woods had escaped development because, like the Fells and Blue Hills, it was part of the rugged ridge that defined the Boston Basin. Located east of the Fells and only a mile and a half from the ocean, the Lynn Woods contained about two thousand acres of pine, oak, maple, and walnut forests that covered its rocky hills and shaded its four ponds. From the top of Mount Gilead, its second highest summit, one could see all the way to Mount Monadnock in southern New Hampshire and—in the opposite direction—to Minot's Ledge Lighthouse in Boston harbor. "This view," Frederick Law Olmsted would later say to the chairman of Lynn's park commissioners, "will make you famous some day."[42]

But, again like the Fells and Blue Hills, this was no primeval forest. The woods had served as a common pasture and source of timber in the early colonial period until the town's landowners divided it among themselves in 1706. They used the area as private woodlots until the advent of coal, although local brick makers continued to forage in the woods for fuel. Attempts at agriculture found little success, and the overgrown cellar holes, orchards, and gardens of abandoned farms testified to the poor quality of the soil. Speculators had tried to grow tourists instead, but the foundation of a never-completed hotel was all that remained of their plans. Although other entrepreneurs built a resort for picnics and dancing that proved quite popular, by the late nineteenth century much of the land lay unused.[43]

In the 1880s, however, a combination of private and public efforts brought much of the Lynn Woods into the public domain. A private group dedicated to preserving the woods as the Free Public Forest acquired 150 acres, which supplemented the area already owned by the water authority. A Park Act passed by the state legislature in 1882, the same year as Wright's Forest Law, provided the mechanism for saving the rest. The act empowered cities and towns to take property for park purposes and issue bonds to cover the expense. Municipalities could keep the land themselves, rather than turning it over to the state as the Forest Law required. When a group of citizens pledged $20,000 for purchasing additional land, the City of Lynn issued $30,000 in bonds under the Park Act and used the money to acquire much of the remaining woods. It took the city several years to sort out the ownership records of some one hundred different parcels of land, but by the end of 1890 it had assembled a forest park of over sixteen hundred acres. Private and public money had come together to create a municipal green space twice as large as New York City's Central Park and second in size only to Philadelphia's Fairmount Park.[44]

Like so many public parks created in the nineteenth century, the Lynn Woods was shaped by class. At least since the fight to preserve Boston Common's flats in the 1820s, park advocates had been insisting that public open space was most important to those who could not afford to purchase their own private pleasure grounds. Lynn's park commissioners adopted the same mantra, but like other park advocates before them, they insisted that use of the woods should focus on the kinds of passive activities preferred by the middle and upper classes. The commissioners did indeed intend to create "a magnificent breathing place for the people," but one that would educate and elevate rather than entertain. The purpose of the new park, wrote Lynn's commissioners, was "*not* to attract multitudes to be amused by merry-go-round shows."[45]

Although created under the Park Act rather than Elizur Wright's Forest Law, the Lynn Woods provided for active forestry just as Wright had envisioned for the Fells. The commissioners hoped to follow the example of Zurich, Switzerland, which earned $20,000 per year from the Sihlwald Forest, almost half from thinning. At the time, the Sihlwald was a poster child for successful municipal forestry and had won many American admirers. It also functioned as a park, which suggested that recreation and forestry were not mutually exclusive. Lynn's park commissioners claimed that park and forest purposes would actually complement each other in the Lynn Woods, since thinning would make the park "more inviting and accessible."[46] With the eyes of the region turned to this new municipal experiment, the city of Lynn had brought to life Elizur Wright's dream of preserving a suburban forest and devoting it to both recreation and production.

Preserving Nature, Preserving History

While protecting the Lynn Woods enabled park advocates to provide for the present, and conservationists to prepare for the future, it also fulfilled a growing interest in preserving the past. In fact, the Lynn community framed their entire park enterprise as a rescue of the old town commons from private hands and a restoration of its ancient form and public purpose. One writer noted that "the fathers with their Aryan ways, their patient oxen, and their demon wolves have gone," but the woods "are being restored to the common inheritance of their children's children."[47] The commissioners' later annual reports provided a visual link to the past by consistently bearing images of the first settlers on their covers. They were seeking to commemorate and even recreate the Puritan wilderness experience.

Writing a decade after the city acquired the area, the park commissioners reported with pride that "the Woods to-day, with the wood-choppers kept out of them for ten years, look more like the forest that the Puritan fathers saw." Despite all the concern about providing adequate recreational space and safeguarding timber resources, the creation of the Lynn Woods was as much about history as it was about nature.[48]

The references to the Puritan errand into the wilderness reflected the event's tremendous cultural importance to nineteenth-century Bostonians, especially those members of the upper classes who could trace their family trees to the founding generation. The "errand" was Boston's creation myth, a story about a small but determined group of people who had used hard work and a superior moral compass to set their city on the path toward perfection. Even the city's enterprising spirit, claimed Elias Derby, descended directly "from those bold ancestors who planted an empire in the wilderness." For the Brahmins, it was the mythical moment when the Puritans had sown the seeds of their descendants' cultural and economic supremacy. That moment gained national resonance after the Revolution, when American historians—half of whom hailed from New England—began linking the new nation's love of freedom and sense of divine mission to the pious settlers of Massachusetts Bay. The idea that American values were born in Boston became part of the national mythology, elevating the status of the Puritans ever further. "No ancestry in the world is half so illustrious," wrote the New Hampshire historian Nathaniel Appleton Haven, "as the Puritan founders of New England."[49]

In the last quarter of the nineteenth century, the entire colonial era assumed a new-found national importance that emerged directly from the tensions created by immigration. Inspired by the centennial celebrations of 1876, America's Anglo-Saxon population launched a colonial revival movement that revitalized public memory of colonial accomplishments and provided a nostalgic refuge for beleaguered natives. The new attraction to all things colonial shaped art, literature, architecture, and even parks like the Lynn Woods into the early years of the twentieth century. In many cases, women rather than men led American culture back in time. They founded house museums, established the Colonial Dames and the Daughters of the American Revolution, and published a large number of books celebrating the people, events, and values of the colonial past. An imagined New England lay at the heart of this national movement, which asked its adherents to see the world as Emily Dickinson did: "New Englandly."[50]

The urge to look backward was particularly strong in Boston, where natives were grappling with the growing presence and power of the Irish. In 1869, the author William Dean Howells took a walk through an immigrant section of Cambridge known as Dublin, where he felt less like a native strolling a few blocks from his own house and more like a traveler in a foreign land. The language, customs, and dress seemed exotic to Howells, and he regretted that the Anglo-Saxon population was "now as extinct in that region as the Pequots." He read the future of his own people in the large number of Irish children playing in the streets. It appeared likely, wrote Howells, that "such increase shall—together with the well-known ambition of Dubliners to rule the land—one day make an end of us poor Yankees as a dominant plurality." The demographic shift from Yankee to Irish would soon become evident in politics as well. In 1884, just fifteen years after Howells's visit to Dublin, Bostonians elected Hugh O'Brien as their first Irish Catholic mayor.[51]

The colonial revival was closely related to the nation's fledgling historic preservation movement, which sought to preserve actual relics of the past rather than producing new works that evoked it. Although some efforts to save historic sites dated to the first half of the century, preservation became a movement after 1853, when the Mount Vernon Ladies' Association of the Union was founded to purchase and preserve George Washington's estate. After that, increasing numbers of middle- and upper-class women extended their traditional role as defenders of home and family to the fight to save historic houses and landscapes. Through their work, local historical societies and house museums proliferated, especially across New England. At the same time, writes historian Van Wyck Brooks, Boston's Brahmins were collecting antiques "as if the race were truly dying and one had to gather the relics before they vanished." Like those trying to remember the colonial period, those trying to preserve its remains were searching for a usable past that could anchor the present against social and environmental change.[52]

Ideas about nature and history had long been intertwined in the American imagination. Self-conscious about their lack of history compared with European nations, nineteenth-century Americans often located a deeper and morally superior past in the wilderness, where primeval trees took the place of ancient columns. "In America," wrote historian Frederick Jackson Turner in 1884, "we have giant cathedrals, whose spires are moss clad pines, whose frescos are painted on the sky and mountain wall, and whose music surges through leafy aisles in the deep toned bass of cataracts." While the wilderness provided America with a sense of rootedness in time, it was also a symbol of present opportunity and future promise. It had always been there, and seemed as if it always would be. The wilderness was what made America "Nature's Nation."[53]

By the end of the century, however, many Americans were coming to see wild and even rural areas as part of a receding past. With agriculture encroaching on wilderness, and cities and suburbs in turn absorbing the countryside, the landscapes that meant the most to Americans were disappearing. Turner's "giant cathedrals" and a host of smaller ones were now threatened, and some Americans—especially urbanites—worked to preserve them as they would any other historical artifact. But doing so required a dramatic shift in the

American relationship to the built and natural environments. Preservation implied permanence, and that was a value that was hard to come by in a nation that equated change with progress.

What's in a Name?

One of the easiest ways to preserve the past in natural places, at least in spirit, was to evoke it through names. When the citizens of Lynn first created their new woodland park, many of its topographical features lacked commonly used designations. The commissioners could have remedied that by naming major natural features after Civil War heroes, biblical places, or famous presidents, but instead they dug deep into the local past for names that suggested the first years of English colonization. Rejecting naming schemes that might remove "memorials of the simple and toilsome life of the pioneers and builders of old Lin," the commissioners instead chose new names that were "simply descriptive or historical." They retained existing names if they were of long usage or memorialized an early settler.[54] Following this method, they restored the former name of Burrill Hill to the park's highest elevation; renamed Mount Tabor "Fuller Hill" after a prominent early family; named a secluded ravine Glen Dagyr after the Welsh colonist who founded Lynn's famous shoe industry; and retained many names that either were of long usage or simply sounded colonial. The commissioners ensured that the names of natural features did everything possible to evoke the past.[55]

Their efforts had been anticipated by Elizur Wright, who several years earlier had suggested commemorating John Winthrop by changing the name of Spot Pond in the Fells to Lake Winthrop. Such a change, however, would have been unfaithful to the historical record. While exploring the Fells in 1631, Winthrop and his companions had sprinkled new names over the hills and streams like seeds in a freshly plowed field, and they had given Spot Pond its name themselves. But the irony was lost on Wright, who was less interested in preserving the actual past than commemorating an imagined one.[56]

Meanwhile, E. G. Chamberlain, a local historian and member of the Appalachian Mountain Club, was using similar criteria to suggest new names for summits in the Blue Hills. Chamberlain spent years researching the historic names of the hills, and after finding that only two carried designations recognized by local residents, he set about assigning names to the rest himself. Chamberlain named a number of hills after former residents and the second highest summit after Chickatawbut, a chief of the Neponset Indians. "I had long desired," he confessed, "to find a nameless but worthy hill" for the chief.[57]

The name Middlesex Fells was itself a recent creation intended to carry stronger historical associations than the commonly used Five Mile Wood. In 1879, a Malden journalist named Sylvester Baxter suggested the name, which cast back in time beyond the roots of settlement to the roots of the settlers themselves. Middlesex was simply the county in which the rocky forest rested, named after a county in England, but Fells was an Old Saxon word that Baxter put to new use. He defined it as meaning "a tract of wild stone hills, corresponding to the German word *felsen.*" Wright approved of the name and helped to publicize it, although its obscurity sent him to his dictionary for a definition. At first, the word would have had little meaning to locals, but in time it conjured an image of ancient and rugged hills. It also suggested an Anglo-Saxon genealogy for the Fells, obscuring the fact that Irish immigrants had been patronizing its private parks since the 1840s. Baxter's exchange of a common name for a more "historical" one fit perfectly alongside similar efforts in the Lynn Woods and Blue Hills—all were attempts to commemorate the past, and all found fertile soil on the rocky rim surrounding Boston.[58]

Preserving Nature and History on a Regional Scale

The scattered efforts to protect nature and history from urban and suburban expansion took an organizational leap forward in 1891 with the establishment of the Trustees of Public Reservations. Less than a year after the creation of the Lynn Woods, the Appalachian Mountain Club gathered its members in Boston to discuss the threat to natural landscapes and historic sites around the state. The landscape architect Charles Eliot had organized the meeting and proposed the establishment of a board of trustees that would acquire by gift or purchase "parcels of real estate possessing natural beauty or historical interest."[59] One hundred enthusiastic members attended the meeting, and four hundred letters of support arrived from such local luminaries as Oliver Wendell Holmes, Francis Parkman, John Greenleaf Whittier, and Frederick Law Olmsted. The group agreed that an organization designed to acquire and manage multiple properties could accomplish much more than the many local historical societies trying to preserve individual sites. Eliot convinced the legislature to incorporate the Trustees of Public Reservations the following year, and the organization received its first gift of land just a few months later. Fanny Tudor, who owned some woods in the Middlesex Fells, wanted to preserve the scenic stretch in memory of her daughter.[60]

Women like Fanny Tudor would be essential to the Trustees' success. Although only three women had served on the large committee that organized the Trustees, and none had leadership positions in the new organization, women provided vital financial support. In the first year, one quarter of those donating money to the Trustees were women, and that quarter provided half of the organization's funds. Just as middle- and upper-class women across urban America were supporting colonial revival and historic preservation movements, they also were playing critical roles in grassroots environmental movements. Whether the issue was smoke pollution, water purity, sanitation, or park development, women were consistently among the most prominent crusaders and benefactors. An organization like the Trustees, which combined advocacy for both nature and history, was bound to attract support from a broad swath of reform-minded women.[61]

What made the Trustees so innovative was their regional rather than local approach to preservation. They existed "for the purpose of acquiring, holding, arranging, maintaining, and opening to the public, under suitable regulations, beautiful and historical places and tracts of land within this Commonwealth."[62] Any site of natural or historical significance in the entire state of Massachusetts was of interest to them, from Beaver Brook Falls in Belmont and the Natural Bridge near North Adams to the Cradock House in Medford and the Wayside Inn in Sudbury. Their ambition went beyond that of previous preservation organizations and governmental bodies alike.

The Trustees quickly inspired the creation of similar groups. In 1895, New Yorkers formed the Trustees of Scenic and Historical Places and Objects in the State of New York. Seeking to build on the preservation of Niagara Falls and the Adirondacks, the group focused on identifying colonial forts, town commons, historic homes, and spectacular natural areas like Watkins Glen and the Palisades that the state legislature might want to purchase. Its members considered the names of towns, villages, and streets to be monuments worth saving as well, and they fought attempts to change historic names or to name new streets in ways that ignored past associations. That same year, a group in England formed the National Trust for Places of Historic Interest or Natural Beauty. The model for preserving history and nature pioneered by the Trustees was gaining an international following.[63]

Legislating Permanence

The regional vision of the Trustees of Public Reservations reflected the realization that many of the environmental challenges faced by developing areas—like providing adequate water, sewer, and park

facilities—transcended municipal boundaries and required metropolitan solutions. Since such problems were often beyond the ability
of private resources to resolve, they also required public funding.
So with ever-greater frequency, governments were asking landscape
architects and engineers to bring the large-scale perspective of the
urban planner to problems that affected adjoining municipalities.
The Boston area became a leader in finding such solutions and
had already created the innovative Metropolitan Sewerage Commission two years before the founding of the Trustees. Park advocates
quickly realized that the commission could serve as a model for preserving green space throughout the region.[64]

Dreams of a park system that cut across municipal boundaries
went back almost fifty years. In 1844, a visiting Scotsman named
Robert Gourlay published a plan of parks and boulevards that
treated nearby communities bordering on the Charles River as part
of an enlarged Boston. In 1869, the landscape gardener Robert Mor-
ris Copeland proposed an expansive park system that included large
green spaces and a scenic boulevard that wound its way through the
suburbs. That same year, Uriel Crocker, a lawyer and park advocate,
suggested the creation of a strip of parkland running from the banks
of the Charles River through Brighton and Brookline to the Chestnut Hill Reservoir. Crocker's four-mile linear park, he claimed,
"would give a golden spoke to the Hub of the Universe."[65]

Any such system would require cooperation among a number of
different municipalities. But the failure of the annexation movement
after 1873 had reinforced an ethic of municipal competition instead.
Like jealous fiefdoms, the towns hesitated to participate in joint
projects that might benefit other communities more than their own.
Many suburbs, for example, remained reluctant to purchase land
under the Park Act as Lynn had done because any new park would
inevitably serve not only residents of the town that paid for it but
also residents from neighboring communities. So the best suburban
land for park development continued to disappear while each town

waited for its neighbor to build a park first.[66] The problem seemed especially daunting to those trying to preserve the Fells and Blue Hills, since the Fells stretched across five different municipalities and the Blue Hills lay in six. The municipal independence that local suburbs valued so highly turned out to be the principal barrier to preserving suburban land for public use.

The park system that would eventually solve this problem was the brainchild of Sylvester Baxter and Charles Eliot, who had both been involved in the various movements to preserve nature and history around Boston. Baxter, the journalist who gave the Middlesex Fells its name, had lobbied for preservation of the Fells from an early date and had written about colonial life and period homes.[67] Eliot's deep love for nature and keen appreciation for the past could be traced back even further, long before he became a prominent landscape architect and founded the Trustees of Public Reservations. As a boy, Eliot had roamed the Cambridge and Boston countryside looking for remnants of colonial times that he had read about in books, and he doubtless remembered his father's efforts to save the Old South Church from demolition. As an adult, he measured the city against what he called the "idyllic landscape" of the pre-urban period. In 1889 and 1890, Eliot wrote a series of articles for *Garden and Forest* that reviewed the history and design of several well-known country estates around Boston and along the Hudson River. Lamenting that the farms and gardens of the pre-Revolutionary period had been "invaded by streets, sewers, and water-pipes," he determined to record the details of the last great estates before they too disappeared. Both men were acutely aware that the natural and historical environments beloved by members of the upper classes were disappearing.[68]

Unlike Eliot, however, Baxter had a larger political goal—to reorient Boston's perfectionist energies toward the establishment of a utopian socialist state. Baxter was a leading disciple of Edward Bellamy, whose utopian novel *Looking Backward* was one of the most popular books of the nineteenth century. Published in 1888 but set in the year 2000, *Looking Backward* described a future Boston in a socialist United States where the government owned all property, controlled all production, and paid all citizens the same salary. Bellamy's philosophy of "Nationalism," which held the economic equality of all people to be the greatest good, resonated powerfully in a country frightened by the possibility of class warfare. More locally, the book reminded Bostonians of their city's historic mission and painted a compelling picture of what Boston could be like if it were freed from class strife.[69]

Baxter wanted to make Bellamy's fictionalized vision a reality. He led the Nationalist Club in Boston and stood ready to apply socialist theories to the injustices created by the Boston area's municipal fragmentation. Borrowing a phrase from Bellamy, Baxter considered Boston and its surrounding municipalities to be "children of one family" and resented the fact that residents of communities like Brookline, which he singled out by name, enjoyed lower taxes and better services than their neighbors simply because of where they lived. He believed that government could correct such injustices and was willing to subordinate private interests to public needs under a new system of metropolitan governance.[70]

In 1890, Baxter proposed the first detailed political solution to the region's park problems by calling on the legislature to reorganize the Boston area into a "federalized metropolis." Drawing on English and German models, and envisioning a Boston the size of such sprawling cities as Philadelphia and Chicago, he wrote a series of articles in the *Boston Herald* urging the legislature to unite twenty-six suburban municipalities with Boston in a way that bypassed the unpopular idea of annexation. Municipalities would retain their borders and some ability to manage their own affairs, but the new metropolitan government would assume responsibility for environmental services, such as drinking water, parks, and public-health monitoring, as well as schools, roads, streetcar lines, lighting, and fire and police protection. Baxter devoted the most space in his plan to the idea of a metropolitan park system, which he envisioned as a chain of public green spaces stretching around the city from the Blue Hills in the south to the Lynn Woods in the north. His scheme would inspire an attempt to consolidate the metropolitan region in the mid-1890s, although the effort ultimately failed.[71]

But Baxter and Eliot did not wait for the debate over municipal consolidation to resolve itself before pushing forward with a plan for metropolitan parks. At their instigation, the Trustees of Public Reservations, the Appalachian Mountain Club, and a number of municipal park commissions lobbied the legislature in 1891 to establish a metropolitan park system owned and managed by the state. The legislature responded by setting up a temporary park commission to explore the matter and make recommendations. Among the commissioners were Charles Francis Adams, Jr., who had defended Boston Harbor against development years before, and Philip Chase, who had played a prominent role in saving the Lynn Woods. Baxter and Eliot did the legwork as secretary and consulting landscape architect and provided most of the ideas as well. In the fall of 1892, the group toured a large number of sites around the metropolitan region and met with local park commissioners and experts in water management and public health. The following year, the commissioners recommended that the state establish a metropolitan system of parks spread over thirty-six municipalities and controlled by a state agency modeled after the Metropolitan Sewerage Commission.[72]

The 1893 plan represented an innovative approach to landscape preservation and an important milestone on the path to environmental permanence. It was also the first attempt to curtail the environmental damage done by what we now call "suburban sprawl." Although we tend to think of sprawl as a product of the post-World War II building boom, Boston began experiencing the rapid spread of low-density development along with its harmful environmental consequences more than half a century earlier. Baxter expressed concern in the plan that suburban growth was already producing "acres and acres of streets and houses where a few years ago were only pastures and woodland." The result of further unplanned construction, he feared, would be "a vast desert of houses, factories and stores, spreading over and overwhelming the natural features of the landscape." The commission's plan would ensure that a selection of significant natural environments would be permanently preserved for the public before they became targets of private development.[73]

Encouraged by popular support for parks, the legislature adopted the committee's plan with few changes. In 1893, the state created a permanent Metropolitan Park Commission and entrusted it with one million dollars for purchasing the necessary parcels of land. Although the state made the initial outlay and would assume responsibility for managing the land, the communities within a newly created metropolitan park district were required to contribute to the system's upkeep. The commissioners first acquired Beaver Brook in Waltham and large swaths of the Fells and Blue Hills, and then purchased a variety of landscapes around the Boston area that included seashores, riverbanks, and rocky hills. They based their final selection of sites on Eliot's belief that geography should dictate the structure of the new park system by highlighting the environmental underpinnings of the entire region. By the early twentieth century, the commission held almost sixteen square miles of land, three quarters of it woodlands. Baxter, Eliot, and the commissioners had combined the values they found in nature and history with the kinds of suburban landscapes that remained undeveloped to produce a park system of incomparable size and variety. Within a dozen years, Baltimore, Chicago, Philadelphia, Portland, Seattle, and many other cities had commissioned their own "outer park systems."[74]

The large woodland areas of the Metropolitan Park System, however, would function only as parks rather than doubling as working forests. By the 1890s, leisure had begun to trump forestry in wooded areas that attracted high levels of recreational use. The commissioners of the Lynn Woods, for example, abandoned the idea of harvesting trees from their park even before the work began, and New York forbid logging in the Adirondacks in 1894. On a national level, Gifford Pinchot's acceptance of the chief forester's office in 1898 began a decline in forest service interest in municipal forestry.[75] Despite the influence of Elizur Wright's ideas and continuing concerns about the nation's dwindling timber supply, active forestry was never a part of Baxter or Eliot's plan. Once preserved, the Boston area's great forest reservations would become places of play.

Recreating the Puritan Wilderness

But the reservations were more than just natural playgrounds. They permanently enshrined history as well. With Eliot's help, the Metropolitan Park Commission immediately began to highlight the reservations' historical value by finding ways to evoke the colonial wilderness. As in the Lynn Woods, one of the easiest ways to do so was through the use of historical names. Eliot's firm devoted considerable study to finding "the oldest or most generally accepted designations" for features that had a name, and invented new names for places that lacked one.[76] Sometimes the commissioners were willing to replace an existing name with one that carried more historical resonance. For example, they changed the name of Taylor's Mountain in the Fells to Winthrop Hill, thereby commemorating a key figure in Boston history and his role as one of the first European explorers to traverse the Fells. In that way, the commissioners were not just giving names to topographical features but also recording stories. Each name suggested a story—and sometimes multiple stories—about the encounter between the first settlers, the local Indians, and the land. Those stories would now enjoy the same permanence as the rocky hills themselves.

Indian names were a favorite. In the Fells, for example, the commissioners assigned the names Nanapeshemet Hill, Squaw Sachem

Rock, and Wenepoykin Hill to three rocky rises. The names commemorated the leader of the local Indians at the time of first contact, the wife who led their people after his death, and one of his
sons, even though these historical figures had no documented connection to the sites that now carried their names. The commissioners also commemorated Hannah Shiner, the last Pawtucket Indian
to live in the area, by naming a ledge after her near the swamp where
she had lived. In the Blue Hills, the commissioners retained the

This nineteenth-century engraving portrays an actual encounter between the Puritan settlers and local Indians on the Charles River in May 1630. In a broader sense, it also captures the historical moment that upper-class Bostonians were trying to commemorate in the Middlesex Fells and Blue Hills. (Author's collection)

name chosen by E. G. Chamberlain for the second highest mount, Chickatawbut Hill, and then gave the Indian leader's brother and grandson, Kitchamakin and Wampatuck, hills of their own.[77]

The commissioners' desire to assign Indian names to natural features was part of a long-standing and national affinity for Indian place names. Nineteenth-century Americans often went out of their way to give Indian names to hills and other topographical features, and when they failed to find a historically sanctioned name, they were not above borrowing one from someplace else or even inventing one. This practice was particularly popular in New England, where Indians were fewer and sentimentalism about their removal was stronger than in other regions. Thomas Starr King, a Boston minister, argued that the "absurd" names given to the peaks of New Hampshire's White Mountains should be replaced with "the names of some great tribes or chiefs," and Edward Hitchcock, a professor from Amherst College, made a practice of rechristening the hills of western Massachusetts with made-up Indian names. What made this practice so common was the close association of Indians with nature. In the public mind, Indians were as much a part of the pre-settlement wilderness as the land itself. So giving a natural place an Indian name seemed like giving it a name that nature itself might have chosen.[78]

A local historian named Albert Kendall Teele had wanted to forge an even stronger connection between the parks and their early Indian inhabitants. Impressed by how well the Blue Hills evoked the pre-settlement landscape, Teele recommended preserving the entire area as a living monument to the Indians. "Let these hills stand in all the wildness of nature," he proposed, "unchanged by art or man's device, a perpetual memorial of the Indian race!" Where a shelving rock jutted out from the southwest slope of Great Blue Hill, Teele envisioned a bronze statue of an Indian gazing forever toward the setting sun. Nature would record history by commemorating the passing of the land's first inhabitants.[79]

Centuries before, the very Indians that Teele wanted to honor had devised a way to inscribe their own history on the Boston area's landscape. Wherever one of their people had performed some great act, the local Indians dug a hole one foot deep and one foot wide. The holes reminded passersby of the stories associated with those places, and the Indians maintained them meticulously lest the stories be lost. The Pilgrims noticed these holes as soon as they began exploring the countryside around Plymouth and marveled at their effectiveness. "Many things of great antiquity," wrote Edward Winslow, "are fresh in memory."[80] In a sense, the holes were filled with memories, and three centuries later Bostonians were trying to create something similar, if on a dramatically larger scale. The Fells and Blue Hills were designed to store information about colonial people and events and prompt visitors to recall the collected stories. The existence of such places implies a relationship of permanence, lest the memories disappear with the monument—as they did for the Indians.

The Metropolitan Park Commission's use of Indian names in the new parks reflected not only a desire to record the colonial past but an effort to grapple with the immigrant present. Toward the end of the century, poetry, plays, photography, and even department store displays across America revealed a new love affair among "native" Americans with all things Native American. By highlighting their own group's historical encounter with the Indians, Anglo-Saxons were connecting themselves with an authentic source of "Americaness" that more recent immigrants lacked. But new immigrants were quick to realize that connecting themselves with Indians was a way to seem more fully assimilated, and by the early twentieth century they were participating in performances of Longfellow's *The Song of Hiawatha* and had even translated it into Yiddish.[81] The Fells and Blue Hills became part of this struggle to define American identity. Preserved at a time when what it meant to be American seemed more uncertain than ever before, the reservations served as giant sketchbooks where anxious Brahmins used history and nature to work out the relationship between Indian, Anglo-Saxon, and immigrant.

The commissioners' preference for using Indian names was therefore connected to their reluctance to use immigrant ones. Boston's immigrant working classes had been visiting the Fells' private parks for half a century and might have expected the commissioners to assign names that would commemorate some of those places. But a new wave of immigration, this time from southern and eastern Europe, was once again inflaming anti-immigrant sentiment. Just a year after the park system's formation, three young Bostonians from prominent families would found the Immigration Restriction League, which quickly spread to other cities. The park commissioners, however, were less concerned with curbing immigrant numbers in the future than with erasing immigrants and their private parks from the past. The chair of the commission remembered the private park north of Spot Pond as "an amusement stand, with merry-go-round, dance hall and cheap music" that was "an offense to eye and ear."[82] As a result, only a single spot in the Fells earned a name that evoked an immigrant experience, and the association was less than positive. Molly's Spring allegedly recalled an elderly Irish squatter, Molly Connors, who lived alone in a hut and demanded payment from anyone wanting a drink from the spring.[83] Just as James Russell Lowell had viewed the Irish as squatters in his city, the new nomenclature in the Fells made them squatters in the pre-settlement wilderness for all time.

The commissioners also evoked the feeling of wilderness by eliminating evidence of culture. In the first few years of managing the parks, they removed many of the buildings that dotted the woods, including factories, farmhouses, and a home that dated to 1690. The reports of the Metropolitan Park Commissioners treated the removal of buildings as routine and did not attempt to explain it. Indeed, unused buildings would have created an unnecessary maintenance and policing burden. But there was something inherently deceptive about the practice, since removing actual historical artifacts to imaginatively recreate a romanticized wilderness past masked the true history of these places. The practice, however, was surprisingly common. The Lynn Woods underwent a similar process, although Lynn's park commissioners took special care to preserve some stone-lined ditches called "wolf pits" that the first settlers were supposed to have constructed. And just a few years later,

William Rockefeller purchased the Adirondack town of Brandon house-by-house and then demolished it to enhance the wilderness qualities of his adjacent estate. Rockefeller's actions earned him the paradoxical nickname "Maker of Wilderness."[84]

Despite the commissioners' efforts to replicate the pre-settlement wilderness, Eliot had no intention of leaving nature to its own devices in the new forest parks. Dismissing the common belief that unmanaged nature produced the most attractive landscape, Eliot claimed instead that nature tended to destroy variety and encourage monotony. He found the Fells interesting because the vegetation varied from place to place, and he attributed the diversity to the area's human history. If the commission were to leave the Fells to the workings of nature alone, he believed, trees would invade the pastures, glades, and fields, block the paths, and grow to a uniform rather than varied height. Such a policy would amount to neglect and diminish the area's beauty. Eliot's ideas are understandable within the context of his profession—he was a landscape architect, so sculpting nature was his work and his art. Like his mentor Frederick Law Olmsted, Eliot held that human artistry could improve the beauty of nature. He did hope, however, that proper management of the woods would "ensure their slow, but ultimate restoration to something like their primitive character and beauty." An imagined and stylized wilderness, not untouched wilderness, was his goal.[85]

From Wilderness Monuments to Emerald Metropolis

The new park system had an extraordinary impact on local development, especially in the cities and towns that bordered the Fells and Blue Hills. The preservation of these two areas alone removed an enormous amount of land from the real estate market in one stroke. Each park was the size of a small town and larger than many nearby municipalities. Rather than hindering real estate development, however, the new parks energized it. Overnight, their new status as permanent green spaces that would never see development transformed the remote lands bordering them into desirable places to live. The parks became magnets attracting development to their edges.[86]

The Metropolitan Park Commission further encouraged development by creating miles of border roads around the parks that became sought-after sites for building. Eliot wanted to surround the Fells and Blue Hills with roads that would serve as fire breaks and facilitate public access. They also would prevent encroachment by establishing clear boundaries for the reservations. Owners of neighboring properties otherwise might be tempted to intrude on the woods, or abutters might construct "road-houses or beer-gardens, which places will appear to lie within the reservation."[87] Many of the border roads were entirely new throughways, not contemplated before the creation of the parks. The commission completed many of the roads well in advance of residential development in the hope that attractive neighborhoods would surround the parks.

Even more extensive were the parkways that the commission built to make the parks more accessible. Parkways had been part of Baxter and Eliot's vision for the metropolitan area from the start, since many of the parks were difficult to get to from Boston. Anyone wanting to visit the Fells, for example, had to depend on minimal streetcar service or navigate through a maze of crowded streets in Charlestown or Cambridge before emerging on unmarked roads in an unfamiliar countryside. Preparing a comprehensive plan for parkways was a daunting task, however, and the commissioners undertook it only when forced to do so by the severe economic depression that followed the Panic of 1893. Since parkway development would generate a large number of jobs, the legislature passed a $500,000 appropriation to begin construction under the commissioners' direction. By 1910, after sixteen years of work, they had completed thirteen parkways comprising thirty-two miles of roads bordered by 864 acres of land. The parkways tied the parks into a single, integrated park system, and they created new transportation links between Boston and its suburbs.[88]

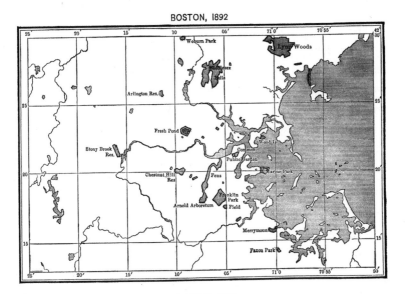

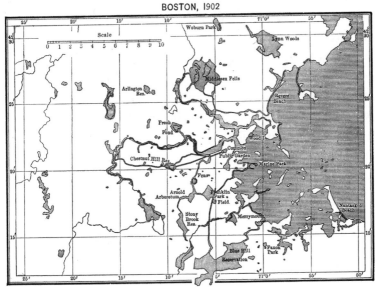

THE OPEN SPACES OF BOSTON IN 1892 AND 1902 COMPARED

The Boston region before and after the establishment of the metropolitan park system. By embracing a new relationship to the natural environment that made room for permanence, Bostonians were able to provide a matrix for future suburban development. (Reproduced from Charles Eliot, *Charles Eliot: Landscape Architect*, 1902, author's collection)

The most important long-term consequence of the parkways was that their permanent presence encouraged and shaped suburban development on an unprecedented scale. Baxter and Eliot were well aware that residential construction would follow the parkways and mold the character of the entire region. Parkways, Baxter wrote, "have the great advantage of being attractive for the best class of residents, and they correspondingly increase the taxable value of property in their neighborhoods." According to Eliot, the likelihood that development would follow the parkways was "not to be counted against them," since the rise in valuation of the property they passed through would finance their construction. He predicted that streetcars traveling along the parkways through undeveloped areas north of the Blue Hills would "tend to populate a large region which has hitherto been inaccessible from the city." The founders of Boston's metropolitan park system expected public roads to encourage private development, making Baxter and Eliot planners as much as preservationists. They not only protected green space but self-consciously shaped the development that would take place around it in years to come. Although sometimes forgotten today, this fact was touted at the time. When the English author H. G. Wells visited Boston in 1906, Baxter took him on a tour of the park system and treated the famous science fiction writer to some real-life time travel. "I suppose no city in all the world (unless it be Washington)," wrote Wells, "has ever produced so complete and ample a forecast of its own future as this Commission's plan of Boston."[89]

The parkways also affected suburban growth in a way that neither Baxter nor Eliot had anticipated. By the early twentieth century, the parkways had become the metropolitan region's first system of automotive highways. Although designed in the 1890s to accommodate bicycles, horses, and carriages, by the 1910s the parkways were serving thousands of automobiles. Even the tour taken by Wells only a few years before was conducted in a "tremulous impatient motor-car." Baxter fully appreciated the irony and moment of this evolution. Built to carry the vehicular traffic of a nineteenth-century city, the parkways had made the automotive-dependent metropolis of the twentieth century possible. "Metropolitan Boston," Baxter insisted in 1913, "could hardly exist" without them. In the space of just a few years, the parkways had unexpectedly evolved into the Boston region's major transportation arteries for recreational vehicles and would retain that role until after World War II.[90]

Change would eventually come to the metropolitan park system, despite its claim to permanence. Over the course of the twentieth century, road widening nibbled away at the green borders of the parkways, the federal government pushed interstate highways through both of the forest reservations, and biologists discovered that the Fells, after a century of protection, contained far fewer native species than when it had first been preserved.[91] The Reverend Lothrop's assertion that "nothing is permanent or enduring upon earth" seemed to retain some merit.

But by then the preserved forests, riverbanks, beaches, and parkways had already done their most important work. They had provided a much-needed template for development in Boston's suburbs, fostered a new commitment across the metropolitan area to publicly-owned open space, given the state government extraordinary influence over regional growth, and created important precedents in urban and suburban planning that other American cities would follow. In the 1890s, the metropolitan park system represented an unprecedented public intrusion into activities usually left to private devices. Today, it remains a fundamental structural component of the metropolitan area.

These accomplishments reflected an important shift in the human relationship to the undeveloped natural areas that still dotted the metropolitan region. Such places had begun to seem like rare and valuable remnants of the past in a way that was impossible in a more rural society. As a result, the residents of greater Boston had rejected an approach to their natural environment—and their built environment as well—that was founded on an assumption of endless change. In its place, they created a new relationship that made room for permanence. The results are visible wherever one finds protected landscapes and restored historic buildings in the metropolitan area. They all owe their existence to the same cultural transformation.

The large reservations also gave the Brahmins their monument to the generation that had first sought to create a city upon a hill. Motivated by the threat of social and environmental change, they had rallied to their cause a battery of ideas about nature and history that could help ameliorate the pain of the present by preserving the past. But even in creating a progressive new park system that seemed perfectly in keeping with the city's perfectionist spirit, they revealed a loss of faith in the vision that their forebears had brought to America. The Brahmin effort to commemorate the Puritan errand into the wilderness was not a forward-looking attempt to mount a beacon that would illuminate future paths. Rather, it was a backward-looking effort to memorialize an ideal before it was forgotten. Their concern for the survival of that ideal, however, was not entirely misplaced. Although Boston's devotion to the vision of a city upon a hill would never disappear entirely, twentieth-century Bostonians would spend less time using it to frame their aspirations and more time remembering it as an artifact of the past.

The City Complete

In his first visit to the United States in 1911, the English novelist Arnold Bennett toured a number of America's greatest cities, including Boston, New York, Philadelphia, Washington, D.C., and Chicago. Out of that group, he identified Boston as the most distinctive. "What primarily differentiates Boston from all the other cities I saw," he wrote, "is this: It is finished." To Bennett, Boston had attained a state of physical and cultural maturity that eluded America's other cities, even those that rivaled it in age. He therefore opposed a proposal to build an artificial island in the Charles River with a large cathedral on it. Such a plan struck him as more appropriate for a still unformed city like Chicago. "It is hoped that Boston," he wrote, "forgetting this infelicitous caprice, will remember in time that she alone among the great cities of America is complete."[1]

Bennett's claim that Boston was "complete," whatever its merits, contained a truth that he probably did not recognize himself: Bostonians had concluded an important stage in their community's development by finishing the places and systems that would thereafter structure their environmental relationships. In fact, Boston's experience suggests that the process of city building was itself a process of inventing new ways of relating to the natural world. Once largely rural and traditional in character, these relationships would become mediated by technology, science, and government, and organized around recreation, domesticity, and an ethic of preservation. By the twentieth century, Boston had become what we recognize today as a modern metropolis, and it had helped to define what that meant from an environmental perspective.

That is not to say that Boston remained stuck in time and never again experienced change. A century later, the cityscape would look very different. But the relationships between Bostonians and the natural world had completed a major and permanent transformation that still influences the daily lives of the city's residents today.

That transformation had been influenced by the natural environment in countless ways. Boston Common's open landscape and access to water had made it an ideal spot for use as both a pasture and a park. The location and quality of fresh water sources had shaped debates about what kind of water system to build. The geographies of country towns had informed their growth and development. The vast tidal flats and complex estuary had affected decisions about how to remake the coastline and the harbor. The topography of suburban land had all but dictated the location of forest preserves and had done much to inspire them in the first place. The list could go on, since Bostonians always had to accommodate very real environmental conditions when building their Eden on the Charles.

Just as important were the competing visions of the Boston ideal produced by different class and ethnic factions, especially the Yankees and the Irish. The tensions between these two groups had animated arguments for a public water system, encouraged the invention of residential suburbs, inspired landmaking schemes to create more ground for middle- and upper-class housing, and influenced the movement to build a monument to the Puritan past in the form of a metropolitan park system. Each vision implied a certain set of social and environmental relationships, and each was expressed through particular ideas about the natural world in which nature took on a variety of meanings. It could be a moral guide, a common good, a relic of the past, a bringer of health, a reflection of the divine, and much more, with each meaning operating in the service of a specific social goal. "Nature is only a mirror," wrote Emerson, "in which man is reflected colossally."[2] Boston's environmental history is the record of its efforts to make sense of that image in the mirror. By the end of the nineteenth century, those efforts had been woven into the city's very fabric.

Although the ideas about nature that Bostonians debated were partly the product of local circumstances, they also reflected a larger evolution in environmental thought that was playing out on a national level. Across America, older ideas about interactions between people and the natural environment were giving way to new ones. Ways of life that treated nature as common property, a place of physical labor, a set of resilient resources, and a symbol of future possibilities were receding before others that emphasized nature's role as private property, a place of recreation, a resource requiring careful management, and a symbol of the nostalgic past. This intellectual shift was not just visible among those who regretted the rise of large cities and preferred the country or the wild, but among those who liked cities and actively furthered their development. In fact, many of the changes that took place in the way Americans thought about the natural world developed hand-in-hand with the invention of the city and the new ways of relating to nature that it brought. The evolutionary path carrying American ideas about nature passed not just around cities but through them.

Boston had also helped to foster a growing national willingness to use the power of government in structuring newly emerging environmental relationships. It was Boston's City Council that decided to transform the Common from a pasture into a park and to take on the burden of constructing a huge public water system. It was the state legislature that first locked Boston permanently behind its present municipal boundaries, creating a belt of independent suburbs beyond it, and then established metropolitan water, sewer, and park systems to bring unity where it had previously encouraged fragmentation. It was also the legislature that created new regulations to control landmaking, although the state often ignored its own rules and even took upon itself the management of landmaking in the Back Bay. Some of these actions pushed back against the culture of privatism, and all were major steps in the increase of governmental control over the metropolitan environment.

Although Boston played a leading role in developing many of the places and systems through which new environmental relationships were expressed, it never held a monopoly on them. Other older cities made important contributions to their creation as well, and younger cities would go on to build their own parks, water works, sewer systems, suburbs, and harbor infrastructure. I have told the story of this process through Boston, but one could tell a similar tale using other cities, even much newer ones. Every community that has become "urban" had to forge new environmental connections to do so. In that sense, every city eventually became Boston. The difference—and it is an important one—was that the trail forward was already blazed. Boston had served as an example to the rest of the nation, even if not in quite the way that its founders had envisioned. As a result, cities that developed later did not have to grapple with the newness of these interactions to the same degree that Bostonians did. They did not have to invent them.

The environmental relationships explored in this book have evolved in mostly small ways since the early twentieth century. Some cities have switched from public to private water systems, or from private to public, and others have restored waterscapes they had previously sought to control. Boston periodically toys with the idea of adding new kinds of recreational facilities to the Common, like a dog park or a restaurant, and most people who hike in the Middlesex Fells or Blue Hills today experience them as generic natural areas rather than remnants of the Puritan wilderness. But these are minor permutations in ways of interacting with nature that have remained remarkably stable over time. They are just as recognizable today as they were over a century ago and continue to define the American metropolis.

They do not, however, always meet the environmental needs of the present. In fact, many have caused serious environmental problems. The allure of life in a thinly settled pastoral suburb has cost the nation millions of acres of productive farmland and animal habitat, replacing them with low-density development accessible only in cars that run on polluting fossil fuels. Our refusal to treat water as anything but abundant has led to the dangerous depletion of water supplies in some of America's largest cities. The confidence that nature can always be controlled through the power of science and technology has contributed to major tragedies, such as the devastation of New Orleans by Hurricane Katrina. We are living twenty-first-century lives through environmental relationships that were designed around nineteenth-century conditions. Many of these relationships fail to recognize limits, and as a result they are failing us today.

Maybe it is time for us to make some changes to them once again. If so, one of the best ways to start will be to reexamine our ideas about the natural world. Raymond Williams recognized that generating new ideas about nature was one of the keys to confronting environmental problems. "We need different ideas," he wrote, "because we need different relationships."[3] Those ideas will be inspired by competing social visions and by the natural world itself, and the way of life we build around them will likely have consequences that we cannot anticipate. But we should aim our sights high, as nineteenth-century Bostonians did, and work to create new environmental relationships that are worthy of a city upon a hill.

In Chapter 1, I argue that social and economic status influenced whether individual Bostonians were for or against removing the cows from Boston Common. That claim is based, in part, on the quantitative analysis outlined in this appendix.

The analysis draws on the 1830 directory for the City of Boston rather than the 1830 federal census, and it does so for two reasons. First, the directory contains information about occupation and the census does not. Second, my data consisted solely of petitions with long lists of names that I could locate more easily in the directory, which is arranged alphabetically by last name. The census, in contrast, is arranged by ward. See Charles Stimpson, *The Boston Directory* (Boston: Charles Stimpson, 1830).

The analysis focuses on the three sets of petitions filed in the spring of 1830. Although Chapter 1 also discusses two sets of petitions filed in 1829 and another in July 1830, I have omitted them from the analysis because they did not directly shape the outcome of the debate over removing the cows.

One of the most labor-intensive parts of this analysis was the process of transcribing the scrawled signatures of the 571 Bostonians who affixed their names to the petitions. The petition bearers who walked the city's streets hunting for signatures probably caught their prey on the fly, and as a result some of the signatures are rushed, others are smudged, and still others contain initials or abbreviations rather than full first names. A number proved impossible to make out at all. I nevertheless transcribed enough of the signatures with sufficient confidence to produce a meaningful sample size.

My method was a simple one. I first assembled the petitions into groups defined by their purpose (either to remove the cows or to prevent their removal) and their timing relative to the City Council's final decision (either before or after it). I then determined the tax burdens and occupational compositions of the groups in order to compare their relative economic and social status. Although modest in size and ambition, the analysis reveals deep economic and social differences between those Bostonians who argued for removal of the cows and those who favored keeping Boston Common a pasture.

The Three Sets of Petitions

I divided the petitions into three groups. Group 1 consists of the five petitions filed in March and April 1830 by those who advocated removing the cows, and Group 2 consists of the two counter petitions filed that April. The City Council then voted in May to remove the cows from the Common. Group 3 consists of the five petitions filed the following June asking the council to rescind its decision. In short, Group 1 is "anti-cow," and Groups 2 and 3 are "pro-cow." Table 1 details for each group the total number of petitioners, the percentage of their signatures that I was able to transcribe, the percentage of the transcribed names that were listed in the city directory, and the percentage for which the directory listed occupations.

It is not surprising that only 61–71 percent of the petitioners whose signatures I was able to transcribe appeared in the Boston directory. Many urban residents went unlisted in city directories at this time, although the names of wealthier residents were far more likely

Table 1. Percentage of names and occupations identified in Groups 1, 2, and 3			
	Group 1	Group 2	Group 3
Number of signatories	181	158	232
Percent of names transcribed	86%	83%	83%
Names listed in city directory (as percent of names transcribed)	61%	66%	71%
Names accompanied by occupation (as percent of names transcribed)	51%	55%	64%

to appear. Peter Knights has calculated that only 81 percent of heads of households in Boston who were recorded in the 1830 federal census were also listed in the city's 1830 directory, and he calculated that later censuses of Boston's population were themselves under-enumerated by 8–10 percent. One should therefore expect one of Boston's directories at this time to contain between two-thirds and three-quarters of the city's heads of households. See Peter R. Knights, *The Plain People of Boston, 1830–1860: A Study in City Growth* (New York: Oxford University Press, 1971), Appendices A and C.

Economic Status Based on Tax Burden

To compare the relative tax burdens among the three groups, I consulted a document produced by the city assessor's office entitled *List of Persons, Co-Partnerships, and Corporations Who Were Taxed Twenty-Five Dollars and Upwards, in the City of Boston, in the Year 1830* (Boston: John H. Eastburn, 1831). As the title suggests, this is not a complete tax roll but rather a list of only the wealthiest residents. The samples are therefore small, although the results are significant. Ten of those petitioning for removal of the cows in Group 1 appear on the list, and their mean tax burden was $115. Ten of the remonstrants in Group 2 also appear in the document, but their mean tax burden is just over half as much: $63. Finally, thirteen of those protesting the city council's removal of the cows in Group 3 appeared on the list, and their mean tax burden was $65, almost exactly the same as that of Group 2. The high correlation between the numbers for Groups 2 and 3 suggests their reliability despite the small samples, and a comparison of the three mean tax burdens points to a strong connection between wealth and the desire to rid Boston Common of its cows. These findings are summarized in Table 2.

Social Status Based on Occupation

There was also a strong correlation between the occupations of petition signers and the side they chose in the war on the cows. As Table 3 shows, pro-cow Group 2 had a higher percentage of people

Table 2. Mean tax burden for petitioners paying more than $25 in taxes in 1830			
	Group 1	Group 2	Group 3
Number of petitioners paying more than $25 in taxes in 1830	10	10	13
Mean tax burden	$115	$63	$65

engaged in a manual labor-related field than the anti-cow Group 1, and the percentage rose even higher in Group 3, which was reacting to the city council's decision to remove the cows. In other words, the groups that favored keeping the Common a pasture included a higher percentage of people engaged in manual labor-related occupations.

The category that I call "manual labor-related occupations" is a collapsed version of the socioeconomic classification scheme developed by Peter Knights (see *Plain People of Boston,* Appendix E). Knights grouped manual laborers into three groups: unskilled and menial service, semi-skilled and service, and skilled. Since these distinctions are not important to my analysis, I have collapsed them into one.

But Knights does indicate that many of the occupations in these three categories could appear instead in categories that include proprietors, managers, and officials if an individual owned the business and had sufficient assets to warrant the shift. In most cases, however, Boston's city directory does not indicate whether a petitioner was a proprietor or an employee, and I lack tax or other information that would tell me how much the individual or his business was worth. As a result, the category as I have constructed it undoubtedly includes petitioners who were involved in manual labor-*related* occupations (hence the name of the category) but no longer engaged in the manual labor part of their businesses themselves. That fact should inflate all three percentages, but not equally. We might reasonably expect to find more proprietors of manual labor-related industries in Group 1 than in Groups 2 and 3, since the anti-cow posi-

Table 3. Petitioners engaged in manual labor-related occupations			
	Group 1	Group 2	Group 3
Number of petitioners with a listed occupation	79	72	122
Number of petitioners engaged in a manual labor-related occupation	39	42	82
Percentage of petitioners engaged in a manual labor-related occupation	49%	58%	67%

tion attracted more people of wealth than the latter two. If that is the case, then the percentage listed above for Group 1 is probably more inflated than those for the other two groups. In short, if it were possible to remove this population from the category, doing so would produce new numbers that showed an even larger difference in the percentage of people engaged in a manual labor-related occupation between Group 1 and Groups 2 and 3 than we see in the present figures.

NOTES

PROLOGUE: TO BUILD A CITY

1 Edward Everett Hale, *A New England Boyhood* (Boston: Little, Brown, 1928), 2; Hale, *Memories of a Hundred Years* (New York: MacMillan, 1904), 125; Hale, *New England Boyhood,* xxi; Hale, *Thirty Years of Boston: An Address Delivered at Hollis-Street Church, January 27, 1861, on Occasion of the Celebration of "The Silver Birthday" of Warrant-street Chapel* (Boston: 1861), 1.

2 Henry P. Tappan, *A Step from the New World to the Old, and Back Again: With Thoughts on the Good and Evil in Both* (New York: D. Appleton, 1852), 2:79. The classic work on anti-urbanism in American thought is Morton and Lucia White, *The Intellectual Versus the City: From Thomas Jefferson to Frank Lloyd Wright* (Cambridge: Harvard University Press, 1962), although it is generally acknowledged that they overstated their argument. For a response to the White's book that explores the ideal of a great city, see Warren I. Susman, "The City in American Culture," in *Culture as History: The Transformation of American Society in the Twentieth Century* (New York: Pantheon Books, 1973), 237–251. Also see Andrew Lees, *Cities Perceived: Urban Society in European and American Thought, 1820–1940* (New York: Columbia University Press, 1985). For Chicago, see Libby Hill, *The Chicago River: A Natural and Unnatural History* (Chicago: Lake Claremont Press, 2000); for Pittsburgh, Edward K. Muller and Joel A. Tarr, "The Interaction of Natural and Built Environments in the Pittsburgh Landscape," in Tarr, ed., *Devastation and Renewal: An Environmental History of Pittsburgh and Its Region* (Pittsburgh: University of Pittsburgh Press, 2003), 11–40; for New Orleans, Craig E. Colten, *An Unnatural Metropolis: Wresting New Orleans from Nature* (Baton Rouge: Louisiana State University, 2005).

3 For an overview of Boston life in the nineteenth century, see Thomas H. O'Connor, *The Hub: Boston Past and Present* (Boston: Northeastern University Press, 2001). For Boston life at the turn of the nineteenth century more specifically, see Jacqueline Barbara Carr, *After the Siege: A Social History of Boston, 1775–1800* (Boston: Northeastern University Press, 2004). Particularly helpful in illuminating the texture of everyday life are reminiscences, such as Hale, *New England Boyhood,* and Caroline Wells Healey Dall, *"Alongside": Being Notes Suggested by "A New England Boyhood" of Doctor Edward Everett Hale* (Boston: Thomas Todd, 1900); also see Justin Winsor, ed., *The Memorial History of Boston, Including Suffolk County, Massachusetts, 1630–1880,* 4 vols. (Boston: James R. Osgood, 1881).

4 See prior note.

5 The literature on the building of nineteenth-century Boston is large and has been approached from a variety of perspectives. See, in particular, Henry C. Binford, *The First Suburbs: Residential Communities on the Boston Periphery, 1815–1860* (Chicago: University of Chicago Press, 1985); Michael P. Conzen and George K. Lewis, *Boston: A Geographical Portrait* (Cambridge: Ballinger, 1976); Mona Domosh, *Invented Cities: The Creation of Landscape in Nineteenth-Century New York and Boston* (New Haven: Yale University Press, 1996); Sarah S. Elkind, *Bay Cities and Water Politics: The Battle for Resources in Boston and Oakland* (Lawrence: University Press of Kansas, 1998); Walter Firey, *Land Use in Central Boston* (Cambridge: Harvard University Press, 1947); Karl Haglund, *Inventing the Charles River* (Cambridge: MIT Press, 2003); Jane Holtz Kay, *Lost Boston* (Boston: Houghton Mifflin, 1980); Lawrence Kennedy, *Planning the City Upon a Hill: Boston Since 1630* (Amherst: University of Massachusetts Press, 1992); Harold and James Kirker, *Bulfinch's Boston: 1787–1817* (New York: Oxford University Press, 1964); Alex Krieger and Lisa J. Green, *Past Futures: Two Centuries of Imagining Boston* (Cambridge: Harvard University Graduate School of Design, 1985); Alex Krieger and David Cobb with Amy Turner, eds., *Mapping Boston* (Cambridge: MIT Press, 1999); William A. Newman and Wilfred E. Holton, *Boston's Back Bay: The Story of America's Greatest Nineteenth-Century Landfill Project* (Boston: University Press of New England, 2006); Anthony N. Penna and Conrad Edick Wright, *Remaking Boston: An Environmental History of the City and Its Surroundings* (Pittsburgh: University of Pittsburgh Press, 2009); Nancy S. Seasholes, *Gaining Ground: A History of Landmaking in Boston* (Cambridge: MIT Press, 2003); Douglass Shand-Tucci, *Built in Boston: City and Suburb, 1800–2000* (Amherst: University of Massachusetts Press, 1999); Nathaniel B. Shurtleff, *A Topographical and Historical Description of Boston,* 2nd ed., rev. (Boston: Noyes, Holmes, 1872); Alexander von Hoffman, *Local Attachments: The Making of an American Urban Neighborhood, 1850 to 1920* (Baltimore: Johns Hopkins University Press, 1994); Sam Bass Warner, Jr., *Streetcar Suburbs: The Process of Growth in Boston, 1870–1900,* 2nd ed. (Cambridge: Harvard University Press, 1978); Walter Muir Whitehill and Lawrence W. Kennedy, *Boston: A Topographical History,* 3rd ed. (Cambridge: Belknap Press of Harvard University Press, 2000); and Cynthia Zaitzevsky, *Frederick Law Olmsted and the Boston Park System* (Cambridge: Belknap Press of Harvard University Press, 1982).

6 For an overview of the Boston Basin's pre-human past, see P. J. Barosh, C. A. Kaye, and D. Woodhouse, "Geology of the Boston Basin and Vicinity," *Civil Engineering Practice: Journal of the Boston Society of Civil Engineers* 4, no. 1 (1989): 39–52; and Newman and Holton, *Boston's Back Bay,* 1–11.

7 For descriptions of early Boston, see Shurtleff, *Topographical and Historical Description of Boston,* especially chapter 2; and Whitehill and Kennedy, *Boston: A Topographical History,* 3–8.

8 Ralph Waldo Emerson, "Boston," in Emerson, *Natural History of Intellect and Other Papers* (Boston: Houghton, Mifflin, 1904), 185.

9 Quote is from Francis Higginson, "New-Englands Plantation" (1630), in *New-Englands Plantation: With the Sea Journal and Other Writings* (Salem: Essex Book and Print Club, 1908), 91. For fish weirs, see Elena B. Décima and Dena F. Dincauze, "The Boston Back Bay Fish Weirs," in *Hidden Dimensions: The Cultural Significance of Wetland Archaeology,* ed. Kathryn Bernick (Vancouver: University of British Columbia Press, 1998), 157–172. For interactions between Native Americans and their environments in New England, see Brian Donahue, *The Great Meadow: Farmers and the Land in Colonial Concord* (New Haven: Yale University Press, 2004); William Cronon, *Changes in the Land: Indians, Colonists, and the Ecology of New England* (New York: Hill and Wang, 1983); and Carolyn Merchant, *Ecological Revolutions: Nature, Gender, and Science in New England* (Chapel Hill: University of North Carolina Press, 1989).

10 Pollard is quoted in Winsor, ed., *Memorial History of Boston,* 521; Emerson, "Boston," in Emerson, *Natural History of Intellect,* 191. For environmental conditions in early Boston, see note 7 above.

11 For the transfer of the colony from Charlestown to Boston and the meaning of "Shawmut," see Shurtleff, *Topographical and Historical Description,* 24–26. For early conditions in the colony, see Darrett B. Rutman, *Winthrop's Boston: Portrait of a Puritan Town, 1630–1649* (Chapel Hill: University of North Carolina Press, 1965); and Francis J. Bremer, *John Winthrop: America's Forgotten Founding Father* (New York: Oxford University Press, 2003).

12 Dolin, *Political Waters;* Elkind, *Bay Cities and Water Politics;* Haglund, *Inventing the Charles River.*

13 Charles Dickens, *American Notes for General Circulation* (Boston: Ticknor and Fields, 1867), 19.

14 John Winthrop, "A Model of Christian Charity," in *The Puritans in America: A Narrative Anthology,* ed. Alan Heimert and Andrew Delbanco (Cambridge: Harvard University Press, 1985), 91 and 90. Winthrop's metaphor was inspired by Matthew 5:14: "Ye are the light of the world. A city that is set on a hill cannot be hid." For a meditation on the place of this metaphor in Boston culture, see Shaun O'Connell, *Imagining Boston: A Literary Landscape* (Boston: Beacon Press, 1990), chapter 1. For a recent use of the metaphor to rally Bostonians around the common good, see Charles C. Euchner and William M. Fowler, Jr., "Embracing That 'City Upon a Hill,'" *Boston Globe,* 4 September 2002, A17.

15 The first use of "Athens of America" is often attributed to William Tudor, although it seems to have been in general use, and Oliver Wendell Holmes, Sr., coined "the hub of the solar system" in Holmes, *The Autocrat of the Breakfast Table* (London: J. M. Dent, 1907), 120; Amos Bronson Alcott, *The Journals of Bronson Alcott,* ed. Odell Shepard (Boston: Little, Brown, 1938), 15; Emerson,

"Boston," in *Natural History of Intellect*, 188. For Boston's literary contributions during this period, see Van Wyck Brooks, *The Flowering of New England: 1815–1865* (New York: E. P. Dutton, 1936). For the city's commitment to social perfectibility in the first half of the nineteenth century, see Thomas H. O'Connor, *Athens of America: Boston, 1825–1845* (Amherst: University of Massachusetts Press, 2006).

16 Winthrop, "A Model of Christian Charity," 89; Theodore Parker, "Theological and Philosophical Development of New England" (delivered in 1855), in Parker, *The Works of Theodore Parker*, vol. 6 (Boston: American Unitarian Association, 1907), 395. Shaun O'Connell considers the "tensions between the one and the many" to be "characteristically Bostonian." O'Connell, *Imagining Boston*, 14. The classic work on the culture of privatism is Sam Bass Warner, Jr., *The Private City: Philadelphia in Three Periods of Its Growth* (Philadelphia: University of Pennsylvania Press, 1968). A number of later works have further developed the theme. See, for example, Robin L. Einhorn, *Property Rules: Political Economy in Chicago, 1833–1872* (Chicago: University of Chicago Press, 1991); Ann Durkin Keating, *Building Chicago: Suburban Developers and the Creation of a Divided Metropolis* (Columbus: Ohio State University Press, 1988); Maureen Ogle, "Water Supply, Waste Disposal, and the Culture of Privatism in the Mid-Nineteenth-Century American City," *Journal of Urban History* 25, no. 3 (March 1999): 321–347; and Harold L. Platt, *City Building in the New South: The Growth of Public Services in Houston, Texas, 1830–1910* (Philadelphia: Temple University Press, 1982). For the tension between individual rights and collective responsibility in American culture more generally, see Robert N. Bellah, Richard Madsen, William M. Sullivan, Ann Swindler, and Steven M. Tipton, *Habits of the Heart: Individualism and Commitment in American Life* (New York: Harper and Row, 1985). For Boston's reform endeavors, see Arthur Mann, *Yankee Reformers in the Urban Age* (Cambridge: Belknap Press of Harvard University Press, 1954); and Nathan Irvin Huggins, *Protestants Against Poverty: Boston's Charities, 1870–1900* (Westport, Conn.: Greenwood Press, 1971).

17 On the evolution of urban government, see especially John C. Teaford, *The Unheralded Triumph: City Government in America, 1870–1900* (Baltimore: Johns Hopkins University Press, 1984). For the creation of Quincy Market and the Back Bay, see John Quincy, Jr., *Quincy's Market: A Boston Landmark* (Boston: Northeastern University Press, 2003); and Newman and Holton, *Boston's Back Bay*.

18 Holmes first used the term "Brahmin" in "The Brahmin Caste of New England," *The Atlantic Monthly* (January 1860). The literature on class in nineteenth-century Boston is large, especially for the upper classes. See E. Digby Baltzell, *The Protestant Establishment: Aristocracy and Caste in America* (New York: Random House, 1964); E. Digby Baltzell, *Puritan Boston and*

Quaker Philadelphia: Two Protestant Ethics and the Spirit of Class Authority and Leadership (New York: Free Press, 1979); Robert F. Dalzell, Jr., *Enterprising Elite: The Boston Associates and the World They Made* (Cambridge: Harvard University Press, 1987); Ronald P. Formisano and Constance K. Burns, eds., *Boston 1700–1980: The Evolution of Urban Politics* (Westport, Conn.: Greenwood Press, 1984); Paul Goodman, "Ethics and Enterprise: The Values of a Boston Elite, 1800–1860," *American Quarterly* 18 (Fall 1966): 437–451; Frederic Cople Jaher, *The Urban Establishment: Upper Strata in Boston, New York, Charleston, Chicago and Los Angeles* (Urbana: University of Illinois Press, 1982); Peter R. Knights, *The Plain People of Boston, 1830–1860: A Study in City Growth* (New York: Oxford University Press, 1971); Peter R. Knights, *Yankee Destinies: The Lives of Ordinary Nineteenth-Century Bostonians* (Chapel Hill: University of North Carolina Press, 1991); Gabriel Kolko, "Brahmins and Business, 1870–1914: A Hypothesis on the Social Basis of Success in American History," in *The Critical Spirit: Essays in Honor of Herbert Marcuse*, ed. Kurt Wolff and Barrington Moore (Boston: Beacon Press, 1967); Edward Pessen, *Riches, Class, and Power Before the Civil War* (Lexington, Mass.: D. C. Heath, 1973); Stephan Thernstrom, *The Other Bostonians: Poverty and Progress in the American Metropolis, 1880–1970* (Cambridge: Harvard University Press, 1973); and Tamara Plakins Thornton, *Cultivating Gentlemen: The Meaning of Country Life among the Boston Elite, 1785–1860* (New Haven: Yale University Press, 1989).

19 Edward Everett Hale, *Letters on Irish Emigration* (Boston: Phillips, Sampson, 1852), 52. For the Boston Irish, see especially Oscar Handlin, *Boston's Immigrants: A Study in Acculturation, 1790–1880* (Cambridge: Belknap Press of Harvard University Press, 1959); and Thomas H. O'Connor, *The Boston Irish: A Political History* (Boston: Northeastern University Press, 1995).

20 C. S. Lewis, *The Abolition of Man* (New York: Macmillan, 1947), 69. For environmental histories of American cities that place particular emphasis on the intersection of power and environment, see Matthew Klingle, *Emerald City: An Environmental History of Seattle* (New Haven: Yale University Press, 2007); Craig E. Colten, *An Unnatural Metropolis: Wresting New Orleans from Nature* (Baton Rouge: Louisiana State University Press, 2005); Ari Kelman, *A River and Its City: The Nature of Landscape in New Orleans* (Berkeley: University of California Press, 2003); Matthew Gandy, *Concrete and Clay: Reworking Nature in New York City* (Cambridge: MIT Press, 2002); and Mike Davis, *Ecology of Fear: Los Angeles and the Imagination of Disaster* (New York: Metropolitan Books, 1998).

21 Ralph Waldo Emerson, "Nature," in Emerson, *Essays: Second Series* (New York: Houghton, Mifflin, 1884), 159. The work of Raymond Williams has done the most to shape my approach to ideas of nature. See particularly Raymond Williams, "Ideas of Nature," in *Problems of Materialism and Culture* (London: Verso, 1980), 67–85; and Williams, *The Country and the City* (New York: Oxford Uni-

versity Press, 1973). Also see Lawrence Buell, *The Environmental Imagination: Thoreau, Nature Writing, and the Formation of American Culture* (Cambridge: Belknap Press of Harvard University Press, 1995); William Cronon, ed., *Uncommon Ground: Rethinking the Human Place in Nature* (New York: W. W. Norton, 1995); Neil Evernden, *The Social Creation of Nature* (Baltimore: Johns Hopkins University Press, 1992); Leo Marx, *The Machine in the Garden: Technology and the Pastoral Ideal in America* (New York: Oxford University Press, 1964); D. W. Meinig, ed., *The Interpretation of Ordinary Landscapes: Geographical Essays* (New York: Oxford University Press, 1979); Simon Schama, *Landscape and Memory* (New York: Vintage Books, 1995); Kate Soper, *What Is Nature? Culture, Politics and the Non-Human* (Cambridge, Mass.: Blackwell, 1995); Yi-Fu Tuan, *Escapism* (Baltimore: Johns Hopkins University Press, 1998); and Yi-Fu Tuan, *Topophilia: A Study of Environmental Perception, Attitudes, and Values* (Englewood Cliffs, N.J.: Prentice-Hall, 1974).

22 Alexander Young, *Chronicles of the Pilgrim Fathers of the Colony of Plymouth, from 1602 to 1625* (Boston: Charles C. Little and James Brown, 1841), 105. For Puritan attitudes toward the wilderness, see Peter N. Carroll, *Puritanism and the Wilderness: The Intellectual Significance of the New England Frontier, 1629–1700* (New York: Columbia University Press, 1969). The social construction of nature has been extensively studied but sometimes pushed to an extreme in which physical nature disappears. For balanced approaches that explore the social content of ideas about nature, see especially Evernden, *The Social Creation of Nature;* and John Rennie Short, *Imagined Country: Environment, Culture and Society* (New York: Routledge, 1991).

23 Thomas Morton, *The New English Canaan,* ed. Charles Francis Adams, Jr. (Boston: John Wilson and Son, 1883), 180, 179; Herman Melville, *Pierre, or the Ambiguities* (New York: Harper and Brothers, 1852), 466.

24 I discuss the battle to bring water to Boston in chapter 2. A number of urban historians and geographers have explored the impact of ideas of nature on nineteenth-century city building, with a special emphasis on romanticism and the pastoral ideal. See especially Peter J. Schmitt, *Back to Nature: The Arcadian Myth in Urban America* (New York: Oxford University Press, 1969); Thomas Bender, *Toward an Urban Vision: Ideas and Institutions in Nineteenth-Century America* (Lexington: University Press of Kentucky, 1975); David Schuyler, *The New Urban Landscape: The Redefinition of City Form in Nineteenth-Century America* (Baltimore: Johns Hopkins University Press, 1986); John Stilgoe, *Borderland: Origins of the American Suburb, 1820–1939* (New Haven: Yale University Press, 1988); and Terence Young, *Building San Francisco's Parks, 1850–1930* (Baltimore: Johns Hopkins University Press, 2004).

25 For Emerson, see Gay Wilson Allen, *Waldo Emerson: A Biography* (New York: Viking Press, 1981), 36–37, 277; for Parkman, see Howard Doughty, *Francis*

Parkman (New York: Macmillan, 1962), 13–19; Oliver Wendell Holmes, Sr., to John Lothrop Motley, February 16, 1861, quoted in John T. Morse, Jr., *Life and Letters of Oliver Wendell Holmes,* vol. 2 (Boston: Houghton, Mifflin, 1896), 157. For the agency of nature, see Linda Nash, "The Agency of Nature or the Nature of Agency?" *Environmental History* 10, no. 1 (January 2005): 67–69; Ted Steinberg, "Down to Earth: Nature, Agency, and Power in History," *American Historical Review* 107, no. 3 (June 2002): 798–820; and Tuan, *Topophilia.*

26 Hale expressed some of his views about environmental relationships in Edward Everett Hale, *Sybaris and Other Homes* (Boston: Fields, Osgood, 1869), especially pages 53–55. For his plans for working-class housing, see the essay in *Sybaris* entitled "Homes for Boston Laborers."

1. Enclosing the Common

1 Historians have never made a detailed study of the transformation of Boston Common from a pasture to a park, or understood the event as an enclosure of common land. For scholarly histories of the Common, see James N. Levitt, "Palladium of the People," Rappaport Institute for Greater Boston, Working Paper 10, December 1, 2003; David Hackett Fischer, "Boston Common," in *American Places: Encounters with History,* ed. William E. Leuchtenburg (New York: Oxford University Press, 2000), 125–143; and Mona Domosh, *Invented Cities: The Creation of Landscape in Nineteenth-Century New York and Boston* (New Haven: Yale University Press, 1996). For popular histories of the Common, see Friends of the Public Garden, *Boston Common* (Charleston, S.C.: Arcadia, 2005); M. A. DeWolfe Howe, *Boston Common: Scenes from Four Centuries,* rev. ed. (Boston: Atlantic Monthly Press, 1921); Samuel Barber, *Boston Common: A Diary of Notable Events, Incidents, and Neighboring Occurrences,* 2nd ed. (Boston: Christopher Publishing House, 1916); Joseph Henry Curtis, *Life of Campestris Ulm, The Oldest Living Inhabitant of Boston Common* (Boston: W. B. Clarke, 1910); Mary Farwell Ayer, *Boston Common in Colonial and Provincial Days* (Boston: privately printed, 1903); and Ayer, *Early Days on Boston Common* (Boston: privately printed, 1910). One of the most useful sources on the history of the Common remains Nathaniel B. Shurtleff, *A Topographical and Historical Description of Boston,* 2nd ed., rev. (Boston: Noyes, Holmes, 1872).

2 Shurtleff, *Topographical and Historical Description,* 25, 294–298.

3 The literature on common lands in England overlaps the literature on enclosure, which I discuss in a later note. For the origins and management of common lands in England, see Martina de Moor, Leigh Shaw-Taylor, and Paul Warde, eds., *The Management of Common Land in North West Europe, c. 1500–1850* (Turnhout, Belgium: Brepols, 2002); Eric Kerridge, *The Common Fields of England* (Manchester: Manchester University Press, 1992); and the classic work by W. G. Hoskins, *The Making of the English Landscape* (London: Hodder and

Stoughton, 1955). For a transnational perspective on common land regimes, see Bonnie J. McCay and James M. Acheson, eds., *The Question of the Commons: The Culture and Ecology of Communal Resources* (Tucson: University of Arizona Press, 1987).

4 See prior note.

5 For the extension of the English common land system to America, see John R. Stilgoe, "Town Common and Village Green in New England: 1620–1981," in *On Common Ground: Caring for Shared Land from Town Common to Urban Park,* ed. Ronald Lee Fleming and Lauri A. Halderman (Harvard, Mass.: Harvard Common Press, 1982), 7–36; J. C. Juergensmeyer, "The Common Lands Concept in American Jurisprudence," *Revue de l'Institute de Sociologie* [Belgium] 2 (1973): 369–389; and Percy Wells Bidwell, *History of Agriculture in the Northern United States, 1620–1860* (Washington, D.C.: Carnegie Institute of Washington, 1925). For the history of proprietary rights in New England, including Boston Common, see Roy Hidemichi Akagi, *The Town Proprietors of the New England Colonies: A Study of Their Development, Organization, Activities and Controversies, 1620–1770* (Philadelphia: University of Pennsylvania Press, 1924). Also see Melville Egleston, *The Land System of the New England Colonies* (New York: Evening Post Print, 1880). The sale of the right to pasture a cow on Boston Common is recorded in a number of contemporary deeds. See, for example, the deed from William Kirby to Richard Gardiner, May 20, 1681, in *Suffolk Deeds,* Liber XII (Boston: Rockwell and Churchill Press, 1902), 57–58. For the more informal use of undeveloped rural land as a common resource in New England, see Richard W. Judd, *Common Lands, Common People: The Origins of Conservation in Northern New England* (Cambridge: Harvard University Press, 1997); and Robert McCullough, *The Landscape of Community: A History of Communal Forests in New England* (Hanover, N.H.: University Press of New England, 1995). Brian Donahue tries to revive the common lands idea in Boston's suburbs in *Reclaiming the Commons: Community Farms and Forests in a New England Town* (New Haven: Yale University Press, 1999).

6 John Winthrop, *Winthrop's Journal,* ed. James Kendall Hosmer, 2 vols. (New York: Charles Scribner's Sons, 1908), 1:143.

7 Boston's early town records, which have been published as City of Boston, *Records Relating to the Early History of Boston,* 39 vols. (Boston: Rockwell and Churchill, City Printers, 1876–1909), also known as *Report of the Record Commissioners,* are filled with references to the Common's management and multiple uses and are the source of the information in this and subsequent paragraphs. For women washing cloths under the Old Elm, see Ayer, *Early Days on Boston Common,* 57. For a detailed description of the buildings erected on the Common, see Thomas Pemberton, "A Topographical and Historical Description of Boston, 1794, by the Author of the Historical Journal of the American

War, with References," Massachusetts Historical Society *Collections,* vol. 3 (Boston: Apollo Press, 1794), 241–304. The wide range of activities on Boston Common made it akin not just to large rural commons but to smaller town commons, which often grew out of meetinghouse lots and served as social centers. See Joseph S. Wood, *The New England Village* (Baltimore: Johns Hopkins University Press, 1997); Richard Ross Cloues, "Where Art Is Combined with Nature: Village Improvement in Nineteenth-Century New England" (Ph.D. diss., Cornell University, 1987); Stilgoe, "Town Common and Village Green"; David D. Brodeur, "Evolution of the New England Town Common: 1630–1966," *The Professional Geographer* 19, no. 6 (November 1967): 313–318; and John D. Cushing, "Town Commons of New England, 1640–1840," *Old-Time New England: The Bulletin of the Society for the Preservation of New England Antiquities* 51, no. 3 (Winter 1961): 86–94.

8 Efforts to regulate Boston Common appear everywhere in City of Boston, *Records.* See in particular the town records for 6 March 1672, and the selectmen's records for 26 March 1705, 15 March 1737, 19 July 1738, 5 March 1740, and 25 February 1783. For the cow tax, see particularly the town records for 1789, pp. 193–194, the selectmen's records for 3 April 1716 and 16 June 1784, and *The Charter of the City of Boston, and Ordinances Made and Established by the Mayor, Aldermen, and Common Council, with such Acts of the Legislature of Massachusetts, as Relate to the Government of Said City* (Boston: True and Greene, City Printers, 1827), 75–77.

9 For New York's pigs, see Hendrick Hartog, "Pigs and Positivism," *Wisconsin Law Review* (July 1985): 899–935.

10 See note 8.

11 Reports of Boston residents strolling along the Common go back as early as 1638. See Paul J. Lindholdt, ed., *John Josselyn, Colonial Traveler: A Critical Edition of the Two Voyages to New-England* (Hanover, N.H.: University Press of New England, 1988), 114. Contemporary poetry reinforced the connection between town commons and the recreational needs of New England children. See "The Village Green," in *Little Poems for Children* (Windsor, Vt.: Printed and Sold by Jesse Cochran, 1815), 11–12. In his essay on Boston Common, David Hackett Fischer categorizes work-related activities like washing clothes and grazing cattle as fulfilling only a private interest, while considering the leisure activities that replaced them to be in the public interest. Early nineteenth-century Bostonians, however, would not have drawn the lines between private and public in that way. Fischer, "Boston Common," 136–137.

12 It is difficult to gauge how much access the city's small African-American population had to the Common. As a matter of custom rather than law, blacks often were excluded from the Common in the early nineteenth century on every day of the year except "Negro Election Day," an annual day of status

reversal. See Nathaniel B. Shurtleff, "Remarks on Negro Election Day," Massachusetts Historical Society *Proceedings,* XIII (1873–1875), 45–46; and Joseph P. Reidy, "'Negro Election Day' and Black Community Life in New England, 1750–1860," *Marxist Perspectives* 1 (Fall 1978): 102–117.

13 For labor relations during this period, see Paul E. Johnson, *A Shopkeeper's Millennium: Society and Revivals in Rochester, New York, 1815–1837* (New York: Hill and Wang, 1978), 43–48; and Jonathan A. Glickstein, *Concepts of Free Labor in Antebellum America* (New Haven: Yale University Press, 1991).

14 For a history of this period, see Jacqueline Barbara Carr, *After the Siege: A Social History of Boston, 1775–1800* (Boston: Northeastern University Press, 2005).

15 Richard L. Bushman, *The Refinement of America: Persons, Houses, Cities* (New York: Vintage Books, 1993).

16 Enoch C. Wines, *A Trip to Boston in a Series of Letters to the Editor of the United States Gazette* (Boston: Charles C. Little and James Brown, 1838), 208.

17 *The Massachusetts Magazine: or, Monthly Museum of Knowledge and Rational Entertainment,* November, 1790; Allen Chamberlain, *Beacon Hill: Its Ancient Pastures and Early Mansions* (Boston: Houghton Mifflin, 1925), 118; Robert Means Lawrence, *Old Park Street and Its Vicinity* (Boston: Houghton Mifflin, 1922), 16–17.

18 Walter Muir Whitehill and Lawrence Kennedy, *Boston: A Topographical History,* 3rd ed., enl. (Cambridge: Belknap Press of Harvard University Press, 2000), 59, 64–66.

19 For the genteel aura created by tree-lined walks and civic buildings, see Bushman, *Refinement of America,* 164–169 and 354–355, respectively. For the history of the garden square, see Phebe S. Goodman, *The Garden Squares of Boston* (Hanover, N.H.: University Press of New England, 2003).

20 Oliver Wendell Holmes, "A Rhymed Lesson," in *The Poetical Works of Oliver Wendell Holmes,* vol. 1 (Boston: Houghton, Mifflin, 1891), 125. Several sources make reference to the cow lanes on Beacon Hill. See, for example, Samuel Eliot Morison, *Harrison Gray Otis, 1765–1848: The Urbane Federalist* (Boston: Houghton Mifflin, 1969), 458. For biographies of the various residents of Park Street, see Lawrence, *Old Park Street and Its Vicinity.* For Otis and the Mount Vernon Proprietors, see Whitehill and Kennedy, *Boston: A Topographical History,* 60–64. For the residential patterns of wealthy Bostonians, see Edward Pessen, *Riches, Class, and Power before the Civil War* (Lexington, Mass.: D. C. Heath, 1973), chapter 9.

21 Frederic Cople Jaher, *The Urban Establishment: Upper Strata in Boston, New York, Charleston, Chicago and Los Angeles* (Urbana: University of Illinois Press, 1982), 21; William Dean Howells, *The Rise of Silas Lapham* (Boston: Ticknor, 1885).

22 For the evolution of gentility in America generally, see Bushman, *Refinement of America.*

23 Ralph Waldo Emerson, *Nature* (1836; New York: Penguin Books, 1995), 47; Emerson, *The Journals and Miscellaneous Notebooks of Ralph Waldo Emerson,* ed. Alfred R. Ferguson, vol. 4 (Cambridge: Belknap Press of Harvard University Press, 1964), 355 (entry for December 8, 1834); Emerson, *Nature,* 6. Emerson was probably referring to Boston Common itself in some of these passages, although there is no direct evidence to support such a claim. See Gay Wilson Allen, *Waldo Emerson: A Biography* (New York: Viking Press, 1981), 36–37, 277. For attitudes toward work during this period, see Glickstein, *Concepts of Free Labor.*

24 Johnson, *Shopkeeper's Millennium,* 38–48.

25 Nehemiah Adams, *Boston Common* (Boston: William D. Ticknor and H. B. Williams, 1842), 55. For some theoretical approaches to thinking about how people use animals to construct identity, see Steve Baker, *Picturing the Beast: Animals, Identity, and Representation* (Manchester: Manchester University Press, 1993), especially chapter 1.

26 Samuel L. Knapp, *Extracts from a Journal of Travels in North America: Consisting of an Account of Boston and its Vicinity, by Ali Bey* (Boston: Printed by Thomas Badger, Jr., 1818), 57 and 56.

27 Shurtleff, *Topographical Description,* 339 and 338. E. P. Thompson made a similar observation of the English laboring classes: "The Plebeian culture is rebellious," he wrote, "but rebellious in defense of custom." E. P. Thompson, "Eighteenth-Century English Society: Class Struggle without Class?" *Social History* 3, no. 2 (May 1978), 154.

28 New England's town meeting system is distinctive to the New England region. John Teaford calls it the "Yankee Anomaly." Teaford, *The Municipal Revolution in America: Origins of Modern Urban Government, 1650–1825* (Chicago: University of Chicago Press, 1975).

29 For Boston's problems with town government and its transition to city government, see Robert A. McCaughey, "From Town to City: Boston in the 1820s," *Political Science Quarterly* 88, no. 2 (June 1973), 191–213; and Francis X. Blouin, Jr., "Boston 1821–1822: The Change from Town to City Government" (master's thesis, University of Minnesota, 1969).

30 Josiah Quincy, *A Municipal History of the Town and City of Boston, During Two Centuries. From September 17, 1630, to September 17, 1830* (Boston: Charles C. Little and James Brown, 1852), 23.

31 For upper-class control of the town government, see Pessen, *Riches, Class, and Power,* chapter 13. The theme of rich versus poor is explored in Blouin, "Boston 1821–1822." McCaughey, "From Town to City," interprets Boston's transition from town to city government as a decisive break with its political past.

32 McCaughey, "From Town to City," 197. For the class background of those holding Boston's new public offices, see Pessen, *Riches, Class, and Power,* chap-

ter 13. For the law that forbids the sale of Boston Common and Faneuil Hall, see *City of Boston Code,* Statutes, Title 3, Section 2 (1975).

33 Quincy, *Municipal History,* 384. For Quincy and his administration, also see Robert A. McCaughey, *Josiah Quincy, 1772–1864: The Last Federalist* (Cambridge: Harvard University Press, 1974); and Matthew H. Crocker, *The Magic of the Many: Josiah Quincy and the Rise of Mass Politics in Boston, 1800–1830* (Amherst: University of Massachusetts Press, 1999).

34 *Boston Columbian Centinel,* 7 June 1823, pp. 2, 3. For the classic statement on the over exploitation of common resources when they go unregulated, see Garrett Hardin, "The Tragedy of the Commons," *Science* 162 (December 1968): 1243–1248.

35 See prior note. Quote is from R. Ben Brown, "The Southern Range: A Study in Nineteenth Century Law and Society" (Ph.D. diss., University of Michigan, 1993), 281, as quoted in Ted Steinberg, *Down to Earth: Nature's Role in American History* (New York: Oxford University Press, 2002), 157. For New York's problem with pigs, see Hartog, "Pigs and Positivism."

36 Barber, *Boston Common,* 137–143.

37 Quincy, *Municipal History,* 113–115.

38 An image of the proposed development can be found in Whitehill and Kennedy, *Boston: A Topographical History,* 145. The image cleverly adopts an elevated perspective to suggest that the construction would not obstruct the view.

39 Roderick Nash, *Wilderness and the American Mind,* 3rd ed. (New Haven: Yale University Press), chapter 4. For landscape painting, also see Barbara Novak, *Nature and Culture: American Landscape and Painting, 1825–1875,* 3rd ed. (New York: Oxford University Press, 2007).

40 Andrew Eliot Belknap, Editorial, 20 July 1824, Boston Common Papers, Massachusetts Historical Society.

41 Belknap, 20, 23 July 1824, Boston Common Papers.

42 Belknap, 23 July and 14, 16 December 1824, Boston Common Papers.

43 Abbott Lawrence to Amos Lawrence, 28 July 1824, Amos Lawrence Papers, Massachusetts Historical Society.

44 John T. Apthorp, *Report of the Committee Chosen by the Inhabitants of the City of Boston, to Take into Consideration the Expediency of Authorizing the City Council to Make Sale of the Upland and Flats, Lying West of Charles Street* (Boston: n.p., 1824), 16, 15, and 14. Apthorp was President of the Suffolk Insurance Company and lived on Boylston Street near the Common.

45 Apthorp, *Report of the Committee,* 17–18.

46 *Boston Columbian Centinel,* 22 December 1824, p. 2.

47 *Boston Courier,* 15 December 1824, p. 2.

48 Quincy, *Municipal History,* 115–116. For vote counts, see the *Boston Columbian*

Centinel, 29 December 1824, p. 2. On Mount Auburn Cemetery, see Blanche Linden-Ward, *Silent City on a Hill: Landscapes of Memory and Boston's Mount Auburn Cemetery* (Columbus: Ohio State University Press, 1989); and William W. Stowe, "Writing Mount Auburn: Language, Landscape, and Place," *Proceedings of the American Philosophical Society* 150, no. 2 (June 2006): 296–317.

49 Minutes of the Common Council, 26 December 1825. The ordinance also appears in *Charter of the City of Boston* (1827), 75–76. For a much earlier version of the ordinance, without the carpet cleaning provision, see *Records Relating to the Early History of Boston,* Boston Town Records, vol. 14 (1757), 326–327.

50 Edward Everett Hale, *A New England Boyhood* (Boston: Little, Brown, and Company, 1928), 64; Hale, "The Story of Boston Common. A Pleasure Ground," in *Wide Awake: An Illustrated Magazine,* vol. AA (Boston: D. Lothrop, 1888), 321. Hale wrote a humorous piece for the *Boston Advertiser* called "The Last Shake" about the last man to clean a carpet on the Common, but I have been unable to locate it. A summary appears in Thomas Wentworth Higginson, *Carlyle's Laugh and Other Surprises* (Boston: Houghton Mifflin, 1909), 162.

51 *Boston Daily Advertiser,* 24 December 1825, p. 2; Hale, "Story of Boston Common," 321.

52 Hale, *New England Boyhood,* 78; "Communication. Boston Common," in *Boston Commercial Gazette* 71, no. 5 (July 3, 1826), 2.

53 Minutes of the Mayor and Aldermen, 10 May 1830, 114.

54 Minutes of the Mayor and Aldermen, 19 May 1828, 152. For elite attempts to control working-class recreation later in the century, see Roy Rosenzweig, *Eight Hours for What We Will: Workers and Leisure in an Industrial City, 1870–1920* (New York: Cambridge University Press, 1983).

55 The literature on the enclosure of common lands in England is vast, and scholars disagree on everything from the chronology and causes of enclosure to its social and economic impact. For a review of the historiography to the early 1980s, see Jerome Blum, "English Parliamentary Enclosure," *Journal of Modern History* 53, no. 3 (September 1981): 477–504. For subsequent revisionist work that paints enclosure as less profitable for landowners and more damaging to commoners than previously thought, see Gregory Clark, "Commons Sense: Common Property Rights, Efficiency, and Institutional Change," *Journal of Economic History* 58, no. 1 (March 1998): 73–102; J. M. Neeson, *Commoners: Common Right, Enclosure and Social Change in England, 1700–1820* (Cambridge: Cambridge University Press, 1993); and Robert C. Allen, *Enclosure and the Yeoman: The Agricultural Development of the South Midlands, 1450–1850* (Oxford: Clarendon Press, 1992). The literature on enclosure in America has focused almost entirely on the informal use of undeveloped rural land and the enclosures that resulted when markets expanded and landowners sought greater control over their properties. For enclosure in the Northeast, see Karl

Jacoby, *Crimes against Nature: Squatters, Poachers, Thieves, and the Hidden History of American Conservation* (Berkeley: University of California Press, 2001); and Judd, *Common Lands, Common People*. For the South, see Shawn Everett Kantor, *Politics and Property Rights: The Closing of the Open Range in the Postbellum South* (Chicago: University of Chicago Press, 1998); R. Ben Brown, "The Southern Range: A Study in Nineteenth-Century Law and Society" (Ph.D. diss., University of Michigan, 1993); and Steven Hahn, *The Roots of Southern Populism: Yeomen Farmers and the Transformation of the Georgia Upcountry, 1850–1890* (New York: Oxford University Press, 1983). For the West, see Louis S. Warren, *The Hunter's Game: Poachers and Conservationists in Twentieth-Century America* (New Haven: Yale University Press, 1997).

56 For the role played by common land in the establishment of England's park system, see Hazel Conway, *People's Parks: The Design and Development of Victorian Parks in Britain* (Cambridge: Cambridge University Press, 1991).

57 Images from the 1820s appear in Ayer, *Early Days on Boston Common*, 31; *Bowen's Picture of Boston, or the Citizen's and Stranger's Guide to the Metropolis of Massachusetts, and Its Environs* (Boston: A. Bowen, 1829), opposite cover page; and Sinclair H. Hitchings and Catherine H. Farlow, *A New Guide to the Massachusetts State House* (Boston: John Hancock Mutual Life Insurance Company, 1964), 108. Another, entitled "The State House and Boston Common," appears in the collections of the Bostonian Society, Case H, EV 23. For earlier views, see especially Ayer, *Early Days on Boston Common*, 20 and 26. Also see Friends of the Public Garden, *Boston Common*.

58 *Boston Columbian Centinel*, 23 May, 1829. The reviewer was commenting on James Kidder's *Boston Common*, published by Abel Bowen in 1829. For the pastoral in American painting, see Sarah Burns, *Pastoral Inventions: Rural Life in Nineteenth-Century American Art and Culture* (Philadelphia: Temple University Press, 1989).

59 For published images of the tableware discussed, see Hitchings and Farlow, *New Guide to the State House*, 78–79. The Bostonian Society and Historic New England house collections of such pieces. The political importance of rural imagery to Boston's upper classes is discussed in Tamara Plakins Thornton, *Cultivating Gentlemen: The Meaning of Country Life among the Boston Elite, 1785–1860* (New Haven: Yale University Press, 1989).

60 Ann Bermingham, *Landscape and Ideology: The English Rustic Tradition, 1740–1850* (Berkeley: University of California, 1986). Also see John Barrell, *The Dark Side of the Landscape: The Rural Poor in English Painting, 1730–1840* (Cambridge: Cambridge University Press, 1980). For the parallel movement in English poetry, see Raymond Williams, *The Country and the City* (New York: Oxford University Press, 1973).

61 For women approaching Otis about removing the cows, see Morison, *Harrison*

Gray Otis, 458. This volume remains the most complete biography of Otis, but it must be used with caution because Morison was not as critical of Otis (who was the author's great-great-grandfather) as he believed himself to be. This is a reworking of his more extensively annotated *The Life and Letters of Harrison Gray Otis, Federalist, 1765–1848* (Boston: Houghton Mifflin, 1913), which is the published form of his dissertation. The two petitions, one sponsored by William Foster and the other by Benjamin Smith, have been lost.

62 Petition of Jacob Kuhn and Others, 29 April 1829, City of Boston Archives.

63 Petition of Amos Lawrence and Others, March 1830, City of Boston Archives.

64 Morison, *Harrison Gray Otis,* 459n.; and Lawrence, *Old Park Street,* 102–103.

65 Petition of B. Smith and Others, 22 March 1830, City of Boston Archives. See the Note on Boston Common Petitions for the statistical analysis that underpins my interpretation of the petitions discussed in this and the following paragraphs.

66 Hale, *New England Boyhood,* 65; Caroline Wells Healey Dall, *"Alongside": Being Notes Suggested by "A New England Boyhood" of Doctor Edward Everett Hale* (Boston: Thomas Todd, 1900), 23.

67 Petition of B. Smith and Others, 22 March 1830, City of Boston Archives.

68 Petition of Daniel Rhodes and Others, 22 March 1830, City of Boston Archives.

69 Petition of Elijah Morse, and Others, 10 April 1830, City of Boston Archives; Petition of Oliver Davis, and Others, 12 April 1830, City of Boston Archives.

70 Petition of Oliver Davis, and Others, 12 April 1830, City of Boston Archives; Petition of Elijah Morse, and Others, 10 April 1830, City of Boston Archives.

71 Minutes of the Mayor and Aldermen, 10 May 1830, 112–113, City of Boston Archives. Echoing Otis, Samuel Eliot Morison considered the cows an "amusing" holdover from a more rural culture. See Morison, *Harrison Gray Otis,* 458–460.

72 Petition of Robert Cummings, 7 June 1830, City of Boston Archives.

73 Petition of James Hendley, 21 June 1830, City of Boston Archives. For the invocation of customary use to protect access to natural resources in England, see E. P. Thompson, *Whigs and Hunters: The Origins of the Black Act* (London: Allen Lane, 1975); and Thompson, "Custom, Law and Common Right," in Thompson, *Customs in Common: Studies in Traditional Popular Culture* (New York: New Press, 1993), 97–184. For a discussion of whether letting pigs run in the streets of nineteenth-century New York City constituted a customary right, see Hartog, "Pigs and Positivism."

74 Minutes of the Mayor and Aldermen, 13 July 1830, 182, City of Boston Archives. Ever Otis's defender, Samuel Eliot Morison called the arrangement "a happy compromise." Morison, *Harrison Gray Otis,* 459. The banning of the cows provided a precedent for later attempts to regulate the use of the Common by military companies. See Clement Hugh Hill, *Opinion of the Assistant*

City Solicitor on the Right of the City Government to Regulate the Use of the Common (1870, City Document No. 52).

75 Shurtleff, *Topographical Description,* 338. The banning of the cows would be Otis' sole legacy as mayor. "The only thing Grandfather Otis did for Boston," joked his grandchildren, "was to exclude cows from the Common" (Morison, *Harrison Gray Otis,* 456).

76 "An Act to Authorize the Enclosing of a Part of Cambridge Common," in Massachusetts General Court, *Laws of the Commonwealth of Massachusetts,* vol. XI (Boston: Dutton and Wentworth, 1831), 503–504; and Commonwealth of Massachusetts, *Report Relating to the Enclosure of Cambridge Common,* Senate No. 23 (Boston: 1832).

77 See Barber, *Boston Common,* 146–161 generally. For the iron fence, also see Shurtleff, *Topographical Description,* 318; and Ayer, *Early Days on Boston Common,* 58.

78 Harrison Gray Otis to William Hayden, Jr., 21? April 1836, Harrison Gray Otis Papers, Massachusetts Historical Society.

79 Nathaniel Hawthorne, *Passages from the American Note-Books,* vol. 18 of *The Complete Writings of Nathaniel Hawthorne,* 22 vols. (Boston: Houghton, Mifflin, 1900), 275 (entry for April 19, 1840); Adams, *Boston Common* (1842), 44.

80 For proposals to change the name of the Common and Frog Pond, see Shurtleff, *Topographical Description,* 328, 348–349. For the confused Londoner, see Barber, *Boston Common,* 150.

81 Nehemiah Adams, *The Boston Common, or Rural Walks in Cities* (Boston: George W. Light, 1838), 19, 13.

82 Oliver Wendell Holmes, *The Poet at the Breakfast-Table: His Talks with His Fellow-Boarders and the Reader* (Boston: James R. Osgood, 1876), 369; Sophia Hawthorne is quoted in Fischer, "Boston Common," 138.

83 Examples of images that adopt this perspective include Hammett Billings' "Boston Common," reprinted in Friends of the Public Garden, *Boston Common,* 35; an anonymous oil painting of Boston Common in the collection of Historic New England (no. 1949.559); and George Harvey's painting "Afternoon Rainbow: Boston Common from Charles Street Mall."

84 Adams, *Boston Common,* 48. Harvey's painting is reprinted in Hitchings and Farlow, *New Guide to the State House,* 87; and in Friends of the Public Garden, *Boston Common,* 29. For haymaking scenes in contemporary paintings, see Burns, *Pastoral Inventions,* 32–34.

85 Domosh, *Invented Cities,* 129. For books devoted to the Old Elm, see John C. Warren, *The Great Elm on Boston Common* (John Wilson and Son, 1855); Robert Cassie Waterston, *Story of the Old Elm on Boston Common* (Boston: John Wilson and Son, 1876); and John W. Hamilton, "Historical Sketch of the Great Tree," in *Memorial of Jesse Lee and the Old Elm* (Boston: J. P. Magee, 1875), 45–55. For

poetry, see *Boston Monthly Magazine,* June 1826, 53; and Eliza, *The Old Elm and the Fountain on Boston Common* (Boston: R. F. Foster, 1853). The special significance attached to elm trees by New Englanders is explored in Thomas J. Campanella, *Republic of Shade: New England and the American Elm* (New Haven: Yale University Press, 2003). Caleb Snow's *A History of Boston, the Metropolis of Massachusetts, from Its Origin to the Present Period* (Boston: A. Bowen, 1825), which was written before the removal of the cows, devotes barely one of its 400 pages to Boston Common. For upper-class efforts to defend the Common from encroachment, see Domosh, *Invented Cities,* 135–141.

86 Curtis, *Life of Campestris Ulm,* 65–67.

87 For the effect of the Common on downtown growth, see Domosh, *Invented Cities,* chapter 5; and Walter Firey, *Land Use in Central Boston* (Cambridge: Harvard University Press, 1947).

88 James N. Levitt, "Palladium of the People," argues that Boston Common also influenced the conservation and preservation movements in America.

89 *Boston Evening Transcript,* 6 August 1850. The expression "nature's nectar" appears in William Bingham Tappan and George Russell, *Celebration Hymns, on the Introduction of the Cochituate Water in Boston, October 25, 1848* (Boston: Old Dickinson Printing Office, 1848).

2. Constructing Water

1 Detailed descriptions of the parade appear in *Celebration of the Introduction of the Water of Lake Cochituate into the City of Boston, October 25, 1848* (Boston: J. H. Eastburn, 1848); and *Illustrated Mail–Extra,* 25 October 1848, Cabot Science Library, Harvard University.

2 For a sampling of histories that explore the creation of urban water systems during the antebellum period, see Martin V. Melosi, *The Sanitary City: Urban Infrastructure in America from Colonial Times to the Present* (Baltimore: Johns Hopkins University Press, 2000); Gerard T. Koeppel, *Water for Gotham: A History* (Princeton: Princeton University Press, 2000); Sarah S. Elkind, *Bay Cities and Water Politics: The Battle for Resources in Boston and Oakland* (Lawrence: University Press of Kansas, 1998); Thomas F. Armstrong, "Not for 'Barter and Speculation': A Comparative Study of Antebellum Virginia Urban Water Supply," *Southern Studies* 18, no. 3 (1979): 304–319; Sam Bass Warner, Jr., *The Private City: Philadelphia in Three Periods of Its Growth* (Philadelphia: University of Pennsylvania Press, 1968); and Nelson M. Blake, *Water for the Cities: A History of the Urban Water Supply Problem in the United States* (Syracuse, N.Y.: Syracuse University Press, 1956).

3 Little specific information about the city's water resources before the construction of the Cochituate works has survived. Questions about who owned particular sources, who used them, and how they used them can be answered

only in broad outline. The most informative sources are Nathaniel B. Shurtl-eff, *A Topographical and Historical Description of Boston* (Boston: Noyes, Holmes, 1872), chapters 29–31, and the town records in City of Boston, *Report of the Record Commissioners of the City of Boston* (Boston: Municipal Printing Office, 1876–1909). The following paragraphs draw largely on these sources.

4 Boston's water debates are discussed briefly in Elkind, *Bay Cities and Water Politics*, 17–27, and Charles David Jacobson, *Ties that Bind: Economic and Political Dilemmas of Urban Utility Networks, 1800–1990* (Pittsburgh: University of Pittsburgh Press, 2000), 32–42, and more extensively in Blake, *Water for the Cities*, and Nathaniel J. Bradlee, *History of the Introduction of Pure Water into the City of Boston, with a Description of Its Cochituate Waterworks* (Boston: Alfred Mudge and Son, 1868).

5 There is little literature on the different meanings that social groups in the United States have assigned to water. For a global perspective, see *A History of Water*, vol. 3: *The World of Water*, ed. Terje Tvedt and Terje Oestigaard (London: I. B. Tauris, 2006).

6 For the Waltham Company and private property owners making their wells accessible to the public, see City of Boston, *Statement of Evidence before the Committee of the Legislature at the Session of 1839, on the Petition of the City of Boston, for the Introduction of Pure Soft Water* (Boston: John H. Eastburn, City Printer, 1839), 25 and 35; and Walter Channing, *A Plea for Pure Water: Being a Letter to Henry Williams, esq., by Walter Channing: With an Address "To the Citizens of Boston," by Mr. H. Williams* (Boston: S. N. Dickinson, 1844), 7. For a discussion of how the antebellum culture of privatism encouraged the use of wells, cisterns, and private water companies over municipal waterworks, see Maureen Ogle, "Water Supply, Waste Disposal, and the Culture of Privatism in the Mid-Nineteenth-Century American City," *Journal of Urban History* 25, no. 3 (1999): 321–347.

7 Melosi discusses private water companies in *Sanitary City*, chapter 4.

8 Boston's power to levy special assessments evolved over the course of the century. For example, assessments on sidewalk construction emerged as early as 1799, but the legislature did not grant permission to levy assessments for street widening until 1866. The one constant seems to have been that Boston was never very good at collecting the money it was owed. See Charles Phillips Huse, *The Financial History of Boston, from May 1, 1822, to January 31, 1909* (Cambridge: Harvard University Press, 1916). For Chicago, see Robin L. Einhorn, *Property Rules: Political Economy in Chicago, 1833–1872* (Chicago: University of Chicago Press, 1991).

9 Josiah Quincy, *A Municipal History of the Town and City of Boston, During Two Centuries. From September 17, 1630, to September 17, 1830* (Boston: Charles C. Lit-

tle and James Brown, 1852), 160 and 176; and John C. Warren to Josiah Quincy, 25 November 1825, Quincy Family Papers, Massachusetts Historical Society.

10 Loammi Baldwin, *Report on Introducing Pure Water into the City of Boston,* 2nd ed., with additions (Boston: Hilliard, Gray, 1835), 75–78. For the quality of cistern water, see Hale, *Proceedings,* 120; and Theodore Lyman, Jr., *Communication to the City Council, on the Subject of Introducing Water in the City* (Boston: J. H. Eastburn, 1834), 7–8. Samuel Eliot estimated the number of cisterns in the city at approximately 2,000. Samuel A. Eliot, *Soft Water,* City Document No. 19 (Boston: 1839), 13.

11 Knapp and Cushing's testimony appear in City of Boston, *Statement of Evidence,* 21 and 3, respectively. See Christopher Hamlin, *A Science of Impurity: Water Analysis in Nineteenth Century Britain* (Berkeley: University of California Press, 1990), for the development of a scientific standard of water purity in Great Britain.

12 For the lack of water generally, see Nathan Hale, *Proceedings Before a Joint Special Committee of the Massachusetts Legislature, Upon the Petition of the City of Boston, for Leave to Introduce a Supply of Pure Water into that City, From Long Pond, February and March, 1845* (Boston: John H. Eastburn, 1845), 68–72; and Baldwin, *Report on Pure Water,* 75–78. For immigrants paying six dollars a pail, see Baldwin, *Report on Pure Water,* 75–77. For the property owner who removed his cistern, see Channing, *Plea for Pure Water,* 7; for the resident of Fort Hill, see City of Boston, *Statement of Evidence,* 35.

13 For praise of London's system, see for example *Practice Against Theory. The Experience of England against the Estimates of Commissioners,* 13 May 1845, Massachusetts Historical Society. For a social and economic analysis of the tension between private and public control of urban water resources in Great Britain, see John Hassan, *A History of Water in Modern England and Wales* (Manchester: Manchester University Press, 1998). For a revisionist interpretation of private water companies in London, see David Sunderland, "'Disgusting to the imagination and destructive of health'? The Metropolitan Supply of Water, 1820–52," *Urban History* 30, no. 3 (2003): 359–380. On the profitability of the Boston Aqueduct Corporation, see L. M. Sargent, *Boston Aqueduct and the City of Boston* (Boston: Dutton and Wentworth, 1849), 7.

14 Prudence, *Another View on the Subject of Water* (Boston: n.d., c. 1846), 3. For a defense of private water in Boston, see L. M. Sargent, *Mr. Sargent's Communication* (Boston: 1838).

15 For complaints about the Boston Aqueduct Corporation, see Hale, *Proceedings,* 35–36 and 71–72; and Channing, *Plea for Pure Water,* 9–10.

16 Samuel A. Eliot, *Soft Water,* City Document No. 25 (Boston: 1839), 14–15. For another critique of private water, see Nathan Hale, *Inquiry into the Best Mode of*

Supplying the City of Boston with Water for Domestic Purposes, in Reply to the Pamphlets of Mr. Wilkins and Mr. Shattuck, and Also to Some of the Representations to the Committee of the Legislature, on the Hearing of the Petition of the City (Boston: Eastburn's Press, 1845).

17 Paul Boyer, *Urban Masses and Moral Order in America, 1820–1920* (Cambridge: Harvard University Press, 1978).

18 For the experience of Irish immigrants in Boston, see Oscar Handlin, *Boston's Immigrants: A Study in Acculturation,* rev. ed. (Cambridge: Belknap Press of Harvard University Press, 1959). For violence, see Jack Tager, *Boston Riots: Three Centuries of Social Violence* (Boston: Northeastern University Press, 2001).

19 Ralph Waldo Emerson to Thomas Carlyle, 30 October 1840, in Joseph Slater, ed., *The Correspondence of Emerson and Carlyle* (New York: Columbia University Press, 1964), 283; Van Wyck Brooks, *The Flowering of New England, 1815–1865* (New York: E. P. Dutton, 1936), 7. For a fuller portrait of the reform impulse in antebellum Boston, see Thomas H. O'Connor, *The Athens of America: Boston 1825–1845* (Amherst: University of Massachusetts Press, 2006).

20 Channing, *Plea for Pure Water,* 6–7. Although urban historians have emphasized the importance of sanitary reform in the antebellum movement for public water, they generally do not embed water movements fully within the broad climate of social reform that defined the era. Scholars of antebellum reform, for their part, rarely discuss debates over urban water supplies, perhaps because water movements drew support from a variety of different causes (temperance, health, charity) and therefore fit awkwardly into the framework traditionally employed to understand the period. In fact, most "environmental" reforms, such as parks and model tenement houses, do not appear in the standard syntheses of antebellum reform, despite the impact they had on urban populations. See Ronald G. Walters, *American Reformers, 1815–1860,* rev. ed. (New York: Hill and Wang, 1997); and Steven Mintz, *Moralists and Modernizers: America's Pre-Civil War Reformers* (Baltimore: Johns Hopkins University Press, 1995).

21 Warner, *Private City,* 109; Koeppel, *Water for Gotham,* 124.

22 Noah Webster, *Collection of Papers on the Subject of Bilious Fevers, Prevalent in the United States for a Few Years Past* (New York: Hopkins, Webb, 1796), iv. For the connection between the sanitary idea and the construction of urban water systems, see Melosi, *The Sanitary City.*

23 Edwin Chadwick, *Report on the Sanitary Condition of the Labouring Population of Great Britain,* ed. M. W. Flinn (1842; Edinburgh: Edinburgh University Press, 1965). For an anthropological perspective on the relationship between ideas of pollution and the social order, see Mary Douglas, *Purity and Danger: An Analysis of Concepts of Pollution and Taboo* (New York: Praeger, 1966). Douglas

argues that "certain moral rules are upheld and certain social rules defined by beliefs in dangerous contagion" (3).

24 Most of Chadwick's biographers have praised him for his contribution to the evolution of modern public health. For a more critical perspective that treats his report as a political document, see Christopher Hamlin, *Public Health and Social Justice in the Age of Chadwick: Britain, 1800–1854* (Cambridge: Cambridge University Press, 1998).

25 Channing, *Plea for Pure Water,* 4; and Eliot, *Soft Water,* City Document No. 19, 9. For Channing's role within the fledgling medical specialty of obstetrics, see Amalie M. Kass, *Midwifery and Medicine in Boston: Walter Channing, M.D., 1786– 1876* (Boston: Northeastern University Press, 2002).

26 Petition of John C. Warren, et al., 4 August 1835, City of Boston Archives; and City of Boston, *Statement of Evidence,* 37–41. Thirteen years later, Bostonians would remember the petition as an important step toward the adoption of municipal water. See *Illustrated Mail–Extra,* 1.

27 Hayward and Randall's opinions are from Lyman, *Communication to the City Council,* 8–13; for New York City, see Blake, *Water for the Cities,* 249–251; for London, see Hamlin, *A Science of Impurity,* 107–109.

28 Hale, *Proceedings,* 16; *Memorial Presented to the Board of Common Councilmen by the Boston Aqueduct Corporation on May 19, 1838* (Boston: 1838), 4–5. Derby's opinion, although uninformed by scientific evidence, was actually closer to the present-day medical understanding. Hard water, which is high in dissolved minerals, especially calcium and magnesium, is a nuisance but not a health hazard. The water-related ailments encountered by Boston's doctors in the nineteenth century likely resulted from groundwater impurities unrelated to its hardness.

29 "Supply of Water to the Metropolis," *Edinburgh Review* 91 (1849), reprinted in *Public Health in the Victorian Age: Debates on the Issue from Nineteenth Century Critical Journals,* ed. Ruth G. Hodgkinson (Farnborough, Hants.: Gregg, 1973), 384. For a social and cultural history of personal cleanliness, see Richard L. Bushman and Claudia L. Bushman, "The Early History of Cleanliness in America," *Journal of American History* 74 (March 1988), 1213–1238. For the origins of moral environmentalism, see Stanley K. Schultz, *Constructing Urban Culture: American Cities and City Planning, 1800–1920* (Philadelphia: Temple University Press, 1989), 112–114.

30 Channing, *Plea for Pure Water,* 14.

31 Channing, *Plea for Pure Water,* 8.

32 For the use of alcohol during this period, see W. J. Rorabaugh, *The Alcoholic Republic: An American Tradition* (New York: Oxford University Press, 1979). Temperance as social control is discussed in Ian R. Tyrrell, *Sobering Up: From*

Temperance to Prohibition in Antebellum America, 1800–1860 (Westport, Conn.: Greenwood Press, 1979); and Paul E. Johnson, *A Shopkeeper's Millennium: Society and Revivals in Rochester, New York, 1815–1837* (New York: Hill and Wang, 1978). For the structure and composition of the temperance movement in Massachusetts during this period, see Robert L. Hampel, *Temperance and Prohibition in Massachusetts, 1813–1852* (Ann Arbor, Mich.: UMI Research Press, 1982).

33 For Tilden, see City of Boston, *Statement of Evidence,* 56; for Channing's friend, see Channing, *Plea for Pure Water,* 15. Historians of temperance have paid little attention to the role played by temperance advocates in bringing municipal water to American cities, and the evidence does not support Rorabaugh's claim that temperance reformers waited until *after* cities improved water supplies before supporting the substitution of water for alcohol. See Rorabaugh, *Alcoholic Republic,* 97.

34 John Pierpont, ed., *The Cold Water Melodies, and Washingtonian Songster* (Boston: Theodore Abbot, 1842), 31 and 37; and Pierpont, "Lift Up, Lift Up the Standard," in *Airs of Palestine, and Other Poems* (Boston: James Munroe, 1840), 197. Pierpont's son, James, inherited his father's musical talent and composed "Jingle Bells" in the 1850s.

35 For Noah, see John Howard Bryant, "Lines Read Before the Princeton, (Bureau County,) Washingtonian Society," in *Poems by John Howard Bryant* (New York: D. Appleton, 1855), 183–184; for Moses, see Pierpont, "In Eden's Green Retreats," in *Airs of Palestine,* 188–189.

36 Anonymous, "Water," in *The Crystal Gem,* ed. John Stowell Adams (Boston: G. W. Cottrell, 1853), 27.

37 Pierpont, "Lift Up, Lift Up the Standard," in *Airs of Palestine,* 197; and William Bingham Tappan and George Russell, *Celebration Hymns, on the Introduction of the Cochituate Water in Boston, October 25, 1848* (Boston: Old Dickinson Printing Office, 1848), Boston Public Library.

38 A Selfish Taxpayer, *Thoughts About Water* (Boston: 1844), 15.

39 Nehemiah Adams, *Boston Common* (Boston: William D. Ticknor and H. B. Williams, 1842), 48 and 49; Channing, *Plea for Pure Water,* 26–27; and Eliot, *Soft Water,* City Document No. 19, 10.

40 Adams, *Boston Common,* 47 and 46. Adams speaks more directly for public water in Nehemiah Adams, "Cochituate Lake," in James T. Fields, ed., *The Boston Book: Being Specimens of Metropolitan Literature* (Boston: Ticknor, Reed, and Fields, 1850), 84–88.

41 Channing, *Plea for Pure Water,* 27. One of the few historical treatments of the social and symbolic roles played by urban fountains is Jean-Pierre Goubert, *The Conquest of Water: The Advent of Health in the Industrial Age,* trans. Andrew Wilson (Princeton: Princeton University Press, 1989), 69–82, 244–245. For An-

drew Jackson Downing's treatment of water generally, see Downing, *A Treatise on the Theory and Practice of Landscape Gardening* (New York: Wiley and Putnam, 1841), 276–295, and for fountains specifically, see 394–401.

42 *Boston Evening Transcript,* 3 September 1844, p. 2.

43 Ibid.

44 For Ware, see Channing, *Plea for Pure Water,* 7–8; for Bowditch, see City of Boston, *Statement of Evidence,* 54–55; for Channing, see Channing, *Plea for Pure Water,* 14. The question of whether water is a right or a privilege remains a subject of heated debate today. See, for example, Ted Steinberg, "Big Is Ugly: Corporate Enclosure and the Global Water Supply," *Technology and Culture* 45, no. 3 (July 2004): 618–623; and Maude Barlow and Tony Clarke, *Blue Gold: The Fight to Stop the Corporate Theft of the World's Water* (New York: New Press, 2002).

45 Adams, ed., *The Crystal Gem,* 5. For other comparisons of water with air and sunshine, see *Illustrated Mail-Extra,* 4; Channing, *Plea for Pure Water,* 35; and Hale, *Inquiry,* 28.

46 *Illustrated Mail-Extra,* 4; Channing, *Plea for Pure Water,* 35. For New York City, see Blake, *Water for the Cities,* 140; for Paris, see André Guillerme, "The Genesis of Water Supply, Distribution, and Sewerage Systems in France, 1800–1850," in *Technology and the Rise of the Networked City in Europe and America,* ed. Joel Tarr and Gabriel Dupuy (Philadelphia: Temple University Press, 1988), 108–109.

47 Walter Channing, *Parliamentary Sketches, and Water Statistics* (Boston: Benjamin H. Greene, 1845), 27. Channing makes a similar case in *Plea for Pure Water,* 24.

48 For the transformation of the physical and legal relationship to water in Lowell, see Theodore Steinberg, *Nature Incorporated: Industrialization and the Waters of New England* (New York: Cambridge University Press, 1991).

49 Hale, *Proceedings,* 12–13.

50 *Boston Courier,* 24 September 1844 and 25 September 1844. Wilkins later republished his views in two pamphlets: John H. Wilkins, *Remarks on Supplying the City of Boston with Pure Water* (Boston: Wilkins, Carter, 1845); and Wilkins, *Further Remarks on Supplying the City of Boston with Pure Water; In Answer Mainly to Inquiry into the Best Mode of Supplying the City of Boston with Water for Domestic Purposes, Etc.* (Boston: Charles C. Little and James Brown, 1845).

51 Selfish Taxpayer, *Thoughts About Water.* The Selfish Taxpayer's "pay for what you get" approach to public services echoes the municipal philosophy explored by Robin Einhorn in *Property Rules.*

52 Hale, *Inquiry,* 5. Henry Williams also opposed a rent-free system. See Channing, *Plea for Pure Water,* 34.

53 L. M. Sargent, *Mr. Sargent's Communication* (Boston: 1838), 8. A reflection of

the popular desire for free water appears in the speech given at the water celebration by Mayor Josiah Quincy, Jr., who twice mentioned the possibility that water would someday be "distributed without cost." Quincy, Jr., in *Celebration of the Introduction of Water,* 40 and 41 (quote is from page 40).

54 Edward Everett Hale, *A New England Boyhood* (Boston: Little, Brown, 1928), xxiii.

55 For opponents of public water and their arguments, see Hale, *Proceedings;* and Elkind, *Bay Cities,* 24.

56 Bradlee, *History of the Introduction of Pure Water,* 17 and 36.

57 Harrison Gray Otis to the Mayor, Aldermen, and Common Council, 9 April 1838, Massachusetts Historical Society.

58 Selfish Taxpayer, *Thoughts About Water,* 5 and 13.

59 For Fletcher, see Hale, *Proceedings,* 111; for his co-counsel, see page 8.

60 Selfish Taxpayer, *Thoughts About Water,* 11.

61 The role of Boston's mayors in the water debates is discussed in Elkind, *Bay Cities,* 22–23. Also see *Mayors of Boston: An Illustrated Epitome of Who the Mayors Have Been and What They Have Done* (Boston: Printed for the State Street Trust Company, 1914).

62 For the testimony of Boston's doctors in support of public water, see City of Boston, *Statement of Evidence,* 37–62. Vote tallies are from Bradlee, *History of the Introduction of Pure Water,* 46–47.

63 For a discussion of the various sources of water available to Boston, see Blake, *Water for the Cities,* chapter 9.

64 Hale, *Inquiry,* 48; and Channing, *Parliamentary Sketches,* 4.

65 Channing, *Parliamentary Sketches,* 22.

66 Ibid., 3.

67 *Boston Daily Argus,* 30 September 1845, quoted in Blake, *Water for the Cities,* 252.

68 "A Drop of Long Pond Water Magnified by the Solar Microscope" (n.p., c. 1845), Massachusetts Historical Society.

69 John H. Wilkins, *A Review of the Report of the Water Commissioners of 1845; with an Examination of Some of Its Statements and Estimates* (Boston: Freeman and Bolles, 1846), 28.

70 Quoted in Hamlin, *A Science of Impurity,* 115.

71 Blake, *Water for the Cities,* 253.

72 Spot Pond Aqueduct Corporation, unsigned broadside (May 1845), Cabot Science Library, Harvard University; Broadside, signed "A Friend to the Best Water" (1845), Cabot Science Library, Harvard University.

73 Broadside, "Water! Water! Now or Never! Vote for the Water Act" (1846), Cabot Science Library, Harvard University.

74 Lemuel Shattuck, *Letter from Lemuel Shattuck, in Answer to Interrogatories of J. Preston, In Relation to the Introduction of Water into the City of Boston* (Boston: Samuel N. Dickinson, 1845), 9. John B. Blake claims that Shattuck's inability to recognize the city's need for water was a major failure of judgment in an otherwise brilliant career. See Blake, "Lemuel Shattuck and the Boston Water Supply," *Bulletin of the History of Medicine* 29, no. 6 (November–December, 1955): 554–562.

75 Lemuel Shattuck, *Report to the Committee of the City Council Appointed to Obtain the Census of Boston for the Year 1845, Embracing Collateral Facts and Statistical Researches, Illustrating the History and Condition of the Population, and Their Means of Progress and Prosperity* (Boston: John H. Eastburn, 1846), 56–57 and Appendix N.

76 Blake, *Water for the Cities,* 206–209.

77 Ibid., 209–211. For the Boston Total Abstinence Society, see Moses Grant to the Mayor and Aldermen of Boston, 6 July 1846, City of Boston Archives.

78 *Illustrated Mail-Extra.*

79 Ibid.

80 *Celebration of the Introduction of Water,* 43.

81 *History of Boston, from 1630 to 1856* (Boston: F. C. Moore, 1856), 153–159.

82 *Illustrated Mail-Extra,* 3.

83 The best source on the celebration and parade is *Celebration of the Introduction of Water.*

84 *Illustrated Mail-Extra,* 3; and *Celebration of the Introduction of Water,* 13–14.

85 Tappan and Russell, *Celebration Hymns.*

86 *Celebration of the Introduction of Water,* 21–22.

87 Ibid., 10–11.

88 Ibid., 5. Quincy's quote appears on p. 30.

89 Ibid., 44–48.

90 Commonwealth of Massachusetts, *Report of the Bureau of Statistics of Labor, Embracing the Account of Its Operations and Inquiries from August 2, 1869, to March 1, 1870, Inclusive* (Boston: Wright and Potter, 1870), 176.

91 Bradlee, *History of the Introduction of Pure Water,* 290 and 261. For a cultural evaluation of the proliferation of domestic plumbing during this period, see Maureen Ogle, *All the Modern Conveniences: American Household Plumbing, 1840–1890* (Baltimore: Johns Hopkins University Press, 1996).

92 Alan Nevins and Milton Halsey Thomas, eds., *The Diary of George Templeton Strong* (New York: MacMillan, 1952), 1: 210.

93 For images of the fountain on Boston Common, see the cover of George Schnapp, *Cochituate Grand Quick Step* (Boston: Stephen W. Marsh, 1848), Boston Athenaeum; *History of Boston, from 1630 to 1856,* 153; and *A Description of*

the Boston Waterworks, Embracing All the Reservoirs, Bridges, Gates, Pipe Chambers, and Other Objects of Interest, from Lake Cochituate to the City of Boston (Boston: George R. Holbrook, 1848), cover page.

94 *Celebration of the Introduction of Water*, 40–41.

95 Peleg W. Chandler, Esq., *City Solicitor's Opinion Upon the Right to Give the Water to the Children's Friend Society,* City Document No. 13 (Boston: 1850), 7. As late as 1856, the city council appointed a committee to investigate the possibility of making water free. The committee reported unfavorably on the proposal, however, and the issue disappeared. See Bradlee, *History of the Introduction of Pure Water,* 175.

96 Roger Lane, *Policing the City: Boston, 1822–1885* (Cambridge: Harvard University Press, 1967; rpt. New York: Atheneum, 1975), 113.

97 James T. Fields, "The Fountain,—Boston Common," in *Poems* (Boston: William D. Ticknor, 1849), 65–66.

98 Eliza, *The Old Elm and the Fountain on Boston Common* (Boston: R. F. Foster, 1853). For additional poetry on water, see Adams, ed., *Crystal Gem.*

99 Eliza, *The Old Elm,* 11.

100 Nathan Hale, in *Celebration of the Introduction of* Water, 29. For the evolving role of government in public health, see John Duffy, *The Sanitarians: A History of American Public Health* (Urbana: University of Illinois Press, 1990); Barbara G. Rosenkrantz, *Public Health and the State: Changing Views in Massachusetts, 1842–1936* (Cambridge: Harvard University Press, 1972); and John B. Blake, *Public Health in the Town of Boston, 1630–1822* (Cambridge: Harvard University Press, 1959).

3. Inventing the Suburbs

1 Nathaniel Hawthorne, *The Blithedale Romance* (Boston: Ticknor, Reed, and Fields, 1852), 173 and 174. For other contemporary works of literature that grappled with the tension between country and city, see particularly Herman Melville, *Pierre; or, The Ambiguities* (New York: Harper and Brothers, 1852); and Cornelius Matthews, *Big Abel and the Little Manhattan* (New York: Wiley and Putnam, 1845). The painters of the Hudson River School best exemplify the parallel effort in art. See Barbara Novak, *Nature and Culture: American Landscape and Painting, 1825–1875,* 3rd ed. (New York: Oxford University Press, 2007).

2 For works on nineteenth-century suburbanization that emphasize pastoral suburbs or the role of ideas about nature in their construction, see especially Margaret Marsh, *Suburban Lives* (New Brunswick, N.J.: Rutgers University Press, 1990); John R. Stilgoe, *Borderland: Origins of the American Suburb, 1820–1939* (New Haven: Yale University Press, 1988); Robert Fishman, *Bourgeois Utopias: The Rise and Fall of Suburbia* (New York: Basic Books, 1987); David Schuy-

ler, *The New Urban Landscape: The Redefinition of City Form in Nineteenth-Century America* (Baltimore: Johns Hopkins University Press, 1986); and Kenneth T. Jackson, *Crabgrass Frontier: The Suburbanization of the United States* (New York: Oxford University Press, 1985). Raymond Williams, *The Country and the City* (New York: Oxford University Press, 1973), discusses the intellectual construction of the rural-urban dichotomy, and James L. Machor traces the deep historical roots of the quest for an urban-rural synthesis in *Pastoral Cities: Urban Ideals and the Symbolic Landscape of America* (Madison: University of Wisconsin Press, 1987).

3 For the process of municipal fragmentation and consolidation in the Boston area, see George H. McCaffrey, "The Political Disintegration and Reintegration of Metropolitan Boston" (Ph.D. diss., Harvard University, 1937); and James Anthony Merino, "A Great City and Its Suburbs: Attempts to Integrate Metropolitan Boston, 1865–1920" (Ph.D. diss., University of Texas at Austin, 1968). The most sustained treatments of municipal fragmentation and consolidation in an American context are Richardson Dilworth, *The Urban Origins of Suburban Autonomy* (Cambridge: Harvard University Press, 2005); Ann Durkin Keating, *Building Chicago: Suburban Developers and the Creation of a Divided Metropolis* (Columbus: Ohio State University Press, 1988); Jon C. Teaford, *City and Suburb: The Political Fragmentation of Metropolitan America, 1850–1970* (Baltimore: Johns Hopkins University Press, 1979); and Jackson, *Crabgrass Frontier*, chapter 8. Also see Henry C. Binford, *The First Suburbs: Residential Communities on the Boston Periphery, 1815–1860* (Chicago: University of Chicago Press, 1985), chapters 4 and 7. For the role played by municipal boundaries in the sorting of population by race and class, see Gregory R. Weiher, *The Fractured Metropolis: Political Fragmentation and Metropolitan Segregation* (New York: State University of New York Press, 1991). For more recent efforts to consolidate cities and suburbs, see David Rusk, *Cities without Suburbs* (Washington, D.C.: Woodrow Wilson Center Press, 1993).

4 For the history of Roxbury, see Sam Bass Warner, Jr., *Streetcar Suburbs: The Process of Growth in Boston, 1870–1900,* 2nd ed. (Cambridge: Harvard University Press, 1978), 39–42; and Alexander von Hoffman, *Local Attachments: The Making of an American Urban Neighborhood, 1850–1920* (Baltimore: Johns Hopkins University Press, 1994). Older, antiquarian histories include Charles M. Ellis, *The History of Roxbury Town* (Boston: Samuel G. Drake, 1847); Francis S. Drake, *The Town of Roxbury: Its Memorable Persons and Places, Its History and Antiquities, with Numerous Illustrations of Its Old Landmarks and Noted Personages* (Roxbury: published by the author, 1878); and *Glimpses of Early Roxbury, Compiled by the "Mary Warren" Chapter Daughters of the Revolution in the Commonwealth of Massachusetts* (Boston: Merrymount Press, 1895). For the history of Brookline, see the work of Ronald Dale Karr, including Karr, "The Evolution

of an Elite Suburb: Community Structure and Control in Brookline, Massachusetts, 1770–1900" (Ph.D. diss., Boston University, 1981); Karr, "Brookline and the Making of an Elite Suburb," *Chicago History* 13, no. 2 (Summer 1984): 36–47; Karr, "The Transformation of Agriculture in Brookline, 1770–1885," *Historical Journal of Massachusetts* 15, no. 1 (January 1987): 33–49; Karr, "Brookline Rejects Annexation, 1873," in *Suburbia Re-examined,* ed. Barbara M. Kelly (New York: Greenwood Press, 1989), 103–110; and Karr, "Two Centuries of Oligarchy in Brookline," *Historical Journal of Massachusetts* 13, no. 2 (June 1985): 117–128. Also see William P. Marchione, "'Uncommon Suburbs': Suburbanization at the Western Edge of Boston, 1820–1873" (Ph.D. diss., Boston College, 1994). Older, antiquarian histories include Charles Knowles Bolton, *Brookline: The History of a Favored Town* (Brookline: C. A. W. Spencer, 1897); John W. Denehy, *A History of Brookline, Massachusetts, From the First Settlement of Muddy River until the Present Time, 1630–1906, Commemorating the Two Hundredth Anniversary of the Town* (Brookline: Brookline Press, 1906); and John Gould Curtis, *History of the Town of Brookline, Massachusetts* (Boston: Houghton Mifflin, 1933).

5 Thomas Jefferson, *Notes on the State of Virginia* (Richmond: J. W. Randolph, 1853), 176; Benjamin Franklin and William Temple Franklin, *Memoirs of the Life and Writings of Benjamin Franklin,* vol. 2 (London: A. J. Valpy, 1818), 117. For the agrarian ideal, see Thomas Bender, *Toward an Urban Vision: Ideas and Institutions in Nineteenth Century America* (Baltimore: Johns Hopkins University Press, 1975), chapter 1; and Tamara Plakins Thornton, *Cultivating Gentlemen: The Meaning of Country Life among the Boston Elite, 1785–1860* (New Haven: Yale University Press, 1989).

6 For the environmental and industrial impact of immigration to Boston, see Oscar Handlin, *Boston's Immigrants: A Study in Acculturation,* rev. ed. (Cambridge: Belknap Press of Harvard University Press, 1959).

7 The classic work on nativism is John Higham, *Strangers in the Land: Patterns of American Nativism, 1860–1925,* 2nd ed. (New Brunswick, N.J.: Rutgers University Press, 1988).

8 For the development of the suburban ideal, see especially Jackson, *Crabgrass Frontier,* chapter 3; Schuyler, *New Urban Landscape,* chapter 8; Stilgoe, *Borderland,* part 1; and John Archer, "Country and City in the American Romantic Suburb," *Journal of the Society of Architectural Historians* 42, no. 2 (May 1983): 139–156.

9 For more detailed descriptions of Boston's nearest neighbors during this period, see John Hayward, *A Gazetteer of Massachusetts, Containing Descriptions of All the Counties, Towns and Districts in the Commonwealth* (Boston: John Hayward, 1847).

10 For the growth of Boston's countryside during the antebellum period, see in

particular Binford, *First Suburbs;* and Peter R. Knights, *The Plain People of Boston, 1830–1860* (New York: Oxford University Press, 1971), chapter 6.

11 McCaffrey, "Disintegration and Reintegration of Metropolitan Boston," 1–9. Municipal organization in New England is different from most other regions of the United States because the area never contained large, unincorporated townships with weak governments. Instead, New Englanders divided newly settled regions into municipalities called towns that exercised corporate powers from a very early date through the direct democracy of town meetings. See Joan C. Williams, "The Invention of the Municipal Corporation: A Case Study in Legal Change," *American University Law Review* 34 (Winter 1985): 369–438.

12 McCaffrey, "Disintegration and Reintegration of Metropolitan Boston," 176–177; Henry David Thoreau, "Slavery in Massachusetts," in *Henry David Thoreau: Collected Essays and Poems* (New York: Library of America, 2001), 339. The process of fragmentation ran in the opposite direction around Chicago: rather than rural areas breaking with developing ones, developing areas broke from rural townships and incorporated as villages to provide themselves with better services. The Midwest's system of large, weak, unincorporated townships helps to explain the difference. See Keating, *Building Chicago,* especially chapter 5.

13 The several antiquarian histories of Roxbury contain descriptions of the town. See Ellis, *History of Roxbury Town;* Drake, *Town of Roxbury;* and *Glimpses of Early Roxbury.*

14 See prior note. For the history of Jamaica Plain, see von Hoffman, *Local Attachments.*

15 On the changing meaning of the word suburb, see Jackson, *Crabgrass Frontier,* chapter 1.

16 Von Hoffman, *Local Attachments,* 2.

17 For summaries of the many efforts to divide the town, see Thomas Gray, *Half Century Sermon, Delivered on Sunday Morning, April 24, 1842, at Jamaica Plain* (Boston: I. R. Butts, 1842), 36–37; and Arthur W. Austin, *Address at Dedication of the Town-House at Jamaica Plain, West Roxbury* (Boston: Alfred Mudge and Son, 1866), 21–23. Also see von Hoffman, *Local Attachments,* 287, n. 4, 5, and 7. There were also attempts to divide Roxbury in the eighteenth-century, but at that time residents of upper Roxbury based their complaints on the inconvenience of traveling several miles to town meetings.

18 City of Roxbury, *Report of the Joint Special Committee on Division and Annexation,* Roxbury City Document No. 5 (Roxbury: Norfolk County Journal Press, 1851), 8–10, 18; Austin, *Address,* 23; Commonwealth of Massachusetts, *Report of the Joint Standing Committee on Towns,* Senate No. 82 (1851), 9.

19 Austin, *Address,* 23–24. For Austin's background, see "Biographical Sketches.

Hon. Arthur W. Austin. Collector of the Port of Boston and Charlestown," in *The United States Democratic Review* n.s. 41, no. 4 (April 1858): 307–310.

20　Austin, *Address*, 23–24.

21　Austin, *Address*, 24. For the petition, see *Report of the Joint Standing Committee*, 16.

22　Austin, *Address*, 27.

23　Rufus Choate, *Application of Samuel D. Bradford and Others, To Set Off Wards Six, Seven and Eight, of the City of Roxbury, as a Separate Agricultural Town. Speech of Hon. Rufus Choate, before the Joint Legislative Committee on Towns, Boston, April 4, 1851* (Boston: George C. Rand, 1851), 27.

24　Ibid., 28. Choate was quoting the English poet Abraham Cowley.

25　Austin, *Address*, 27.

26　Hayward, *A Gazetteer of Massachusetts*, 254–255; and Gray, *Half Century Sermon*, 31–32.

27　Choate, *Application of Samuel D. Bradford*, 5 and 31; and Ralph Waldo Emerson, "Farming," in *Society and Solitude. Twelve Chapters* (Boston: Fields, Osgoods, 1870), 124.

28　Choate, *Application*, 29, 39.

29　*Report of the Joint Standing Committee*, 4.

30　The names of the committee members appear in *Report of the Joint Standing Committee*, 4 and 19. The towns they represented can be found in Nahum Capen, ed., *The Massachusetts State Record, New England Register, and Year Book of General Information. 1851*, vol. 5 (Boston: James French, 1851), 12–16.

31　*Report of the Joint Standing Committee*, 19; and Choate, *Application*, 10.

32　*Report of the Joint Standing Committee*, 15.

33　Town of Roxbury, *Report of the Physician to the Almshouse* (n.p., 1846–51); and Hawthorne, *Blithedale Romance*, 286.

34　*Report of the Joint Standing Committee*, 15.

35　Choate, *Application*, 41. Choate was not alone in claiming a moral purpose for urban-suburban transportation systems. See Joel A. Tarr, "From City to Suburb: The 'Moral' Influence of Transportation Technology," in Tarr, *The Search for the Ultimate Sink: Urban Pollution in Historical Perspective* (Akron, Ohio: University of Akron Press, 1996), 309–322.

36　Austin, *Address*, 29–30 and 35. Several years later, officials restored the name to Centre Street, an act that Austin found unpardonable (p. 38). A resident named Charles MacKintosh claimed to have made the motion to change the name back. See MacKintosh, *Some Recollections of the Pastors and People of the Second Church of Old Roxbury* (Salem, Mass.: Newcomb and Gauss, 1901), 68.

37　Town of West Roxbury, *Report of the Selectmen of West Roxbury, April 3, 1854* (n.p.), 34. See p. 32 for the town paupers.

38 From Mayor Frederick Prince's 1881 inaugural address, quoted in Charles Phillips Huse, *The Financial History of Boston: From May 1, 1822, to January 31, 1909* (Cambridge: Harvard University Press, 1916), 227.

39 William Dean Howells, *Suburban Sketches* (New York: Hurd and Houghton, 1871), 16.

40 City of Roxbury, *Report of the Joint Special Committee to Oppose the Petition of Isaac T. Allard and Others, for the Annexation of Roxbury to Boston,* Roxbury City Document No. 7 (Roxbury: Thomas Prince, 1852), 17.

41 Samuel Guild, *A Word for Old Roxbury* (Boston: 1851). The committee appointed to oppose annexation claimed that Guild's pamphlet, together with another he authored, titled *Another Word for Old Roxbury; In Reply to the Report of a Committee in Favor of Annexation* (Boston: J. M. Hewes, 1852), "were largely instrumental in settling, for the present at least, the question of our annexation to Boston." *Report of the Joint Special Committee,* 31. For a response to Guild, see City of Roxbury, *Report of the Committee in Favor of the Union of Boston and Roxbury* (Boston: Eastburn's Press, 1851).

42 For Chelsea, see Teaford, *City and Suburb,* 55; for Charlestown, see Merino, "A Great City and Its Suburbs," 4–5.

43 George Morey and Others, *Annexation of Roxbury and Boston. Remonstrance of Bostonians Against the Measure. Opinion of Josiah Quincy, Governor Andrew, and Others* (Boston: Press of Geo. C. Rand and Avery, 1865), 3 and 4. For the city in American thought, see Andrew Lees, *Cities Perceived: Urban Society in European and American Thought, 1820–1940* (New York: Columbia University Press, 1985); and Morton and Lucia White, *The Intellectual versus the City: From Thomas Jefferson to Frank Lloyd Wright* (Cambridge: Harvard University Press, 1962).

44 John C. Clifford, *Argument on the Question of the Annexation of Roxbury to Boston, Before the Legislative Committee, Thursday, February 23, 1865* (Boston: Wright and Potter, 1867), 4.

45 Jackson, *Crabgrass Frontier,* 142–143. For municipal annexation in other countries during this period, see for example, A. F. Weber, "Suburban Annexations," *North American Review* 166 (May 1898): 612–617; and Greg Stott, "Enhancing Status through Incorporation: Suburban Municipalities in Nineteenth-Century Ontario," *Journal of Urban History* 33, no. 6 (November 2007): 885–910.

46 The trend in Massachusetts toward requiring suburbs to vote on annexation began in 1866, when the governor vetoed an act of union between Roxbury and Boston and forced the legislature to revise the act to require a referendum. Governor Alexander H. Bullock, *Veto and Explanation of an Act to Unite the Cities of Boston and Roxbury,* Senate No. 290 (Boston: Wright and Potter, 1867). For the evolution of local self-determination in general, see Jackson, *Crabgrass*

Frontier, 147–152; and Teaford, *City and Suburb,* 34–39. For Baltimore, see Joseph L. Arnold, "Suburban Growth and Municipal Annexation in Baltimore, 1745–1918," *Maryland Historical Magazine* 73, no. 2 (1978), 113.

47 For the migration of Bostonians to the countryside, see Binford, *First Suburbs,* 126–142.

48 City of Roxbury, *Report of the Commissioners Appointed by the City Councils of the Cities of Boston and Roxbury, Respectively, on the Union of the Two Cities Under One Municipal Government,* Roxbury City Document No. 3 (Boston: Wright and Potter, 1867), 26.

49 Nathaniel B. Shurtleff, *A Topographical and Historical Description of Boston,* 2nd ed., rev. (Boston: Noyes, Holmes, 1872), 34. For a summary of the several attempts to annex Roxbury, see Clifford, *Argument on the Question,* 6–7.

50 J. S. Potter, *Speech of Hon. J. S. Potter, of Arlington, on the Subject of Uniting Certain Cities and Towns with the City of Boston: Delivered in the Massachusetts Senate, Thursday, April 24, 1873* (Boston: Wright and Potter, 1873), 72. The argument that density rather than size produces urban problems was understandably popular among annexationists. It also appears in M. E. Ingalls, *Argument of Hon. M. E. Ingalls, in Favor of Annexation to Boston of Brighton, Brookline & W. Roxbury, Before Committee on Towns, Monday, April 18, 1870* (Boston: Alfred Mudge and Son, 1870), 11.

51 Von Hoffman, *Local Attachments,* 173–177.

52 Ingalls, *Argument in Favor of Annexation,* 7–8.

53 Von Hoffman, *Local Attachments,* 177–180.

54 Ibid.; and McCaffrey, "Disintegration and Reintegration of Metropolitan Boston," 267.

55 For the environmental racism faced by the Irish, see Handlin, *Boston's Immigrants;* David R. Roediger, *The Wages of Whiteness: Race and the Making of the American Working Class* (New York: Verso, 1991); and Charles E. Rosenberg, *The Cholera Years: The United States in 1832, 1849, and 1866* (Chicago: University of Chicago Press, 1962). For the relationships between urban immigrants and nature more generally, see Adam Rome, "Nature Wars, Culture Wars: Immigration and Environmental Reform in the Progressive Era," *Environmental History* 13, no. 3 (July 2008): 432–453.

56 Andrew Eliot Belknap [unsigned], *Boston Daily Times and Bay State Democrat,* 22 July 1850, in Boston Common Papers, Massachusetts Historical Society.

57 James Boyd, "Centennial Anniversary Address," in *The Constitution and By-Laws of the Charitable Irish Society of Boston* (Boston: James F. Cotter, 1876), 51.

58 There was some effort mid-century to ship Irish immigrants out of Boston to work in the countryside, which supposedly offered a more wholesome environment. See Edward Everett Hale, *Letters on Irish Emigration* (Boston: Phillips,

Sampson, 1852), 35–37. For the immigrant vote in West Roxbury, see von Hoffman, *Local Attachments,* 180.

59 *Daily Boston Globe,* 8 October 1873, 5; Branch Alliance of the All Souls Unitarian Church, *The Roxbury Magazine* (Boston: George H. Ellis, 1899), 28.

60 West Roxbury's development after 1870 is explored in Warner, *Streetcar Suburbs,* chapter 6.

61 Warner, *Streetcar Suburbs,* 45; Branch Alliance, *Roxbury Magazine,* 29.

62 For the development of the Emerald Necklace, see Cynthia Zaitzevsky, *Frederick Law Olmsted and the Boston Park System* (Cambridge: Belknap Press of Harvard University Press, 1992).

63 Residents of Brookline based their claim to being "the richest town in the world" on real estate valuation. See, for example, Denehy, *A History of Brookline,* 5.

64 Karr, "Evolution of an Elite Suburb," 176–179, contains useful population statistics. To gain a visual sense for how quickly the northern part of Brookline developed after the coming of the railroad, and how long the south remained rural, consult the property maps created by Theodore F. Jones in *Land Ownership in Brookline from the First Settlement,* Publication No. 5 of the Brookline Historical Society (Brookline, Mass.: Riverdale Press, 1923). The maps detail the town's development from 1636 to 1916.

65 Frederick Law Olmsted et al., *Report to the Staten Island Improvement Commission of a Preliminary Scheme of Improvements* (1871), in *Landscape into Cityscape: Frederick Law Olmsted's Plans for a Greater New York City,* ed. Albert Fein (Ithaca: Cornell University Press, 1967), 180. For the development in the 1850s of the idea that suburbs should be a blend of city and country, see Archer, "Country and City."

66 Mary W. Poor, *Recollections of Brookline* (Brookline, Mass.: The Riverdale Press, 1903), 6; William B. Tappan, "Brookline," *Littell's Living Age,* no. 42 (1 March 1845): 576; see Longfellow's "A Gleam of Sunshine"; Taylor is quoted in Edward Atkinson, *Edward Atkinson, His "Egotistigraphy"* (unpublished ms., Massachusetts Historical Society), 15.

67 Andrew Jackson Downing, *A Treatise on the Theory and Practice of Landscape Gardening* (New York: Wiley and Putnam, 1841), 56. Downing was a major force in the development and popularization of the suburban ideal in America. See David Schuyler, *Apostle of Taste: Andrew Jackson Downing, 1815–1852* (Baltimore: Johns Hopkins University Press, 1996).

68 For elite control over Brookline's environment, see Karr, "Evolution of an Elite Suburb," chapter 6; and Karr, "Brookline and the Making of an Elite Suburb," 46.

69 Cynthia Zaitzevsky, "Frederick Law Olmsted in Brookline: A Preliminary

Study of His Public Projects," in *Proceedings of the Brookline Historical Society for 1977* (Brookline, Mass.: Brookline Historical Society, 1977), 46.

70 See the statistical analysis of Brookline's class structure in Karr, "Evolution of an Elite Suburb," 214–223. Karr attributes Brookline's early and persistent commitment to urban services to an ideology he calls "compulsory excellence," which emerged from the progressive spirit embedded in the Unitarian faith and Whig politics of the ruling elite. Karr, "Evolution of an Elite Suburb," 133–134.

71 *Brookline Transcript,* 27 January, 1872, as quoted in Ronald Dale Karr, "Brookline Rejects Annexation, 1873," 106. Karr's article also contains a statistical analysis of the participants in the annexation debate.

72 *Brookline Independent,* 25 July 1873, and N. G. Chapin, *Brookline Transcript,* 22 March 1873, both as quoted in Karr, "Brookline Rejects Annexation," 106–107. Karr identifies a tension between "ruralists" and "urbanists" over development of the town. See Karr, "Evolution of an Elite Suburb," 233–239. Sam Bass Warner, Jr., attributes the ultimate collapse of Boston's annexation movement in part to the attractions of the small town ideal. See Warner, *Streetcar Suburbs,* 163–164.

73 Karr, "Brookline Rejects Annexation," 105.

74 Alfred Chandler, "Brookline," in *Brookline: The Chronicle Souvenir of the Bicentennial* (Brookline, Mass.: Riverdale Press, 1905), 4.

75 Ibid., 5–6; Karr, "Evolution of an Elite Suburb," 239–250; and Karr, "Brookline Rejects Annexation," 105.

76 For the influence of Frederick Law Olmsted on Brookline's landscape, see Zaitzevsky, "Frederick Law Olmsted in Brookline."

77 Wakefield is quoted in *The Brookline Magazine* (Brookline, Mass.: Riverdale Press, 1897), 42, 41, 41–42.

78 From an interview with Olmsted's son, cited in Laura Wood Roper, *FLO: A Biography of Frederick Law Olmsted* (Baltimore: Johns Hopkins University Press, 1973), 383.

79 For the history of the country club, see John Steele Gordon, "The Country Club," *American Heritage* 41, no. 6 (September/October 1990): 75–84; and James M. Mayo, *The Country Club: Its Origins and Development* (New Brunswick, N.J.: Rutgers University Press, 1998).

80 Town of Brookline, *Report of the Committee of Twenty-Five on Brookline Town Government* (Brookline, Mass.: Riverdale Press, 1900), 2–3. For concerns about representative government, see Chandler, "Brookline," 23. For the evolution of government in neighboring Cambridge and Charlestown, see Binford, *The First Suburbs,* chapter 4.

81 Robert Wood has argued that attachment to small-town government ener-

gized suburban resistance to annexation into the twentieth century. See
Wood, *Suburbia: Its People and Their Politics* (Boston: Houghton Mifflin, 1958).

82 Herbert Baxter Adams, *The Germanic Origin of New England Towns*, Johns Hopkins University Studies in Historical and Political Science, 1st ser., no. 2 (Baltimore: Johns Hopkins University, 1882). The historical roots of the New England Town meeting are still unclear. For the competing theories, see John
Fairfield Sly, *Town Government in Massachusetts (1630–1930)* (Cambridge: Harvard University Press, 1930), 52–74; and Joseph F. Zimmerman, *The Massachusetts Town Meeting: A Tenacious Institution* (Albany: State University of New
York, 1967), 12–14. For a contemporary disquisition on the historical benefits
of town government, see Robert C. Winthrop, *Address at the Dedication of the
New Town Hall of Brookline, on the 22nd of February, 1873* (Cambridge: John Wilson and Son, 1873).

83 Alfred D. Chandler, Esq. *Local Self-Government: Elective Town Meetings for Large
Towns, with a General Legislative Bill Therefor [sic], and the Recent Charter of the
City of Newport, Rhode Island, Based Thereon* (Brookline, Mass.: Riverdale Press,
1908), 17 and 51.

84 Chandler explains the representative town meeting in *Local Self-Government*.
Also see Chandler, "Brookline: A Study in Town Government," in *The New England Magazine* 14, no. 6 (August 1893): 777–797; Sly, *Town Government in Massachusetts*, 165–192; and Zimmerman, *The Massachusetts Town Meeting*, 51–56.
Another perspective appears in Arthur W. Spencer, "Back to the Town Meeting: Brookline's Solution of the Problem of Municipal Government," *Government Magazine* 2, no. 4 (January 1908): 249–258. Support for the town meeting
among progressives appears in B. O. Flower, "Brookline: A Model Town under
the Referendum," *Arena* 19 (April 1898): 505–519; and Flower, "Democracy
and Municipal Government; or, How the Richest Town in the World Is Ruled
by the Referendum," *Arena* 32 (October 1904): 377–391. Newport, Rhode Island—not Brookline—was the first municipality in America to adopt Chandler's representative town meeting.

85 Howard Allen Bridgman, "The Suburbanite," *The Brookline Magazine* (Brookline, Mass.: Riverdale Press, 1897), 37.

86 "The Suburbanite's Opportunity," *Brookline Magazine*, 69.

87 "The Advantages and Obligations of Residence in Brookline. A Symposium,"
Brookline Magazine, 59–66; Chandler, "Brookline," 780.

88 Jackson, *Crabgrass Frontier*, 148–153; and Teaford, *City and Suburb*, chapter 5.

89 For the growth of metropolitan services, see Sarah S. Elkind, *Bay Cities and
Water Politics: The Battle for Resources in Boston and Oakland* (Lawrence: Univer-
sity Press of Kansas, 1998). For efforts to consolidate the municipalities around
Boston after Brookline's rejection of annexation, see James A. Merino, "Coop-

erative Schemes for Greater Boston: 1890–1920," *New England Quarterly* 45, no. 2 (1972): 196–226.

4. Making the Harbor

1 The definitive study of landmaking in Boston is Nancy S. Seasholes, *Gaining Ground: A History of Landmaking in Boston* (Cambridge: MIT Press, 2003).

2 For general histories of Boston Harbor, see Work Projects Administration, *Boston Looks Seaward: The Story of the Port, 1630–1940* (Boston: Bruce Humphries, 1941); Samuel Eliot Morison, *The Maritime History of Massachusetts, 1783–1860* (Boston: Houghton Mifflin, 1941); and W. H. Bunting, *Portrait of a Port: Boston, 1852–1914* (Cambridge: Belknap Press of Harvard University Press, 1971). For the history of pollution in the harbor, see Eric Jay Dolin, *Political Waters: The Long, Dirty, Contentious, Incredibly Expensive but Eventually Triumphant History of Boston Harbor—A Unique Environmental Success Story* (Amherst: University of Massachusetts Press, 2004); and Charles M. Haar, *Mastering Boston Harbor: Courts, Dolphins, and Imperiled Waters* (Cambridge: Harvard University Press, 2005).

3 Carolyn Merchant, "The Theoretical Structure of Ecological Revolutions," in *Out of the Woods: Essays in Environmental History*, ed. Char Miller and Hal Rothman (Pittsburgh: University of Pittsburgh Press, 1997), 20. The literature on the social construction of science is large. For an overview, see Ian Hacking, *The Social Construction of What?* (Cambridge: Harvard University Press, 1999). Also see, for example, I. G. Simmons, *Interpreting Nature: Cultural Constructions of the Environment* (New York: Routledge, 1993); Gregg Mitman, *The State of Nature: Ecology, Community, and American Social Thought, 1900–1950* (Chicago: University of Chicago Press, 1992); Donna Haraway, *Primate Visions: Gender, Race, and Nature in the World of Modern Science* (New York: Routledge, 1989); and Noretta Koertge, ed., *A House Built on Sand: Exposing Postmodernist Myths about Science* (New York: Oxford University Press, 1998).

4 Urban and environmental historians have paid little attention to the history of harbor engineering in America. Harbors do receive some attention in Todd Shallat, *Structures in the Stream: Water, Science, and the Rise of the U.S. Army Corps of Engineers* (Austin: University of Texas Press, 1994), but most environmental historians interested in navigable waterways have focused on rivers, particularly the Mississippi. See, for example, George S. Pabis, "Subduing Nature through Engineering: Caleb G. Forshey and the Levees-only Policy, 1851–1881," in *Transforming New Orleans and Its Environs: Centuries of Change*, ed. Craig E. Colten (Pittsburgh: University of Pittsburgh Press, 2000), 64–83; Pabis, "Delaying the Deluge: The Engineering Debate over Flood Control on the Lower Mississippi River, 1846–1861," *Journal of Southern History* 64, no. 3 (Au-

gust 1998): 421–454; Martin A. Reuss, "Andrew A. Humphreys and the Development of Hydraulic Engineering: Politics and Technology in the Army Corps of Engineers, 1850–1950," *Technology and Culture* 26, no. 1 (January 1985): 1–33; and Martin A. Reuss, "The Art of Scientific Precision: River Research in the United States Army Corps of Engineers to 1945," *Technology and Culture* 40, no. 2 (April 1999): 292–323. Urban historians, for their part, assume too often that cities stop at the water's edge. Two exceptions, both studies of New York City, are Kevin Bone, ed., *The New York Waterfront: Evolution and Building Culture of the Port and Harbor* (New York: Monacelli Press, 1997); and Ann L. Buttenwieser, *Manhattan Water-Bound: Planning and Developing Manhattan's Waterfront from the Seventeenth Century to the Present* (New York: New York University Press, 1987). The Army Corps of Engineers has produced a number of factual histories that explore various American harbors and the engineering works designed to make them navigable, but there is more critical literature on Great Britain, whose poor natural harbors often required massive engineering works to make them navigable. See Gordon Jackson's classic study, *The History and Archaeology of Ports* (Tadworth, U.K.: World's Work Limited, 1983); and Adrian Jarvis, ed., *Port and Harbour Engineering,* Studies in the History of Civil Engineering, vol. 6 (Aldershot, U.K.: Ashgate, 1998). For a more international perspective, see Josef W. Konvitz, *Cities and the Sea: Port City Planning in Early Modern Europe* (Baltimore: Johns Hopkins University Press, 1978); and Nicholas C. Kraus, ed., *History and Heritage of Coastal Engineering: A Collection of Papers on the History of Coastal Engineering in Countries Hosting the International Coastal Engineering Conference, 1950–1996* (New York: American Society of Civil Engineers, 1996).

5 Descriptions of journeys through Boston Harbor in the nineteenth century appear in Nathaniel B. Shurtleff, *A Topographical and Historical Description of Boston,* 2nd ed. (Boston: Noyes, Holmes, 1872), 582–585; and M. F. Sweetser, *King's Handbook of Boston Harbor,* 3rd ed. (Boston: Moses King Corporation, 1888), 23–28. For the harbor islands, see Edward Rowe Snow, *The Islands of Boston Harbor: Their History and Romance, 1626–1935* (Andover, Mass.: Andover Press, 1935); and David Kales, *The Boston Harbor Islands: A History of Urban Wilderness* (Charleston: History Press, 2007).

6 See prior note. For boasts about the size of the harbor, see for example Elias H. Derby, "Commercial Cities and Towns of the United States: City of Boston," in *Hunt's Merchants' Magazine and Commercial Review* 23, no. 5 (November 1850): 483.

7 Commonwealth of Massachusetts, *Fifth Annual Report of the Board of Harbor Commissioners. January, 1871,* House No. 53 (1871), 78–79.

8 For an overview of the harbor's hydraulics as understood by nineteenth-

century engineers, see C. W. Raymond, "Boston Harbor," in Massachusetts Institute of Technology, Society of Arts, *Abstract of the Proceedings* 23 (Boston: W. J. Schofield, 1885), 34–62.

9 Aubrey Parkman, *History of the Waterways of the Atlantic Coast of the United States* (Alexandria, Va.: U.S. Army Corps of Engineers Institute for Water Resources, 1983), 9–12.

10 For Boston's "Sacred Codfish," see Commonwealth of Massachusetts, Committee on History of the Emblem of the Codfish, *A History of the Emblem of the Codfish in the Hall of the House of Representatives* (Boston: Wright and Potter, 1895).

11 Snow, *Islands of Boston Harbor,* 325–341; *Fifth Annual Report of the Harbor Commissioners,* House No. 53 (1871), 82; and Commonwealth of Massachusetts, *Report of the Commissioners for Fixing the Line of Private Property in Boston Harbor,* Senate No. 8 (1840), 8–10.

12 William Wood, *New England's Prospect,* ed. Alden T. Vaughan (Amherst: University of Massachusetts Press, 1977), 61 and 27. Also see Julie A. Richburg and William A. Patterson III, "Historical Description of the Vegetation of the Boston Harbor Islands: 1600–2000," *Northeastern Naturalist* 12, no. 3, Boston Harbor Islands National Park Area: Natural Resources Overview (2005): 13–30.

13 Snow, *Islands of Boston Harbor,* 312–313. For interactions between the first New England settlers and the region's forests, see Charles H. W. Foster, ed., *Stepping Back to Look Forward: A History of the Massachusetts Forest* (Cambridge: Harvard University Press, 1998); William Cronon, *Changes in the Land: Indians, Colonists, and the Ecology of New England* (New York: Hill and Wang, 1983); and Carl Bridenbaugh, "Yankee Use and Abuse of the Forest in the Building of New England, 1620–1660," in Bridenbaugh, *Early Americans* (New York: Oxford University Press, 1981), 92–120. Frederick Law Olmsted proposed a plan to reforest the islands in "Report of the Landscape Architect Advisory," in City of Boston, *Thirteenth Annual Report of the Board of Commissioners of the Department of Parks for the City of Boston, for the Year 1887,* City Doc. No. 14 (1888), 38–46. Also see Charles Eliot, *Charles Eliot: Landscape Architect* (Boston: Houghton, Mifflin, 1902), 699–701.

14 For the removal of stone and gravel for ballast, see City of Boston, *Report on Memorial of the Boston Marine Society,* reprinted in Commonwealth of Massachusetts, Senate No. 4 (1847), 4–5; Benjamin A. Gould, *Boston Harbor: A Series of Communications to the Boston Daily Advertiser* (Boston: J. E. Farwell, 1863), 36–37; *Fifth Annual Report of the Harbor Commissioners,* House No. 53 (1871), 82; and Commonwealth of Massachusetts, Committee on the Judiciary, Senate No. 39 (1862). The estimate of the amount of ballast removed is from William A. Baker, *A History of the Boston Marine Society, 1742–1981,* 2nd ed. (Boston: Boston Marine Society, 1982), 172. For the imbalance between imports

and exports, see Commonwealth of Massachusetts, *Report of the Commissioners in Relation to the Flats in Boston Harbor, January 1850,* Senate No. 3 (1850), 59–60.

15 Gould, *Boston Harbor,* 32–37.

16 *Report of the Commissioners,* Senate No. 3 (1850), 22, 58, 64, and 66; and William Whiting, *The Destruction of Boston Harbor. Argument of William Whiting, Esq., Before the Committee of the Legislature, April 17, 1851, Against an Application for Leave to Fill Up Flats in Mystic River* (Boston: J. M. Hewes, 1852). Whiting's pamphlet appeared the year before under the title *Application of John C. Tucker and Others for a Charter for the Mystic River Rail Road* (Boston: J. M. Hewes, 1851).

17 For the decline of shipping and the rise of railroads, see Bunting, *Portrait of a Port,* 7–17.

18 Commonwealth of Massachusetts, *Report of the Commissioners for the Survey of Boston Harbor,* Senate No. 47 (1837), 21. For the Saco River, see Parkman, *History of the Waterways of the Atlantic Coast,* 45. For the Thames, see Michael S. Reidy, *Tides of History: Ocean Science and Her Majesty's Navy* (Chicago: University of Chicago Press, 2008), 72–77. One of the more detailed discussions of the theory of tidal scour as applied to Boston Harbor appears in Whiting, *The Destruction of Boston Harbor.* For more recent analyses of water circulation in Boston Harbor, see G. B. Gardner, R. F. Chen, and S. Rudnick, "Estuarine Circulation in Boston Inner Harbor," *Eos Trans. AGU 79* (17), Spring Meet. Suppl. (1998), S187; and Richard P. Signell, "Tide- and Wind-Driven Flushing of Boston Harbor, Massachusetts," *Estuarine and Coastal Modeling: Proceedings of the 2nd International Conference sponsored by the Waterway, Port, Coastal and Ocean Division of the American Society of Civil Engineers* (New York: American Society of Civil Engineers, 1992), 594–606.

19 Thomas Stevenson, *The Design and Construction of Harbours: A Treatise on Maritime Engineering,* 2nd ed. (Edinburgh: Adam and Charles Black, 1874), 223. For the history of hydraulics, see Enzo Levi, *The Science of Water: The Foundation of Modern Hydraulics,* trans. Daniel E. Medina (New York: American Society of Civil Engineers, 1995). For the challenges faced by engineers trying to understand river flow, see Reuss, "Art of Scientific Precision."

20 John S. Sleeper, *Address on the Encroachments in the Harbor of Boston* (Boston: Rockwell and Churchill, 1872), 11. Sleeper spent much of his career in the merchant service sailing ships out of Boston. He retired in 1830 at the age of thirty-six and subsequently worked as a newspaper editor and author of sea tales under the pseudonym "Hawser Martingale."

21 *Report of the Commissioners,* Senate No. 3 (1850), 68.

22 Seasholes, *Gaining Ground,* 3–8.

23 Seasholes, *Gaining Ground,* 6, 92–96, 169, 244–248.

24 Seasholes, *Gaining Ground,* 7–8. A small number of Bostonians—including

some doctors—believed that made land was itself unhealthy. See Commonwealth of Massachusetts, *Report Relative to the Flats and Water Areas of the Commonwealth, by the Committee Appointed under the Order of the House of Representatives, June 17, 1869,* House No. 240 (1870), 48–49; and Walter Muir Whitehill and Lawrence W. Kennedy, *Boston: A Topographical History,* 3rd ed. (Cambridge: Belknap Press of Harvard University Press, 2000), 164. Such worries did little to curb landmaking.

25 Jose L. Fernandez, "Untwisting the Common Law: Public Trust and the Massachusetts Colonial Ordinance," *Albany Law Review* 62, no. 2 (December 1998), 623–665; and Mark Cheung, "Rethinking the History of the Seventeenth-Century Colonial Ordinance: A Reinterpretation of an Ancient Statute," *Maine Law Review* 42 (1990): 115–158. For the kinds of legal problems that the ordinance had created by the nineteenth century, see Nathaniel I. Bowditch, *Wharf Property; or, The Law of Flats; being Remarks before the Judiciary Committee of the Senate of Massachusetts, April 14, 1852* (Boston: J. Wilson and Son, 1852).

26 Seasholes, *Gaining Ground,* 420. Also see, especially, Matthew Klingle, "Changing Spaces: Nature, Property, and Power in Seattle, 1880–1945," *Journal of Urban History* 32, no. 2 (January 2006): 197–230; Anne-Marie Cantwell and Diana diZerega Wall, *Unearthing Gotham: The Archaeology of New York City* (New Haven: Yale University Press, 2001), chapter 13; and Lois Wille, *Forever Open, Clear, and Free: The Struggle for Chicago's Lakefront,* 2nd ed. (Chicago: University of Chicago Press, 1991).

27 *Report of the Commissioners,* Senate No. 3 (1850), 49, 59–60.

28 *Report of the Commissioners,* Senate No. 8 (1840), 24; and City of Boston, *Report on Memorial of the Boston Marine Society,* in Commonwealth of Massachusetts, Senate No. 4 (1847), 6–7, 13.

29 *Report of the Commissioners,* Senate No. 3 (1850), 28.

30 *Report of the Commissioners,* Senate No. 3 (1850), 27–28; and Commonwealth of Massachusetts, Joint Committee on Mercantile Affairs and Insurance, Senate No. 119 (1850), 9–10.

31 *Letters to His Excellency, George S. Boutwell, on His Veto of the Bill to Create the Eastern Avenue Corporation, in the Session of 1851* (Boston, Printed at the Office of the Daily Courier, 1851), 17.

32 *Report on Memorial of the Boston Marine Society,* Senate No. 4 (1847), 11. For the Boston Marine Society, see Baker, *History of the Boston Marine Society.*

33 Aubrey Parkman, *Army Engineers in New England: The Military and Civil Work of the Corps of Engineers in New England, 1775–1975* (Waltham, Mass.: U.S. Army Corps of Engineers, New England Division, 1978), 44–45. In 1824, the Supreme Court concluded in *Gibbons v. Ogden* that the federal government had the power to support internal improvements under the commerce clause of the Constitution. The decision opened the door to a deep and lasting engage-

ment between the Army Corps of Engineers and America's waterways. On the Army Corps of Engineers, see Shallat, *Structures in the Stream;* Forest G. Hill, *Roads, Rails and Waterways: The Army Engineers and Early Transportation* (Norman: University of Oklahoma Press, 1957); and David A. Clary, *Fortress America: The Corps of Engineers, Hampton Roads, and United States Coastal Defense* (Charlottesville: University Press of Virginia, 1990).

34 Seasholes discusses the South Bay project in *Gaining Ground,* 261–274. For criticism of the city, see *Report of the Commissioners,* Senate No. 3 (1850), 45–46. The city's response to such accusations is recorded in Commonwealth of Massachusetts, Joint Committee on Mercantile Affairs and Insurance, Senate No. 119 (1850), 4.

35 Commonwealth of Massachusetts, Committee on Mercantile Affairs and Insurance, Senate No. 117 (1848), 4.

36 Senate No. 39 (1862), 2–4.

37 *Report of the Commissioners,* Senate No. 47 (1837). For a sample of subsequent efforts to draw new harbor lines and amend existing ones, see Commonwealth of Massachusetts, *An Act to Preserve the Harbor of Boston and to Prevent Encroachments Therein,* House No. 63 (1837); *Report of the Commissioners,* Senate No. 8 (1840); Commonwealth of Massachusetts, Senate No. 25 (1847); and Commonwealth of Massachusetts, Senate No. 53 (1849). The courts upheld the legality of harbor lines as part of the state's police power in *Commonwealth v. Alger,* 61 Mass. 53 (1851). The drawing of harbor lines became a federal responsibility in 1888.

38 Commonwealth of Massachusetts, Committee on Mercantile Affairs and Insurance, Senate No. 134 (1848), and Senate No. 119 (1849), 2.

39 For the legislature ignoring its own harbor lines see, for example, *Report of the Commissioners,* Senate No. 8 (1840), 21. The Mystic River Corporation and the Boston Wharf Company are discussed in Seasholes, *Gaining Ground,* 292–295 and 397–401. For resistance to the Mystic River Corporation's project, also see Whiting, *The Destruction of Boston Harbor.*

40 The most detailed history of the Back Bay is William A. Newman and Wilfred E. Holton, *Boston's Back Bay: The Story of America's Greatest Nineteenth-Century Landfill Project* (Boston: Northeastern University Press, 2006). Also see Whitehill, *Boston: A Topographical History,* chapter 7; Seasholes, *Gaining Ground,* chapter 7; and Bainbridge Bunting, *Houses of Boston's Back Bay: An Architectural History, 1840–1917* (Cambridge: Belknap Press of Harvard University Press, 1967).

41 *Letters to His Excellency,* 4.

42 For the history of the police power, see Stanley K. Schultz, *Constructing Urban Culture: American Cities and City Planning, 1800–1920* (Philadelphia: Temple University Press, 1989), chapters 3 and 4.

43 *Commonwealth v. Alger,* 61 Mass. 53 (1851), 85.

44 Baker, *History of the Boston Marine Society,* 172.

45 Senate No. 39 (1862) and *Commonwealth v. Tewksbury,* 11 Met. 55 (1846). Tewksbury was well known at the time for the number of lives he had saved off the coasts of Port Shirley and Deer Island. See Snow, *Islands of Boston Harbor,* 280–284.

46 Senate No. 39 (1862) and Senate No. 25 (1847), 9–10.

47 Senate No. 39 (1862).

48 Senate No. 119 (1850), 3.

49 Senate No. 119 (1850), 1–4; and *Report of the Commissioners,* Senate No. 3 (1850), 4–12 and 33–35. Also see Seth Adams, *A Protest Against the Claim of the Commonwealth to a Vendible Interest in the Flats; with Remarks upon the Law and Custom that Govern the Use of the Sea-Shore* (Boston: n.p., 1868). For the different conceptions of public property and governmental authority over it, see Carol M. Rose, *Property and Persuasion: Essays on the History, Theory, and Rhetoric of Ownership* (Boulder: Westview Press, 1994), especially chapter 5.

50 *Report of the Commissioners,* Senate No. 3 (1850), 28.

51 Ibid., 34.

52 Commonwealth of Massachusetts, Commissioners on Harbors and Flats, Senate No. 244 (1864), especially 2–3; and *Fifth Annual Report of the Harbor Commissioners,* House No. 53 (1871), 84.

53 City of Boston, *The Mayor's Communication in Relation to a Scientific Survey of Boston Harbor,* City Doc. No. 64 (1859).

54 Gould, *Boston Harbor,* 12. General Richard Delafield replaced Totten after the latter's death in 1864.

55 *Tenth Report of the United States Commissioners on Boston Harbor,* City Doc. No. 50 (1866), 84.

56 Quoted in *Fifth Annual Report of the Harbor Commissioners,* House No. 53 (1871), 90–91.

57 The recommendations of the Unites States Commissioners on Boston Harbor are scattered throughout their ten reports. See *Preliminary Report of the Commissioners on Boston Harbor,* City Doc. No. 37 (1860); *Second Report of United States Commissioners on the Condition of Boston Harbor,* City Doc. No. 97 (1860); *Special Report of United States Commissioners on Boston Harbor, on the Relation of Mystic Pond and River to Boston Harbor,* City Doc. No. 12 (1861); *Fourth Report of the United States Commissioners on Boston Harbor,* City Doc. No. 62, (1861); *Fifth Report of United States Commissioners on Boston Harbor,* City Doc. No. 35 (1863); *Sixth Report of United States Commissioners on Boston Harbor,* City Doc. No. 53 (1863); *Seventh Report of the United States Commissioners on Boston Harbor,* City Doc. No. 33 (1864); *Eighth Report of the United States Commissioners on Boston Harbor,* City Doc. No. 34 (1864); *Ninth Report of the U.S. Commissioners on Boston Harbor on the Subject of Compensation,* City Doc. No. 28 (1865); and *Tenth*

Report of the United States Commissioners on Boston Harbor, City Doc. No. 50 (1866).

58 See prior note. The kinds of harbor works suggested by the U.S. Commissioners were more common in Great Britain and its colonies. For a taste of the political, economic, and engineering problems posed by such works, see Adrian Jarvis, "Beyond the River Wall: The Attack on the Mersey Bar, 1890–1923"; and L. Twyman, "The First Harbour Works at Port Natal: The Role of John Milne from 1849–1857," reprinted as chapters 14 and 15 in Jarvis, ed., *Port and Harbour Engineering.*

59 *Special Report of the United States Commissioners on Boston Harbor, on the Relation of Mystic Pond and River to Boston Harbor,* City Doc. No. 12 (1861), 60.

60 *Tenth Report of the United States Commissioners,* 43–44. The U.S. Commissioners devoted their entire ninth report to the issue of compensation.

61 Thomas Lamb, *Plan and Suggestions for Improving Boston Harbor and, Incidentally, the Vicinity* (Boston: E. P. Dutton, 1867). For a brief biographical sketch of Thomas Lamb, see Baker, *History of Boston Marine Society,* 204.

62 See prior note.

63 Gould, *Boston Harbor,* 6.

64 Charles Francis Adams, Jr., "Boston," *The North American Review* 106, no. 218 (January 1868): 15, 16.

65 *Tenth Report of the United States Commissioners,* 48.

66 Commonwealth of Massachusetts, Acts of 1866, Chapter 149.

67 United States Advisory Council to the Board of Harbor Commissioners of Massachusetts, *Report of the United States Advisory Council to the Board of Harbor Commissioners upon Recent Changes in the Bed of Boston Harbor, to which is Added an Opinion upon Compensation,* in Commonwealth of Massachusetts, *Second Annual Report of the Board of Harbor Commissioners. January, 1868,* House No. 10 (1868), 32–38.

68 Ibid.

69 Commonwealth of Massachusetts, *Report of the Committee Appointed under Chapter 93 of the Resolves of 1867, in Relation to the Commonwealth Flats near South Boston,* House No. 76 (1868), 56.

70 Ibid., 64.

71 Ibid.

72 Ibid., 75.

73 Ibid., 83.

74 Commonwealth of Massachusetts, *Report Relative to the Flats and Water Areas of the Commonwealth, by the Committee Appointed Under the Order of the House of Representatives, June 17, 1869,* House No. 240 (1870).

75 Thomas Kuhn notes that, "once it has achieved the status of paradigm, a scientific theory is declared invalid only if an alternate candidate is available to

take its place." Thomas S. Kuhn, *The Structure of Scientific Revolutions* (Chicago: University of Chicago Press, 1962), 77. Those who preferred land to water failed to suggest a new paradigm based in science.

76 Senate No. 25 (1847); and *Fourth Report of United States Commissioners,* City Doc. No. 62 (1861), 10.

77 Commonwealth of Massachusetts, *Third Annual Report of the Board of Harbor Commissioners. January 1869,* House No. 13 (1869), 9.

78 Commonwealth of Massachusetts, *Seventh Annual Report of the Board of Harbor Commissioners. January, 1873,* House No. 65 (1873), 31–38.

79 Commonwealth of Massachusetts, *Ninth Annual Report of the Board of Harbor Commissioners,* House No. 61 (1874), 14–16; Commonwealth of Massachusetts, *Tenth Annual Report of the Board of Harbor Commissioners,* House No. 75 (1876), 10.

80 *Fifth Annual Report of the Harbor Commissioners,* House No. 53 (1871), 16–17.

81 Commonwealth of Massachusetts, *Annual Report of the Board of Harbor Commissioners for the Year 1878,* House No. 33 (1879), 16.

82 Commonwealth of Massachusetts, *Fourth Annual Report of the Board of Harbor Commissioners. January, 1870,* House No. 55 (1870), 106–109; and *Fifth Annual Report of the Harbor Commissioners,* 12–15.

83 *Seventh Annual Report of the Harbor Commissioners,* 42–48.

84 *Annual Report of the Board of Harbor Commissioners for the Year 1878,* House No. 33 (1879), 17.

85 *Fifth Annual Report of the Harbor Commissioners,* 90.

86 For dredging in the harbor, see Commonwealth of Massachusetts, *Annual Report of the Board of Harbor and Land Commissioners for the Year 1895,* Public Doc. 11 (1896), 15; *Annual Report of the Board of Harbor and Land Commissioners for the Year 1900,* Public Doc. 11 (1901), 7; *Annual Report of the Board of Harbor and Land Commissioners for the Year 1901,* Public Doc. 11 (1902), 7; and *Addresses Delivered at the Fifteenth Annual Banquet of the Boston Merchants Association, November 15, 1895, on the Improvement of Boston Harbor* (Boston: Robinson Press, 1896). More recent dimensions for the harbor's main channels and deepwater anchorage can be found in United States Army Corps of Engineers, *The Port of Boston, Massachusetts,* Port Series No. 3, Revised 1994 (Washington, D.C.: United States Government Printing Office, 1994).

87 Gould, *Boston Harbor,* 45.

88 Maritime historian Gordon Jackson claims correctly that modern ports "are only as good as their dredgers," yet historians have yet to give the history of dredging the attention it deserves. Jackson, *History and Archaeology of Ports,* 110. For the early evolution of the dredge, see David F. Bastion, "The Development of Dredging through the 1850's," in *National Waterways Roundtable Pa-*

pers: *Proceedings on the History and Evolution of U.S. Waterways and Ports* (Norfolk, Va.: U.S. Army Engineer Water Resources Support Center, Institute for Water Resources, 1980), 1–21.

89 Sweetser, *King's Handbook of Boston Harbor,* 23. Also see James H. Stark, *Illustrated History of Boston Harbor* (Boston: The Photo-Electrotype Company, 1879); and *A Descriptive and Historical Sketch of Boston Harbor and Surroundings, Giving All the Islands, Ledges, Shoals, Buoys, Channels, and Towns from Nahant to Minot's with Their Location and History* (Boston: W. M. Tenney, 1885). For the larger cultural processes drawing urbanites to the sea for leisure, see Alain Corbin, *The Lure of the Sea: The Discovery of the Seaside in the Western World, 1750–1840,* trans. Jocelyn Phelps (Berkeley: University of California Press, 1994).

90 City of Boston, *Sixth Annual Report of the Board of Health,* City Doc. No. 68 (1878), 3, quoted in Karl Haglund, *Inventing the Charles River* (Cambridge: MIT Press, 2003), 110. For pollution in the Charles River, see Haglund, 107–114.

91 Commonwealth of Massachusetts, *Report of the Joint Board Consisting of the Metropolitan Park Commission and the State Board of Health,* House No. 775 (1894), 18–22.

92 *Annual Report of the Board of Harbor and Land Commissioners for the Year 1894,* Public Doc. 11 (1895), 21, 18.

93 Commonwealth of Massachusetts, *Report of the Committee on Charles River Dam Appointed Under Resolves of 1901, Chapter 105, to Consider the Advisability and Feasibility of Building a Dam Across the Charles River at or Near Craigie Bridge* (Boston: Wright and Potter, 1903), 20.

94 Ibid., 22–24, 100–102. Freeman's findings came at the tale end of a period when civilian engineers were questioning the competence of military engineers. See Reuss, "Andrew A. Humphreys and the Development of Hydraulic Engineering," 23–26.

95 *Report of the Committee on Charles River Dam,* 22. For an earlier perspective, see William O. Crosby, *Physical History of the Boston Basin* (Boston: Press of J. Allen Crosby, 1889). I am using the freighted term "paradigm shift" purposefully, because the replacement of one scientific model by another in the case of Boston Harbor closely parallels the path described in Kuhn, *The Structure of Scientific Revolutions.* The existing scientific model, in this case the theory of tidal scour, was growing progressively incapable of explaining the observable facts. Yet, as Kuhn predicts, it was judged invalid only after someone suggested a new model that better explained the facts.

96 *Report of the Committee on Charles River Dam,* 21.

97 S. O. Edwards to John Freeman, June 29, 1903, in Freeman Papers, Massachusetts Institute of Technology Archives, Box 91, quoted in Deborah A. Cozort,

"John R. Freeman and the Honest Doubters of Boston: How the Charles River Dam Was Won," *Journal of the Boston Society of Civil Engineers* 67, no. 4 (Summer 1981), 212, n. 28.

98 "Must We Lose Boston?" *New York Times,* 20 June 1903, 6.

99 Bunting, *Portrait of a Port,* 48.

100 Sleeper, *Address on the Encroachments,* 12.

5. RECREATING THE WILDERNESS

1 Samuel K. Lothrop, *Memorial of the Church in Brattle Square, A Discourse Preached in the Church in Brattle Square, on the Last Sunday of Its Use for Public Worship, July 30, 1871* (Boston: John Wilson and Son, 1871), 27. For the tension between change and continuity in the urban environment, see Michael Holleran, *Boston's "Changeful Times": Origins of Preservation and Planning in America* (Baltimore: Johns Hopkins University Press, 1998).

2 James Russell Lowell, "The Place of the Independent in Politics," in Lowell, *Complete Works of James Russell Lowell: Literary and Political Addresses,* vol. 7 (Boston: Houghton, Mifflin, 1904), 265–266. For some suggestive reading on the relationship between nature and history, see Paul A. Shackel, *Myth, Memory, and the Making of the American Landscape* (Gainesville: University Press of Florida, 2001); Arnold R. Alanen and Robert Z. Melnick, *Preserving Cultural Landscapes in America* (Baltimore: Johns Hopkins University Press, 2000); Simon Schama, *Landscape and Memory* (New York: Vintage Books, 1995); and David Lowenthal, "The Place of the Past in the American Landscape," in *Geographies of the Mind: Essays in Historical Geosophy in Honor of John Kirtland Wright,* ed. Lowenthal and Martyn J. Bowden (New York: Oxford University Press, 1976), 89–117.

3 Barrett Wendell to Colonel Robert Thomson, 17 December 1893, in M. A. DeWolfe Howe, *Barrett Wendell and His Letters* (Boston: Atlantic Monthly Press, 1924), 108.

4 For historical memory generally, see especially Michael Kammen, *Mystic Chords of Memory: The Transformation of Tradition in American Culture* (New York: Alfred A. Knopf, 1991); and David Lowenthal, *The Past Is a Foreign Country* (Cambridge: Cambridge University Press, 1985).

5 Charles W. Eliot, *Charles Eliot, Landscape Architect* (Boston: Houghton, Mifflin, 1902), 317.

6 Much of the existing scholarship on Boston's Metropolitan Park System emphasizes the influence of the park and planning movements on its formation. See especially Karl Haglund, "Emerald Necklace," *Arnoldia* 53, no. 4 (1993): 2–17; Keith N. Morgan, "Held in Trust: Charles Eliot's Vision for the New England Landscape," *National Association for Olmsted Parks Workbook Series,* vol. 1:

Biography (Bethesda: National Association for Olmsted Parks, 1991); Norman T. Newton, "Charles Eliot and His Metropolitan Park System," in *Design on the Land: The Development of Landscape Architecture* (Cambridge: Belknap Press of Harvard University Press, 1971), 318–336; and Steven T. Moga, "Marginal Lands and Suburban Nature: Open Space Planning and the Case of the 1893 Boston Metropolitan Parks Plan," *Journal of Planning History* 8, no. 4 (November 2009): 308–329.

7 For the topography of the Boston region, see Commonwealth of Massachusetts, *Report of the Board of Metropolitan Park Commissioners, January 1893,* House No. 150 (1893), 83–89. For the view from the Blue Hills in the nineteenth century, see E. G. Chamberlain, "The Blue Hills," *Appalachia* 3, no. 2 (April 1883).

8 Quoted in Medford Historical Society, *Round About Middlesex Fells: Historical Guide-Book* (Medford, Mass.: Medford Historical Society, 1935), 4.

9 Commonwealth of Massachusetts, *Report of the Board of Metropolitan Park Commissioners, January 1895,* Public Doc. 48 (1895), 86.

10 Sylvester Baxter, *The Metropolitan Park System* (Boston: Massachusetts Horticultural Society, 1894), 15–16.

11 Medford Historical Society, *Round About Middlesex Fells,* 8–9; Ellen Levin and Thomas Mahlstedt, *Middlesex Fells Reservation Historic Land-Use Study* (Boston: Metropolitan District Commission, 1990), 11; and *Report of the Board of Metropolitan Park Commissioners, 1895,* 91–93.

12 Levin and Mahlstedt, *Middlesex Fells Reservation,* 12–15, 18–20, 30.

13 Ibid., 15–16.

14 Ibid., 10, 18, 30. For Tudor's Grove, see "Upper Forest Street Sixty Years Ago," *Medford Historical Register* 31, no. 2 (1928), 35; and for the spiritualists see George B. Davenport, *A Lecture on the Middlesex Fells* (Medford, Mass.: Press of the Medford City News, 1893), 11. For immigrant use of parks in the Fells, see Oscar Handlin, *Boston's Immigrants: A Study in Acculturation,* rev. ed. (Cambridge: Belknap Press of Harvard University Press, 1959), 156.

15 *Report of the Metropolitan Park Commissioners, 1895,* 70–78. Quote is from page 74.

16 Medford Historical Society, *Round About Middlesex Fells,* 6.

17 Albert Kendall Teele, *The Blue Hills* (Boston: 1884), 11.

18 George Perkins Marsh, *Man and Nature; or, Physical Geography as Modified by Human Action,* ed. David Lowenthal (1864; Seattle: University of Washington Press, 2003); and David Lowenthal, *George Perkins Marsh: Prophet of Conservation* (Seattle: University of Washington Press, 2000).

19 Wilson Flagg, *The Woods and By-Ways of New England* (Boston: James R. Osgood, 1872), 434.

20 Statistics are from Sylvester Baxter, *Greater Boston: A Study for a Federalized Metropolis Comprising the City of Boston and Surrounding Cities and Towns* (Boston: A. J. Philpott, 1891), 10.

21 Elizabeth Hope Cushing, "'So Near the Metropolis': Lynn Woods, A Sylvan Gem in an Urban Setting," in *No Race of Imitators: Lynn and Her People, an Anthology,* ed. Cushing (Lynn, Mass.: Lynn Historical Society, 1992), 142–143; Fred L. Cushing, "Medford's Water Supply," *Medford Historical Register* 13, no. 3 (1910): 51–62; and Levin and Mahlstedt, *Middlesex Fells Reservation,* 20–23.

22 Wright's life is chronicled in Lawrence B. Goodheart, *Abolitionist, Actuary, Atheist: Elizur Wright and the Reform Impulse* (Kent, Ohio: Kent State University Press, 1990).

23 Elizur Wright, *Elizur Wright's Appeals for the Middlesex Fells and the Forests, with a Sketch of What He Did for Both by His Daughter, Ellen Wright* (1893; reprint, with a preface by Ellen Wright, Boston: George H. Ellis, 1904), xxvii. For the creation of urban parks in the nineteenth century, see Terence Young, *Building San Francisco's Parks, 1850–1930* (Baltimore: Johns Hopkins University Press, 2004); Roy Rosenzweig and Elizabeth Blackmar, *The Park and the People: A History of Central Park* (Ithaca: Cornell University Press, 1992); David Schuyler, *The New Urban Landscape: The Redefinition of City Form in Nineteenth-Century America* (Baltimore: Johns Hopkins University Press, 1986); and Galen Cranz, *The Politics of Park Design: A History of Urban Parks in America* (Cambridge: MIT Press, 1982).

24 For the development of a conservation ethic during this period, see Richard W. Judd, *Common Lands, Common People: The Origins of Conservation in Northern New England* (Cambridge: Harvard University Press, 1997); Robert McCullough, *The Landscape of Community: A History of Communal Forests in New England* (Hanover, N.H.: University Press of New England, 1995); and Roderick Nash, *Wilderness and the American Mind,* 3rd ed. (New Haven: Yale University Press, 1982).

25 Wright, *Elizur Wright's Appeals,* 116. The details of Wright's plans evolved considerably over time. Some of the earlier ones recommended developing part of the Fells to pay for purchasing the rest or preserving the entire area for scientific study. By the 1880s, however, he was emphasizing sustainable forestry.

26 Ibid., 87. For opposition to Wright's plan, see pp. 108–110, 116–118, and 129–131.

27 Ibid., 61, 70–71, 73.

28 Ibid., 29.

29 Ibid., 71.

30 Ibid., 62.

31 Ibid., 109.

32 Ibid., 39.

33 Ibid., 27.

34 Ibid., 85. For attitudes toward immigrant uses of nature in the urban environment, see Adam Rome, "Nature Wars, Culture Wars: Immigration and Environmental Reform in the Progressive Era," *Environmental History* 13, no. 3 (July 2008): 432–453.

35 Flagg, *Woods and By-Ways,* 68–69. Flagg detailed his proposal for the Fells in Wilson Flagg to Colonel T. W. Higginson, 10 December 1879, Cabot Science Library, Harvard University. Also see Wright, *Elizur Wright's Appeals,* 33–34. He laid out his larger plan for conserving forests nationally in Flagg, *Woods and By-Ways,* 68–73 and 426–436. Flagg was not the first to notice the Fells' potential as a park: the landscape architect H. W. S. Cleveland suggested that the Fells be preserved as early as 1849 or 1850. *Charles Eliot,* 323.

36 Flagg to Higginson, 10 December 1879, 5.

37 Higginson is quoted in Wright, *Elizur Wright's Appeals,* xli. Flagg admitted that his reserved personality and poor public speaking skills rendered him unable to explain and defend his own plan. Flagg to Higginson, 10 December 1879, 4–5, and 14 December 1879, Cabot Science Library, Harvard University.

38 Ellen Wright, "Elizur Wright and the Middlesex Fells," *Medford Historical Register* 4, no. 3 (July 1901): 81–82. Quotes are from Wright, *Elizur Wright's Appeals,* 55 and 58.

39 Rosewell B. Lawrence, "Middlesex Fells," *Appalachia* 4, no. 3 (March 1886): 199–214, supplemented and republished as Lawrence, *Middlesex Fells* (Boston: Appalachian Mountain Club, 1892); Chamberlain, "The Blue Hills"; and Wright, *Elizur Wright's Appeals,* 97–100. Quote is from Lawrence, *Middlesex Fells,* 213.

40 The legislature passed the Forest Law, also called the Public Domain Act, as Chapter 255 of the Acts of 1882. A reprint appears in Wright, *Elizur Wright's Appeals,* 93–95. Also see Franklin Hough, "The New Forestry Law of Massachusetts," *The American Journal of Forestry* 1 (April 1883): 304–307.

41 For the history of the Lynn Woods, see Cushing, "'So Near the Metropolis.'" Cushing writes that the residents of Lynn who worked to preserve the town woods "considered themselves to be pioneers in the effort to preserve forest lands in the tradition espoused by Elizur Wright." Cushing, 145.

42 Quoted in Sylvester Baxter, *Lynn's Public Forest: A Hand-Book Guide to the Great Woods Park in the City of Lynn* (Boston: Authors' Mutual Publishing Company, 1891), 34.

43 Baxter, *Lynn's Public Forest,* 2, 41, 47, 48.

44 City of Lynn, *First Annual Report of the Park Commissioners of the City of Lynn, for the Year Ending December 31, 1889* (Lynn, Mass.: Whitten and Cass, 1890), 5–8. The legislature passed the Park Act as Chapter 154 of the Acts of 1882.

45 City of Lynn, *Eleventh Annual Park Commissioners' Report, Lynn, Massachusetts, 1899,* 11.

46 City of Lynn, *Second Annual Report of the Park Commissioners of the City of Lynn, for the Year Ending December 20, 1890* (Lynn, Mass.: Whitten and Cass, 1891), 7. For the Sihlwald, see McCullough, *Landscape of Community,* 105–109.

47 Quoted in Sylvester Baxter, *Lynn's Public Forest,* 60.

48 City of Lynn, [*Tenth Annual] Park Commissioners' Report, Lynn, Massachusetts, 1898,* 18. For a detailed analysis of efforts to restore the Puritan Wilderness in the Lynn Woods, see Donald Jones, "Recreating the Wilderness: The Cultural Landscape of Lynn Woods, a Late Nineteenth-Century Public Park in Lynn, Massachusetts" (Ph.D. diss., Boston University, 1994).

49 Elias H. Derby, "Commercial Cities and Towns of the United States: City of Boston," in *Hunt's Merchants' Magazine and Commercial Review* 23, no. 5 (November 1850): 496; Nathaniel Appleton Haven, "The First Settlers of New Hampshire," in *The New Hampshire Book. Being Specimens of the Literature of the Granite State,* ed. Charles James Fox and Samuel Osgood (Nashville: Charles T. Gill, 1844), 15. For New England's attachment to the Puritan past, especially as reflected in literature, see Lawrence Buell, *New England Literary Culture from Revolution through Renaissance* (Cambridge: Cambridge University Press, 1986). Bostonians also rejected many aspects of the Puritan past. See Jan C. Dawson, *The Unusable Past: America's Puritan Tradition, 1830–1930* (Chico, Calif.: Scholars Press, 1984).

50 Emily Dickinson, *The Complete Poems of Emily Dickinson,* ed. Thomas H. Johnson (Boston: Little, Brown, 1960), 132. Most scholars who study the environmental aspects of the colonial revival movement focus on houses and gardens rather than parks and wilderness areas. For an overview of the movement, see Alan Axelrod, ed., *The Colonial Revival in America* (New York: W. W. Norton, 1985). For the movement's New England context, see Joseph A. Conforti, *Imagining New England: Explorations of Regional Identity from the Pilgrims to the Mid-Twentieth Century* (Chapel Hill: University of North Carolina Press, 2001), especially chapter 5.

51 William Dean Howells, *Suburban Sketches* (New York: Hurd and Houghton, 1871), 69 and 68.

52 Van Wyck Brooks, *New England: Indian Summer, 1865–1915* (New York: E. P. Dutton, 1940), 330. For the development of preservationist thought in Boston, see Michael Holleran, *Boston's 'Changeful Times.'* The classic history of preservation in America remains Charles B. Hosmer, Jr., *Presence of the Past: A History of the Preservation Movement in the United States before Williamsburg* (New York: G. P. Putnam's Sons, 1965). For the role of women, see Patricia West, *Domesticating History: The Political Origins of America's House Museums* (Washington, D.C.: Smithsonian Institution Press, 1999).

53 Frederick Jackson Turner, "Architecture Through Oppression," *University Press* 15, June 21, 1884, reprinted in Steven Conn and Max Page, eds., *Building the Nation: Americans Write About Their Architecture, Their Cities, and Their Landscape* (Philadelphia: University of Pennsylvania Press, 2003), 22.

54 *Second Annual Report of the Park Commissioners of the City of Lynn,* 6.

55 Sylvester Baxter discusses some of the name changes in Baxter, *Lynn's Public Forest,* 49–53, and attributes many of them to Cyrus M. Tracy, a local historian and naturalist who played a prominent role in preserving the Lynn Woods. For the importance of names to the recreation of a sense of wilderness in the Lynn Woods, see Jones, "Recreating the Wilderness," 267–269.

56 Wright, *Elizur Wright's Appeals,* 32. For Winthrop's journey north of Boston, see the entry for February 7, 1632, in John Winthrop, *The History of New England from 1630 to 1649,* ed. James Savage (Boston: Little, Brown, 1853), 83–84. For the place-naming strategies used by colonial New Englanders, see the classic work by George R. Stewart, *Names on the Land: A Historical Account of Place-naming in the United States,* 4th ed. (1945; reprint, with an introduction by Wallace Stegner, San Francisco: Lexikos, 1982), 38–39, 44–57; and Eugene Green, "Naming and Mapping the Environments of Early Massachusetts, 1620–1776," *Names: Journal of the American Name Society* 30, no. 2 (June 1982): 77–92.

57 E. G. Chamberlain, "Names of the Blue Hills," *Boston Transcript,* 4 June, 1895, reprinted in *Appalachia Bulletin* (May 1973): 175.

58 Quoted in William B. de las Casas, "The Middlesex Fells," *The New England Magazine* 18, no. 6 (August 1898): 703; Wright, *Elizur Wright's Appeals,* 23. Baxter takes credit for the name "Middlesex Fells" in Baxter, *Boston Park Guide, Including the Municipal and Metropolitan Systems of Greater Boston* (Boston: published by the author, 1895), 50–51.

59 *First Annual Report of the Trustees of Public Reservations, 1891* (Boston: George H. Ellis, 1892), 7.

60 For the history of the Trustees, see Gordon Abbott, Jr., *Saving Special Places: A Centennial History of the Trustees of Reservations, Pioneer of the Land Trust Movement* (Ipswich, Mass.: Ipswich Press, 1993).

61 The names of those who gave money to the Trustees in its first years appear in *Second Annual Report of the Trustees of Public Reservations, 1892* (Boston: George H. Ellis, 1893), 4–7. For the role of gender in nineteenth-century environmental reform see, for example, Adam Rome, "'Political Hermaphrodites': Gender and Environmental Reform in Progressive America," *Environmental History* 11, no. 3 (July 2006): 440–463; David Stradling, *Smokestacks and Progressives: Environmentalists, Engineers, and Air Quality in America, 1881–1951* (Baltimore: Johns Hopkins University Press, 1999), particularly chapter 3; and Suellen M. Hoy, "'Municipal Housekeeping': The Role of Women in Improving Urban Sanitation Practices, 1880–1917," in *Pollution and Reform in American Cities,*

1870–1930, ed. Martin V. Melosi (Austin: University of Texas Press, 1980), 173–198.

62 *First Annual Report of the Trustees of Public Reservations,* 11.

63 *Annual Report of the Trustees of Scenic and Historical Places and Objects in the State of New York* (Albany: Wynkoop Hallenbeck Crawford, 1896); and *Annual Report of the Society for the Preservation of Scenic and Historic Places and Objects to the Legislature of the State of New York. 1900* (Albany: James B. Lyon, 1900).

64 For the evolution of urban planning in the nineteenth century, see Jon A. Peterson, *The Birth of City Planning in the United States, 1840–1917* (Baltimore: Johns Hopkins University Press, 2003); Robert Fishman, ed., *The American Planning Tradition: Culture and Policy* (Baltimore: Johns Hopkins University Press, 2000); Stanley K. Schultz, *Constructing Urban Culture: American Cities and City Planning, 1800–1920* (Philadelphia: Temple University Press, 1989); and Daniel Schaffer, ed., *Two Centuries of American Planning* (Baltimore: Johns Hopkins University Press, 1988).

65 "Letter from Uriel Crocker," in City of Boston, City Document No. 123 (1869), 93, quoted in Karl Haglund, *Inventing the Charles River* (Cambridge: MIT Press, 2003), 83. For an overview of these plans, see Haglund, 80–88.

66 *Charles Eliot,* 354–357.

67 See Sylvester Baxter, "The Hotel Cluny of a New England Village," in *Publications of the Ipswich Historical Society* X (Salem, Mass.: Salem Press, 1901), 1–11.

68 For Eliot, see Keith N. Morgan, "Charles Eliot, Landscape Architect: An Introduction to His Life and Work," *Arnoldia* 59, no. 2 (Summer 1999): 2–22; Newton, "Charles Eliot and His Metropolitan Park System"; and *Charles Eliot.* Quotes are from *Report of the Metropolitan Park Commissioners, 1893,* 88; and *Charles Eliot,* 240.

69 For an overview of Baxter's socialist thought, see Baxter, "The Author of 'Looking Backward,'" in Edward Bellamy, *Looking Backward, 2000–1887* (New York: Grosset and Dunlap, 1898), v–xvii; and Baxter, "How the Bills of Socialism Will Be Paid," *The Forum* 17 (August 1894): 699–709.

70 The phrase "children of one family" appears in both Sylvester Baxter, *Greater Boston,* 19; and Bellamy, *Looking Backward,* 312. Baxter takes aim at Brookline in *Greater Boston,* 19.

71 Baxter, *Greater Boston.* Baxter had studied urban planning at the universities of Leipzig and Berlin, and his plan provided an important model for the metropolitan park system as it subsequently developed. Yet historians have emphasized Eliot's contributions at the expense of Baxter's. Eliot's father began the trend by editing the works of his deceased son in such a way that Eliot appeared the sole inspiration for the system. For a sampling of Baxter's many other forays into planning, see Baxter, "The German Way of Making Better Cities," *Atlantic Monthly* 104 (July 1909): 72–95. For the movement to con-

solidate the metropolitan region inspired by Baxter's proposal, see James A. Merino, "Cooperative Schemes for Greater Boston: 1890–1920," *New England Quarterly* 45, no. 2 (June 1972): 196–226.

72 The preliminary committee's report and recommendations were published as *Report of the Metropolitan Park Commissioners, 1893*.

73 Ibid., 9 and 2–3. The environmental impact of nineteenth-century suburbanization remains understudied. For the second half of the twentieth century, see Adam Rome, *The Bulldozer in the Countryside: Suburban Sprawl and the Rise of American Environmentalism* (New York: Cambridge University Press, 2001).

74 The work of the Metropolitan Park Commissioners is traceable through their annual reports, which appear in state records beginning in 1895 as Public Document No. 48.

75 McCullough, *Landscape of Community,* 114.

76 *Charles Eliot,* 513.

77 To get a sense for the sheer volume of new names created by Eliot's firm and approved by the Commissioners, compare the map prepared for the Appalachian Mountain Club in 1886 (attached to Lawrence, *Middlesex Fells*) with the earliest map published by the Metropolitan Park Commission (attached to *Report of the Board of Metropolitan Park Commissioners, 1895*).

78 Thomas Starr King, *The White Hills: Their Legends, Landscape, and Poetry* (1859; reprinted Boston: Estes and Lauriat, 1887), 29. For Hitchcock, and the use of Indian names generally, see Jared Farmer, *On Zion's Mount: Mormons, Indians, and the American Landscape* (Cambridge: Harvard University Press, 2008), chapter 7.

79 Albert Kendall Teele, *The Blue Hills* (Boston: n.p., 1884), 11.

80 Alexander Young, ed., *Chronicles of the Pilgrim Fathers of the Colony of Plymouth, from 1602 to 1625* (Boston: Charles C. Little and James Brown, 1841), 367.

81 See Alan Trachtenberg, *Shades of Hiawatha: Staging Indians, Making Americans, 1880–1930* (New York: Hill and Wang, 2004).

82 De las Casas, "Middlesex Fells," 719.

83 Edwin M. Bacon, *Walks and Rides in the Country Round About Boston* (Boston: Houghton, Mifflin, 1897), 56.

84 For the removal of buildings from the new reservations, see Bacon, *Walks and Rides,* 341; Commonwealth of Massachusetts, *Report of the Board of Metropolitan Park Commissioners, January 1897,* Public Document No. 48 (Boston: Wright and Potter Printing, 1897), 36 and 59; and Commonwealth of Massachusetts, *Report of the Board of Metropolitan Park Commissioners, January 1898,* Public Document No. 48 (Boston: Wright and Potter Printing, 1898), 85. For Rockefeller, see Karl Jacoby, *Crimes Against Nature: Squatters, Poachers, Thieves, and the Hidden History of American Conservation* (Berkeley: University of California Press, 2001), 43. For past and present efforts to "rewild" natural areas, see

Mark David Spence, *Dispossessing the Wilderness: Indian Removal and the Making of the National Parks* (New York: Oxford University Press, 1999); Justin Reich, "Re-Creating the Wilderness: Shaping Narratives and Landscapes in Shenandoah National Park," *Environmental History* 6, no. 1 (January 2001): 95–117; Christopher McGrory Klyza, ed., *Wilderness Comes Home: Rewilding the Northeast* (Hanover, N.H.: University Press of New England, 2001); and William Cronon, "The Riddle of the Apostle Islands," *Orion* (May/June 2003): 36–42.

85 For Eliot's ideas on the importance of wilderness management, see *Charles Eliot, 554–555*, and 657. The quote appears on p. 514.

86 Today, the Middlesex Fells contains 2,575 acres and the Blue Hills over 7,000 acres. For comparison, the City of Chelsea contains 1,589 acres, Belmont 3,009 acres, Everett 2,346 acres, and Watertown 2,664 acres.

87 *Charles Eliot*, 616.

88 For the earliest discussion of parkways, see *Report of the Metropolitan Park Commissioners, 1893*, 62–67. For a summary of parkway work in the first five years, see Commonwealth of Massachusetts, *Report of the Board of Metropolitan Park Commissioners, January, 1899*, Public Doc. No. 48 (1899), 12–13. The statistics for 1910 are from Walter A. Webster, *Report on Metropolitan Park Commission*, House No. 1985 (1911), 9 and 14–15. For the history of parkways, see Norman T. Newton, "Parkways and Their Offspring," in *Design on the Land*, 596–619.

89 *Report of the Metropolitan Park Commissioners, 1893, 63*; *Charles Eliot, 606*; *Report of the Metropolitan Park Commissioners, 1895, 43*; and H. G. Wells, *The Future in America: A Search After Realities* (London: Chapman and Hall, 1906), 68. Other cities also situated their parkways with an eye toward future development. See, for example, State of Rhode Island, *Sixth Annual Report of the Board of Metropolitan Park Commissioners* (Providence: E. L. Freeman, 1910), 10. Also see Elizabeth Macdonald, "Suburban Vision to Urban Reality: The Evolution of Olmsted and Vaux's Brooklyn Parkway Neighborhood," *Journal of Planning History* 4, no. 4 (November 2005): 295–321.

90 Wells, *Future in America*, 68; and Sylvester Baxter, "A Vast Metropolitan Province: A Forecast of the Greater Boston of 1950," *Boston Evening Transcript*, Spring Real Estate Supplement, 5 April 1913, p. 2. Also see James C. O'Connell, "How Metropolitan Parks Shaped Greater Boston, 1893–1945," in *Remaking Boston: An Environmental History of the City and Its Surroundings*, ed. Anthony N. Penna and Conrad Edick Wright (Pittsburgh: University of Pittsburgh Press, 2009), 168–197.

91 Brian Drayton and Richard B. Primack, "Plant Species Lost in an Isolated Conservation Area in Metropolitan Boston from 1894–1993," *Conservation Biology* 10, no. 1 (February 1996): 30–39.

Epilogue: The City Complete

1 Arnold Bennett, *Your United States: Impressions of a First Visit* (New York: George H. Doran, 1912), 57, 62.

2 Ralph Waldo Emerson, *Natural History of Intellect and Other Papers* (Boston: Houghton, Mifflin, 1904), 165.

3 Raymond Williams, "Ideas of Nature," in Williams, *Problems in Materialism and Culture* (London: Verso, 1980), 85.

ACKNOWLEDGMENTS

The extent of a debt becomes clear only after it is tallied, and mine is large. I received generous support in the form of a Carter Manny Award from the Graham Foundation for Advanced Studies in the Fine Arts, a Mary C. Mooney Fellowship from the Boston Athenaeum, an Andrew W. Mellon Fellowship from the Massachusetts Historical Society, and fellowships from the Stanford Humanities Fellows Program and the Mrs. Giles Whiting Foundation. Several travel fellowships and grants from the University of Wisconsin-Madison helped to lighten the financial burden of research trips to Boston, and a Professional Staff Congress-City University of New York Research Award paid for illustration permissions. I also benefited from the generous release time policies of Brooklyn College, which invests heavily in the success of its junior faculty.

My research led me to dozens of libraries and archives that serve as the custodians of Boston's past. I owe particularly large debts to the Boston Athenaeum, the Boston Public Library, the Bostonian Society, Historic New England, the Massachusetts Historical Society, and the State Library of Massachusetts. One of the many joys of doing archival research on the history of Boston derives from the proximity of these institutions. They are all located in downtown Boston, giving researchers the opportunity to visit the places they are writing about while walking from one archive to another. I also ventured into nearby Cambridge to take advantage of the collections at Harvard University's Cabot Science and Frances Loeb Libraries, and I relied heavily on the libraries of the State Historical Society of Wisconsin, the University of Wisconsin-Madison, and Stanford University. Countless librarians and archivists helped me to locate the material I was looking for, but I owe special thanks to Kristen Swett of the City of Boston Archives, who tracked down the petitions at the heart of chapter 1; the special collections archivists at the State Library of Massachusetts, who tolerated my endless requests for photocopies; and Sean Fisher, archivist for the Massachusetts Department of Conservation and Recreation, who provided me with a number of sources that strengthened chapter 5.

A large number of colleagues contributed their insights to this book. For offering suggestions on various parts of the manuscript, I am indebted to William Barnett, Greg Bond, Emily Brock, James Feldman, David Herzberg, Hiroshi Kitamura, William Meyer, Martin Reuss, Adam Rome, Steven Rudnick, Nancy Seasholes, Kendra Smith, Joel Tarr, Lissa Wadewitz, Carolyn Winterer, and Christopher Wells. Herbert Klein generously agreed to review the statistical work in my Note on Boston Common Petitions. I am particularly grateful to Matthew Klingle, Thomas Robertson, Carl Smith, and Conrad Wright, who spent considerable time and effort reading later versions of the manuscript. Their comments were invaluable. I also owe special thanks to my mentors at the University of Wisconsin-Madison, where I was fortunate to work with a gifted and supportive group of scholars. William Cronon has been a model mentor and friend, and Paul Boyer, Stanley Schultz, and William Reese shared their time and wisdom with unstinting generosity. Much of what I know about history I learned from them. I also benefited from the guidance of Arne Alanen and Steven Kantrowitz.

Special notes of appreciation go to Kathleen McDermott, Susan Wallace Boehmer, and the staff at Harvard University Press, and to David Stradling and an anonymous reader, who reviewed the manuscript for Harvard. Some of the material in this book appeared previously in *Environmental History* and the *Journal of Urban History,* copyright 2009 by Sage Publications, Inc. I am grateful for permission to reprint it here.

My greatest debt, however, is to my wife and daughters, who remind me every day that life must be lived in the present rather than the past. For that priceless gift, I dedicate this book to them.

INDEX